THE THIRD COAST

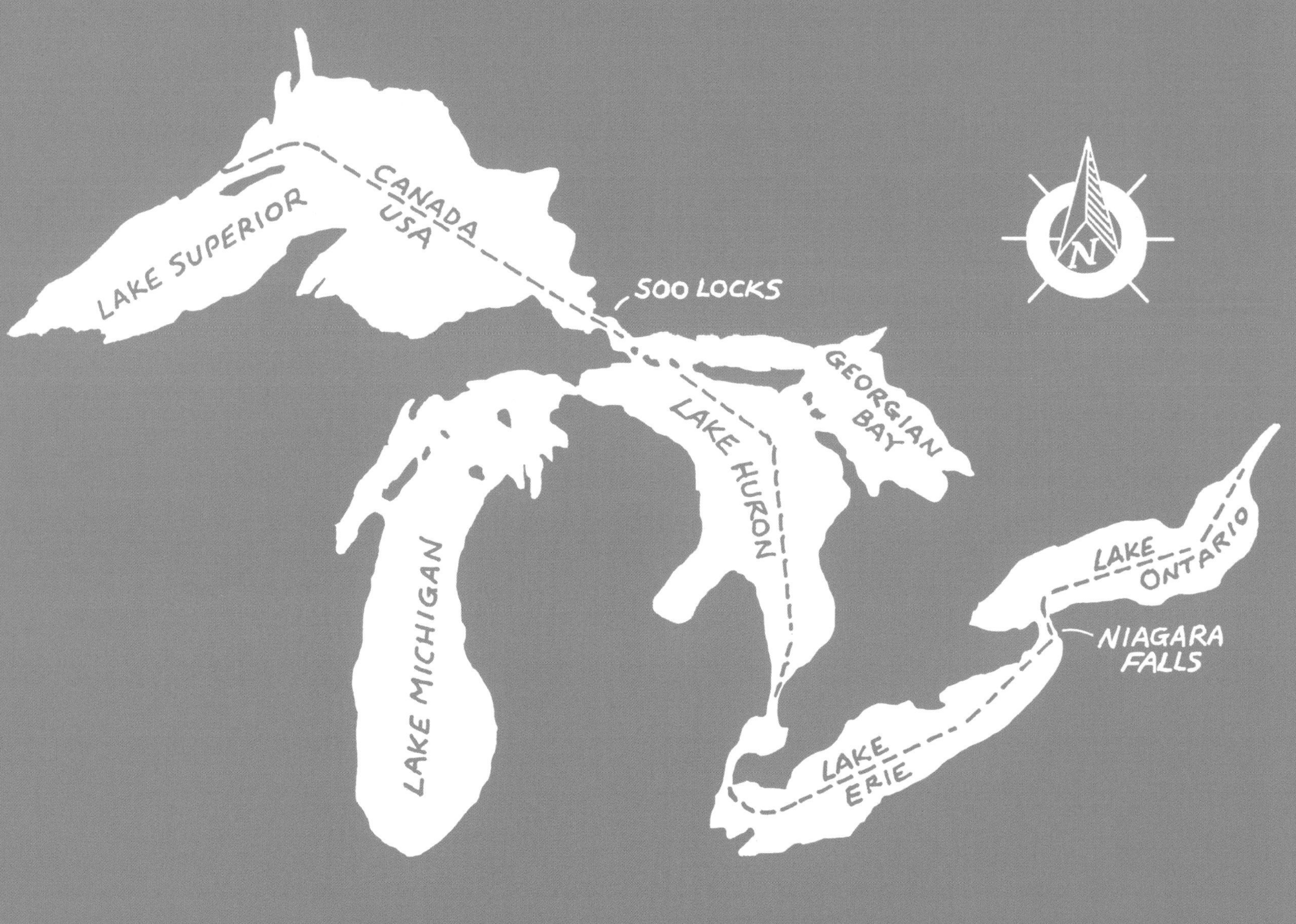
LAKE SUPERIOR
CANADA
USA
SOO LOCKS
GEORGIAN BAY
LAKE HURON
LAKE MICHIGAN
LAKE ONTARIO
NIAGARA FALLS
LAKE ERIE
N

THE THIRD COAST

AMERICA'S GREAT LAKES SHORELINE

DAVID ZURICK

FOREWORD BY JERRY DENNIS

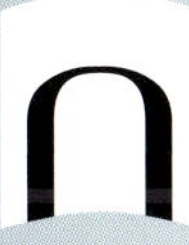

NORTHWESTERN UNIVERSITY PRESS / EVANSTON, ILLINOIS

Northwestern University Press
www.nupress.northwestern.edu

Map of the Great Lakes (opposite the title page) by Doug Zurick.

Printed in Canada

10 9 8 7 6 5 4 3 2 1

ISBN 978-0-8101-4867-3 (paper)

Library of Congress Cataloging-in-Publication Data
Names: Zurick, David photographer author | Dennis, Jerry, 1954– author of introduction, etc.
Title: Third coast : America's Great Lakes shoreline / David Zurick ; foreword by Jerry Dennis.
Description: Evanston : Northwestern University Press, 2025.
Identifiers: LCCN 2025011047 | ISBN 9780810148673 paperback
Subjects: LCSH: Great Lakes (North America)—Pictorial works | LCGFT: Illustrated works
Classification: LCC F551 .Z87 2025 | DDC 977.00222—dc23/eng/20250312
LC record available at https://lccn.loc.gov/2025011047

CONTENTS

FOREWORD

JERRY DENNIS

For most of my life I've been trying to find what for lack of a better word let's call the soul of the Great Lakes. I've been trying to find the soul of many other things as well, but the Great Lakes are special. They're where I grew up, and where many of my ideas of the world were formed, and where, despite a restless nature, I have chosen to stay. I've found no place so consistently engaging.

Even after sixty years my earliest memories of the lakes remain vivid—and flooded with contradictions. When I was five years old my family lived for a summer on the shore of Lake Michigan, in the village of Empire, Michigan, within sight of Sleeping Bear Dunes. I remember the dunes as a brilliant mountain of sand sloping to the lake, and the lake itself shredded by the wind, with whitecaps to the horizon and furious breakers hurling themselves against the shore. The lake was so vast and powerful that I assumed it must be an ocean.

But that same beach was fouled with millions of the small fish called alewives that had died and washed to shore in rotting heaps as high as my waist. We had to wade through them to get to the water's edge. Their stench carried far inland.

The house we lived in that summer had a telescope mounted on a pedestal in front of the picture window. At night my father would aim the telescope at the lights of freighters passing on the horizon, and as I stood on a chair watching them he would tell me they were bound for New York, London, Tokyo. And he told me that these lakes that connected us to the world were sick to death with pollutants that he could never have imagined when he was a child.

He told me about fishing for lake trout in the 1940s and '50s, and how the fish rose from the depths and hit the lures anglers trolled on wire lines, and how there was always a chance of catching a monster of thirty or forty pounds. And he said that now the fish were nearly gone, their numbers decimated by an invasion of predatory lamprey that seemed like creatures from a horror film. In their place was this other invader, the alewife, which, with few predators left to check it, had exploded in population until it accounted for 90 percent of the biomass of everything living in the lakes.

He told stories about my grandfather, my mother's father, who died shortly before I was born, and who as a young man worked for the U.S. Life-Saving Service on Lake Michigan's South Manitou Island and helped rescue crews of ships that had foundered on the sandbars of the Manitou Passage.

He talked about the storms that swept the lakes and made boating of every kind so risky that only a fool would venture out without checking the forecast and keeping an eye on the sky.

But few people went out in pleasure boats anymore. There was no reason to. The water stank, and the fish were gone.

I was with my father in 1967 when the first runs of coho salmon, which had been introduced to Lake Michigan as fingerlings a year and a half earlier, returned to Platte Bay and revitalized the Great Lakes. We caught them until our arms ached and went home day after day drunk on this exotic bounty that was unlike anything we had ever experienced. And I was with him when a squall swept in from the west and sent a fleet of upwards of a thousand small boats racing in panic to the shore. I was just a boy, but I joined my father and others on the beach as they tried to rescue anglers who had gone into the water when their boats swamped and capsized in the surf. And though my father tried to protect me from seeing it, I watched some of those men die.

≈

I've spent much of my writing career, nearly forty years now, studying the Great Lakes and their surroundings and trying to tell the story of this amazing, beautiful, and heartbreaking place. It's a big story. A complex story. And it's changing all the time.

I've tried to tell it in books, essays, stories, and poems. In one book I tell the story from the decks of boats—sailing, motoring, and paddling through all five lakes and helping to deliver a schooner from Lake Michigan to Bar Harbor, Maine. In another book I tell a more personal story while living for a winter on the shores of Lakes Michigan and Superior and thinking about the philosophical questions that we face as stewards in this era of great change.

I'm in a dilemma familiar to everyone. The more we learn, the more there is to learn. The more we see, the more there is to see. The more we do, the more that remains to be done.

Is the story of the Great Lakes the story of enormous ice sheets plowing the earth, then melting to fill the basins they dug?

Is it the story of the ancient people who migrated here as the ice receded to hunt woolly mammoths and elk and who formed sophisticated societies that thrived for thousands of years?

Is it the story of the Europeans who followed, and the furs, forests, and minerals they plundered, and the cities they built on the shores?

Is it the story of Cleveland's Cuyahoga River catching fire in 1969 and igniting the environmental conscience of a nation?

Is it the story of the world's greatest freshwater fishery—its collapse and resurgence—and perhaps its impending collapse yet again?

Is it the story of dead zones in the lakes and avian botulism?

Is it the story of organisms that have inhabited the lakes since the Ice Age, like the amphipod *Diporeia*, which until zebra and quagga mussels invaded a few decades ago was found in concentrations of ten thousand per square meter of lake bottom, and now has disappeared entirely from most of Lakes Huron and Michigan?

Is it the story of the water itself, *our* water, which will become increasingly precious, and is now being pumped from our aquifers, sealed in plastic bottles, and sold back to us?

Is it the story of cities yoked with outdated, inadequate, or flat-out poisonous water supplies?

Is it the story of voyageur canoes and sailboat regattas? Of sea kayakers and surfers? Of factories and farms? Of pristine beaches and sand dunes and rock formations and national parks that are among the most beautiful in America? Of the impact of global warming on the Great Lakes and the communities that surround them?

The answer, of course, is yes. It's all those stories and countless others. They are diverse stories, and messy. They include the heartening and the discouraging, the entertaining and the distressing, those that deliver good news and those that deliver bad. Taken together, they are the story of one of the most interesting and complicated of our planet's natural wonders—and one of the least appreciated.

≈

Think of the Great Lakes as five beautiful and moody sisters: willful, tempestuous, enigmatic, frequently charming, impossible to ignore. You can set out to know them, but it's a difficult task. Getting to know a small place is hard enough—

you can spend a lifetime learning your own backyard. But the Great Lakes are probably impossible. They're too big, too varied, they sprawl across too large a swath of continent.

Those of us who live near them have gained a basic understanding, but most people around the world don't get it. They don't know the most fundamental things about the lakes.

They don't know that you can't see across them.

Or that for nearly four centuries the lakes have been critical to the economic and political fortunes of not just the United States and Canada, but of much of the world.

Or that the five lakes collect the runoff of a drainage basin encompassing an area bigger than France that is home to more than thirty million people—one in ten Americans and more than 30 percent of all Canadians.

Or that the lakes contain 95 percent of the surface freshwater in the United States—and nearly 20 percent of the world's.

Or that they are encircled by ten thousand miles of shoreline, more than the Atlantic and Pacific coasts of the United States combined.

Or that these lakes that were once declared dead are still alive and kicking—and still in need of our protection.

And of course they don't know—even many of us who live here don't know—that these vast lakes that are so important globally must be protected locally.

Often I'm asked what I think are the biggest problems facing the Great Lakes. Is it climate change? Invasive species? Nutrient loading from agricultural runoff and municipal waste? Petroleum and chemical spills and the threat of rupture from submerged pipelines? Airborne deposition of heavy metals? The threat of diversion, sale, or theft of the water itself?

All of those are big problems and they all need our attention.

But I think there's a bigger danger. One that makes many of the problems looming over the lakes even more threatening. One that might have made many of them possible in the first place.

I fear the greatest threat to the Great Lakes—and the greatest threat to the environmental health of the world—is anything that causes us to turn our backs, become cynical, lose hope. It's anything that makes us think it's too late to make a difference. Anything that makes us prefer to stay inside our houses. Anything that makes us accept the insidious message beamed to us countless times every day by every medium: that our value is not as compassionate and inquisitive human beings, but as consumers. Anything that makes us believe the battles are already lost and that we might as well grab what we can for ourselves before somebody else gets it.

≈

And yet there remain many reasons to be hopeful. We face profound challenges, as we always have and always will. But you don't have to look far around the Great Lakes to find encouraging stories.

For those who find themselves losing hope, it helps to visit the wild shores of Lake Superior and its biggest island, Isle Royale. Or the North Channel of Lake Huron's Georgian Bay. Or the dunes that stretch from Indiana Dunes at the south end of Lake Michigan to Sleeping Bear Dunes and beyond in the north. Or the islands of Lake Erie. Or Lake Ontario near Toronto and Kingston and the St. Lawrence downriver through the Thousand Islands. Those and many other places will convince you that large portions of the lakes remain healthy and beautiful, even, on the surface at least, pristine.

It helps also to see the lakes through the eyes of artists, like David Zurick, who have immersed themselves deeply in the subject. When David set out to document the Great Lakes region in all its beautiful and messy grandeur, he paired his global perspective with memories of growing up on the shore of Lake Huron. The result is an honest, unique, and absolutely unsentimental portrait of the lakes, their surrounding communities, and the people who live, work, and play here.

Finally, I'm hopeful because of the people I've met. Everywhere I've gone in my travels around the lakes I've listened to them share their concerns. Some are discouraged and some have quit trying. Many are indifferent. Or, rather, *most* are indifferent. But most always have been.

It's the ones who speak up who make a difference. And what I've heard from them, young and old, college graduates and high school dropouts, from every race and religion and social class, is the same message: We care.

We care about the water, the land, the air, and every living thing that shares them with us.

We care about the decisions made about our land and water—and demand that those decisions not be made by people who have a vested interest in plundering and profiting from them.

We care so much that we will rise up and block locust industries that would harvest our natural resources and then move on.

We care when the place where we live is abused, because what happens to it, happens to us. And we damned well take it personally.

They might not use these words but every one of them is saying what I've been trying to say and what David Zurick clearly knows: There's a soul to this place. And it touches our souls.

THE THIRD COAST

WINTER

LAKE SUPERIOR

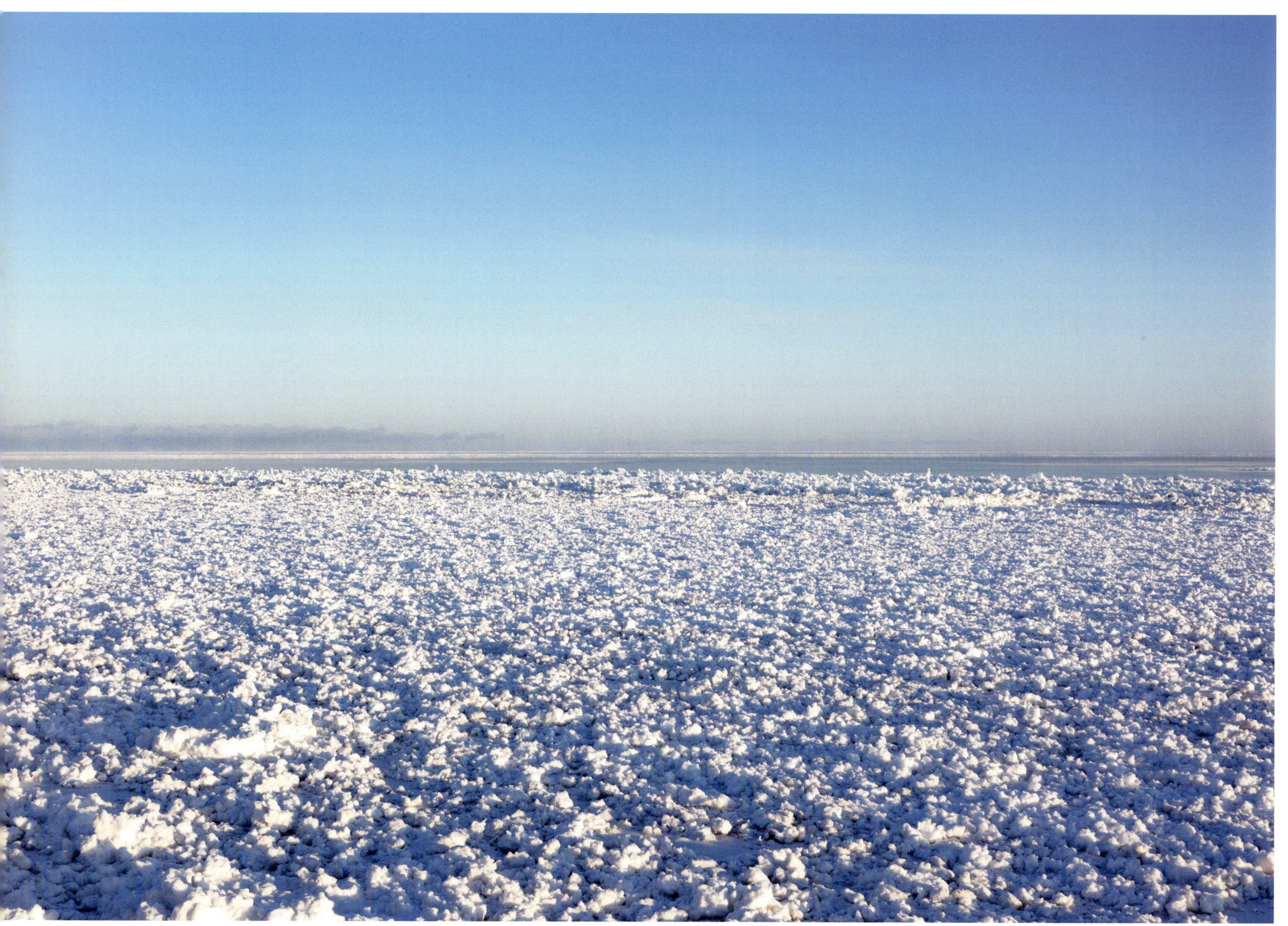

Shipwreck Coast, Michigan, 2022

Ice road to Madeline Island, Wisconsin, 2022

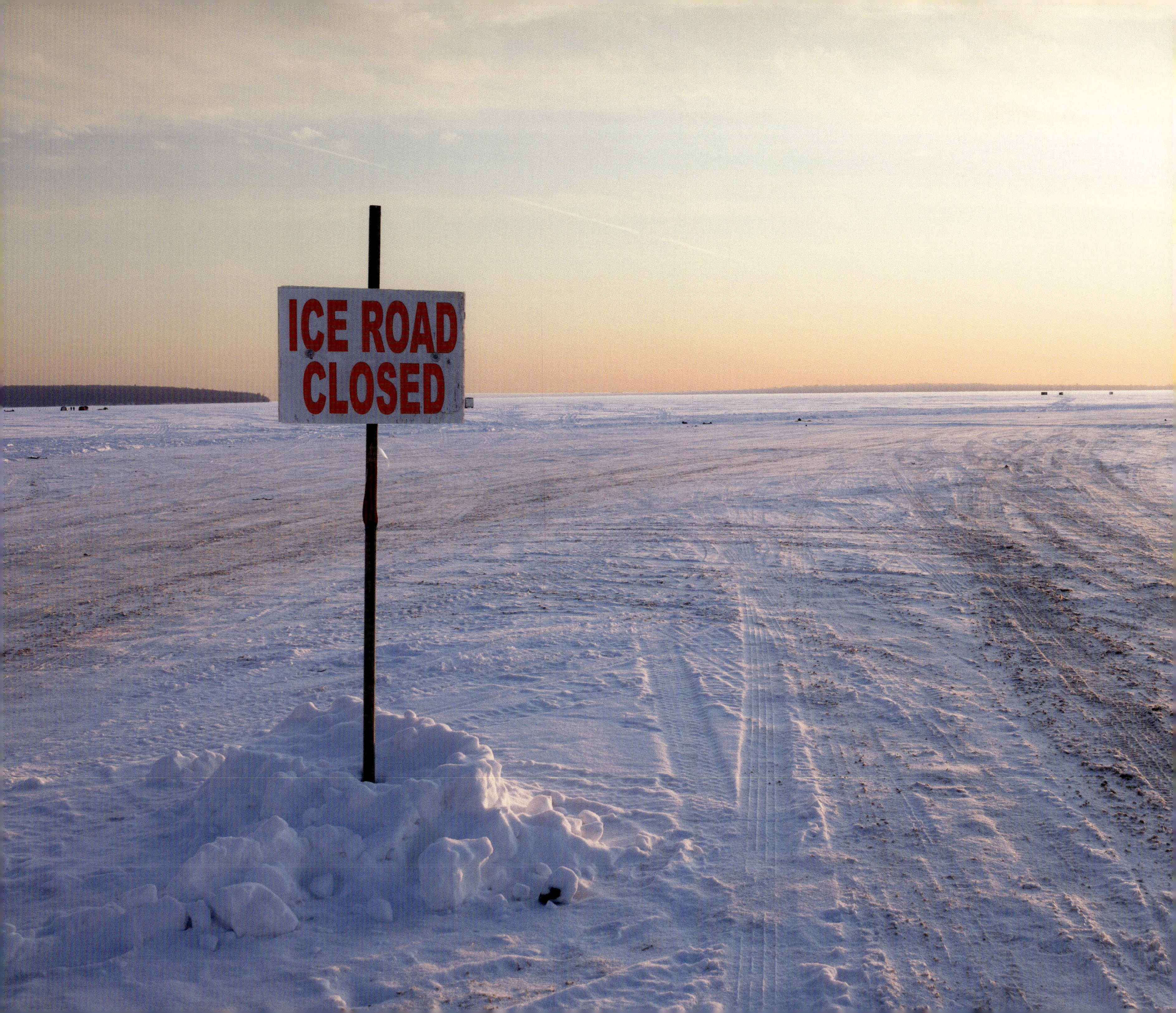
ICE ROAD
CLOSED

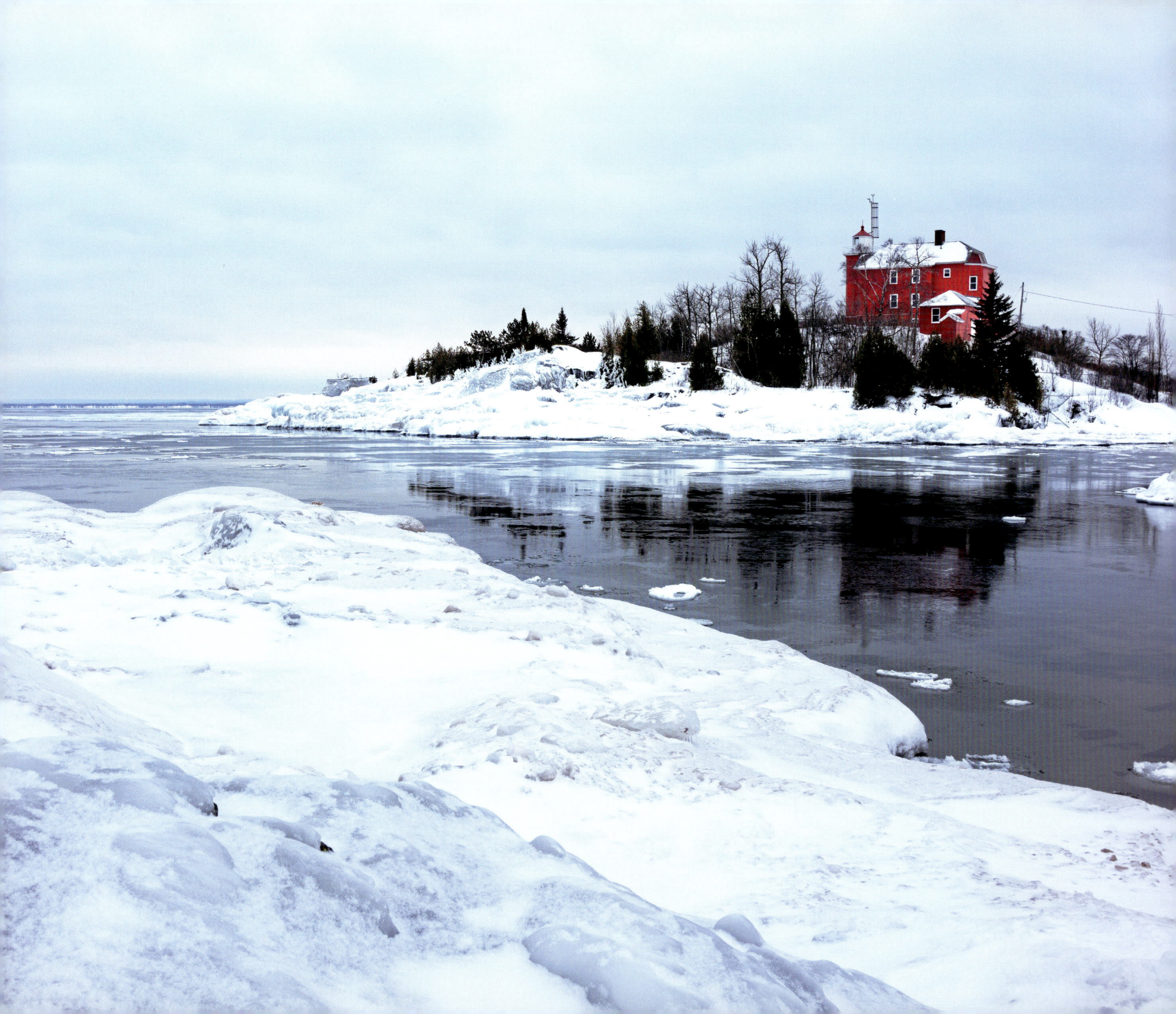

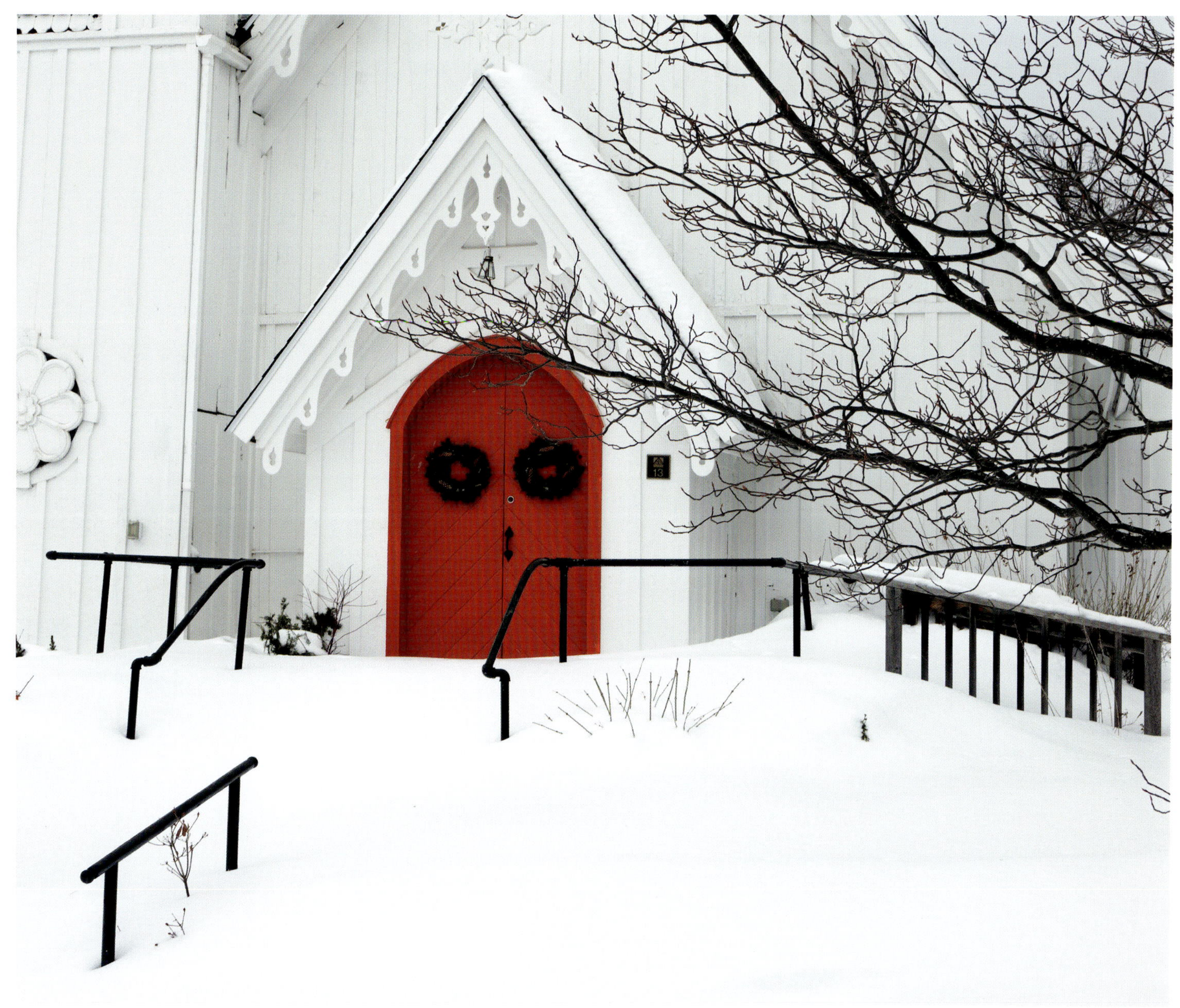

Church with red door, Houghton County, Michigan, 2022

Lighthouse, Marquette Harbor, Michigan, 2022

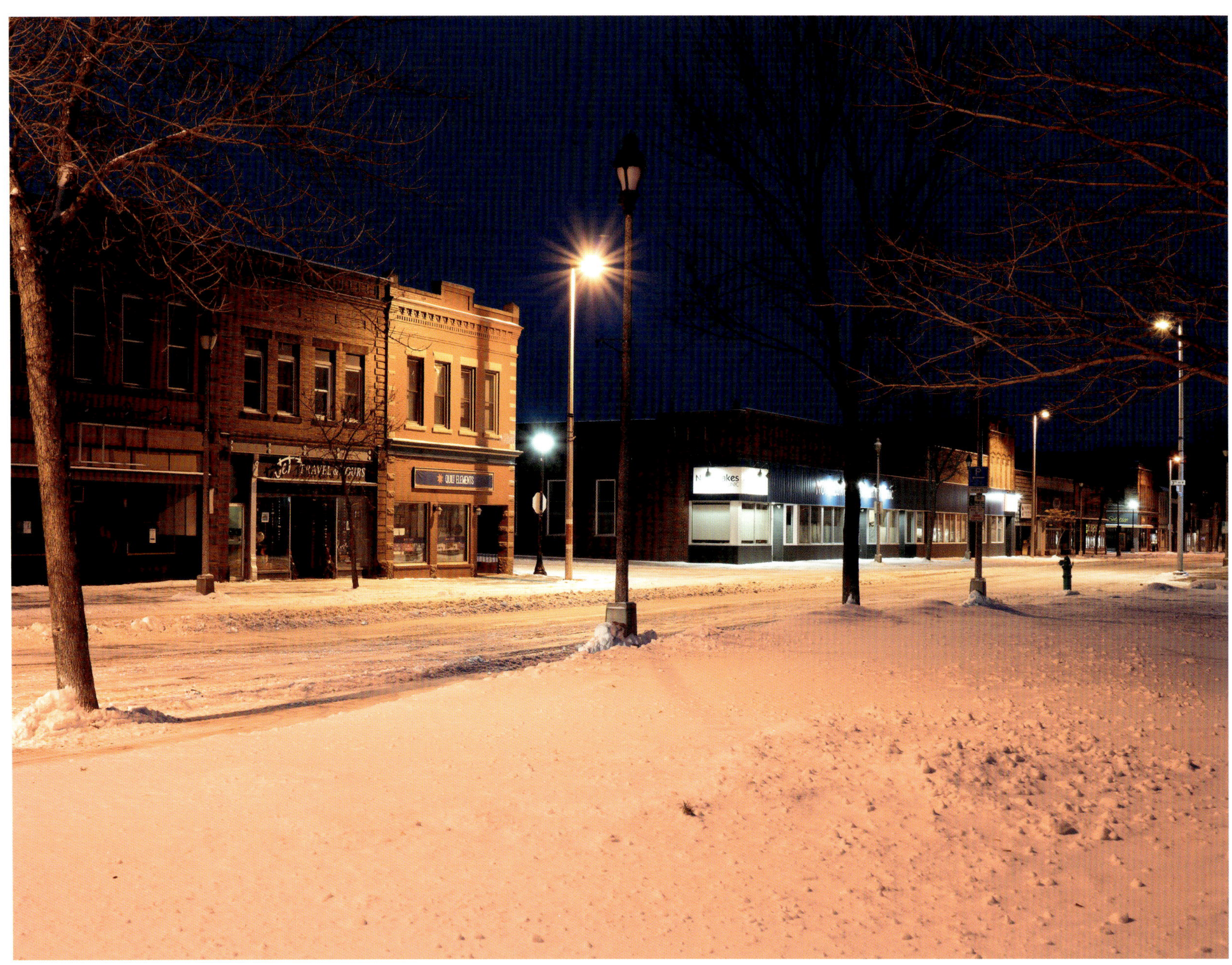

Ashland, Wisconsin, 2022

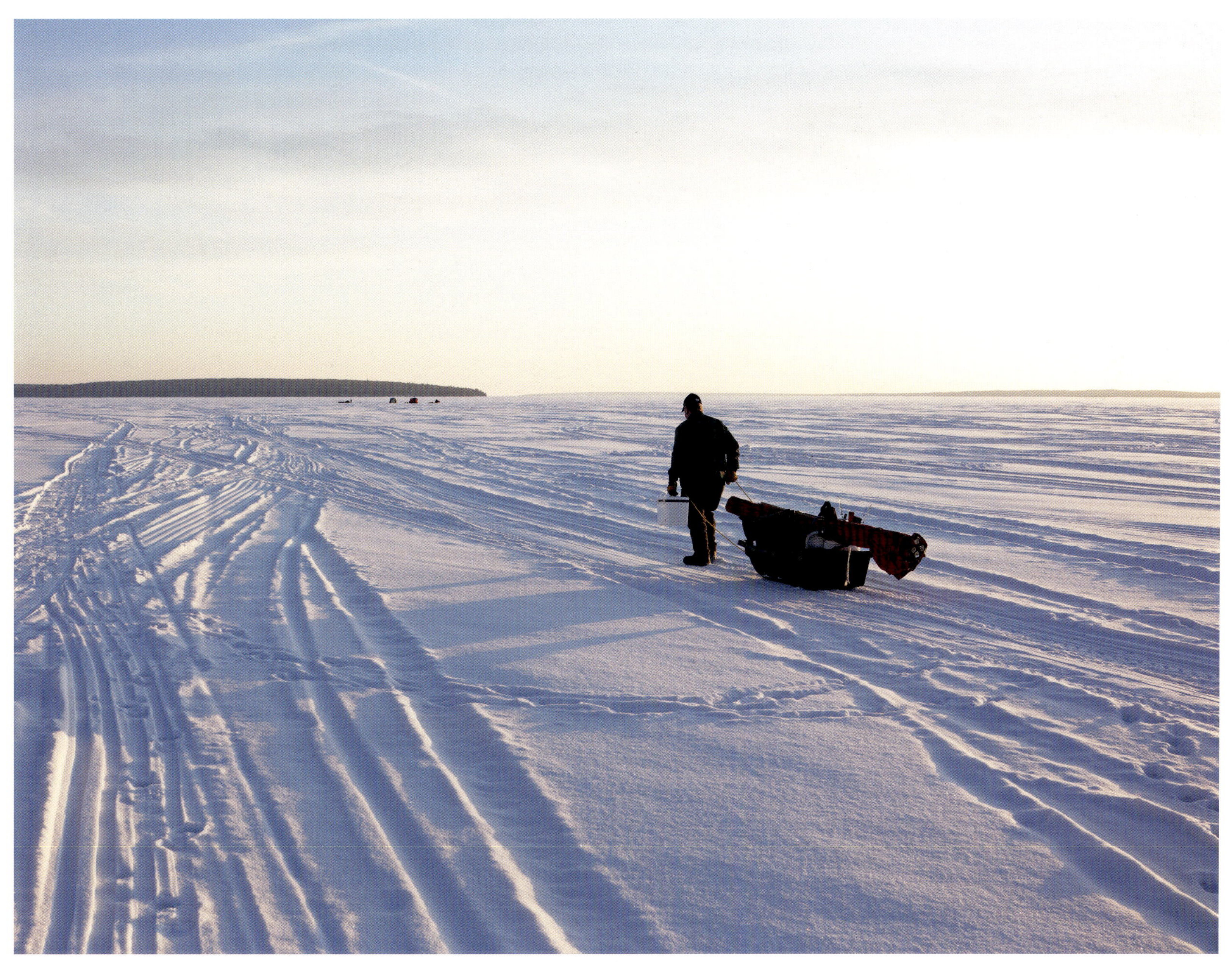

Ice fisherman, Apostle Islands, Wisconsin, 2022

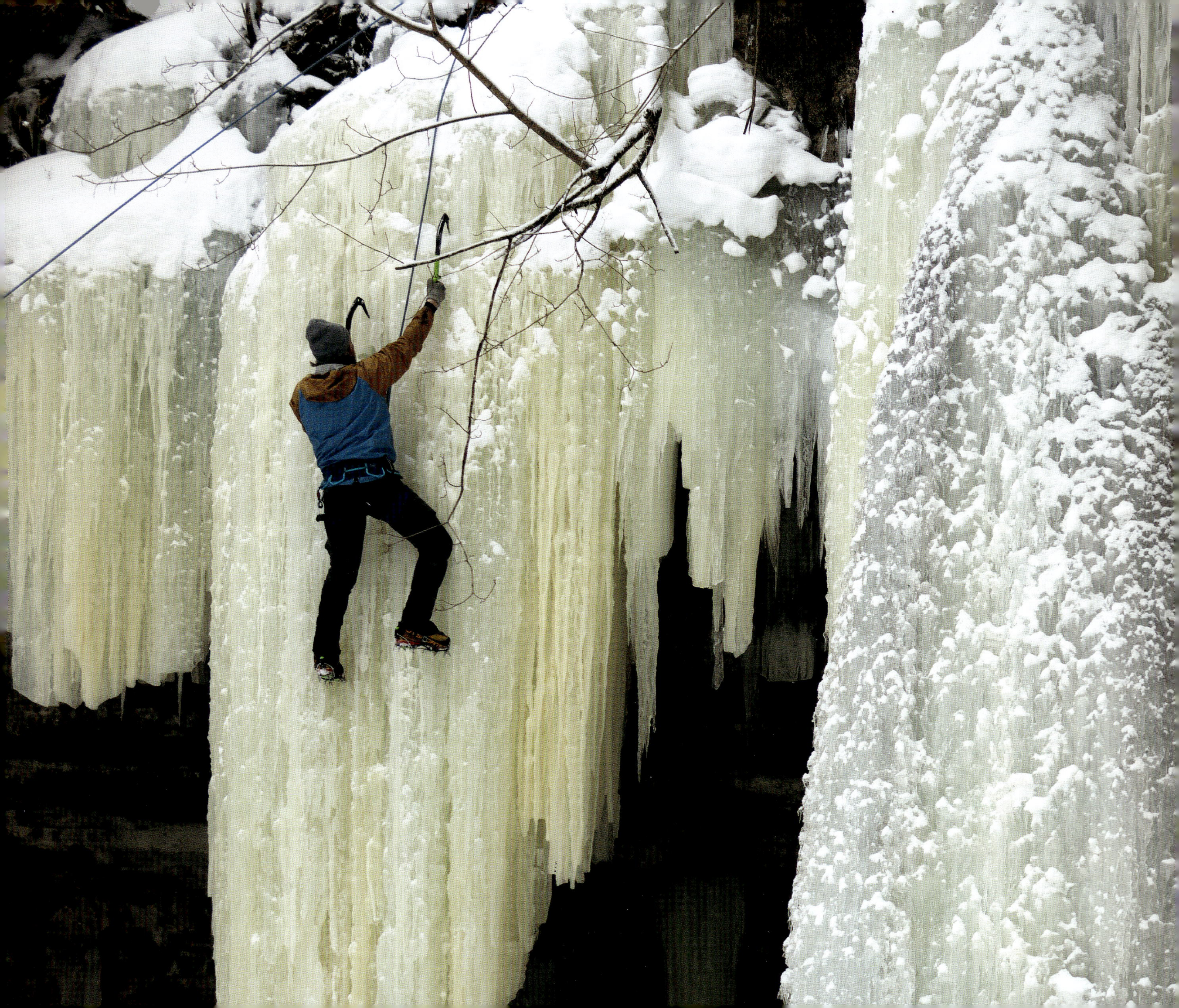

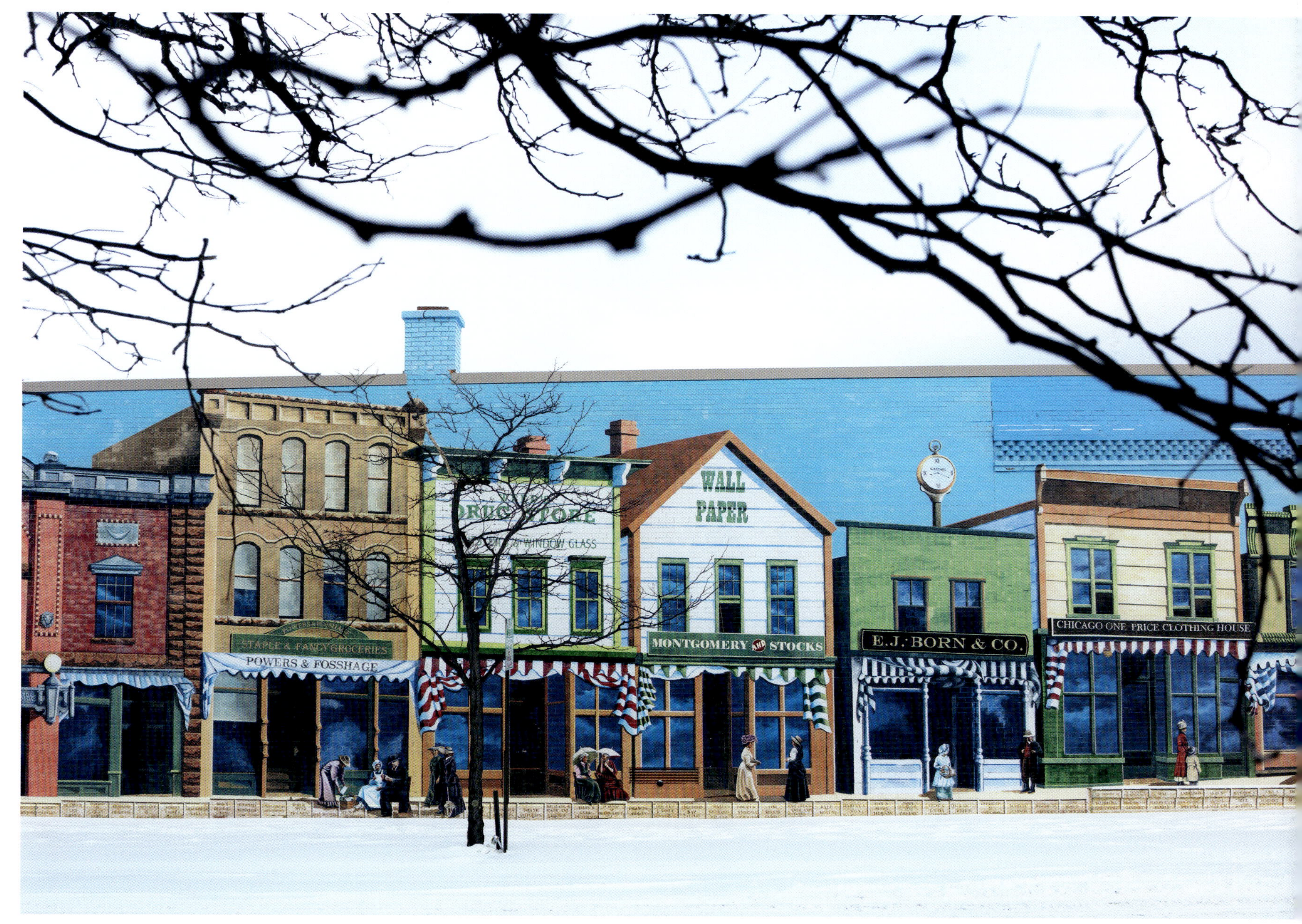

Mural, Ashland, Wisconsin, 2022

Ice climber, Munising, Michigan, 2022

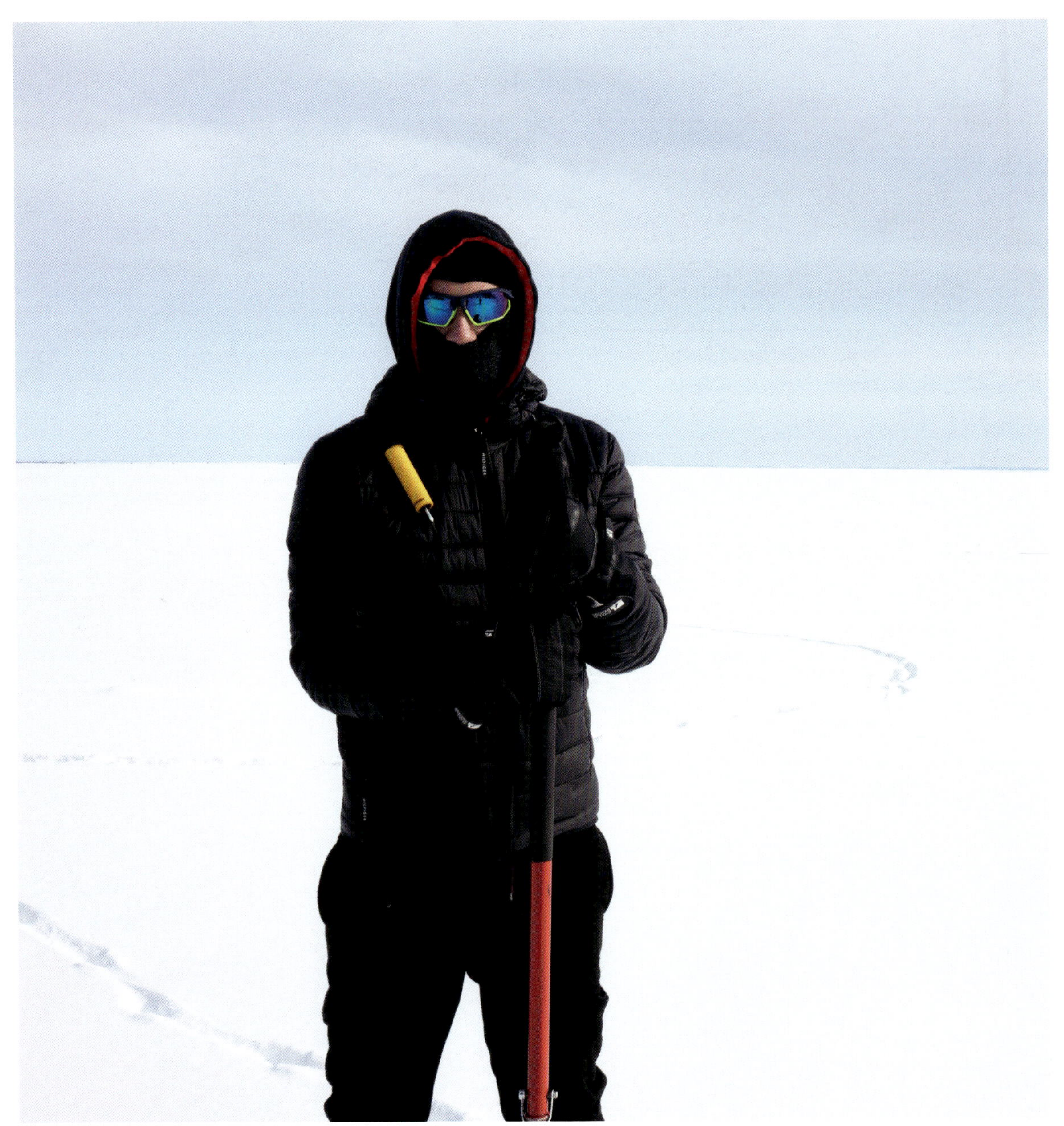

Dallas (ice guide), Apostle Islands, Wisconsin, 2022

South Channel, Bayfield County, Wisconsin, 2022

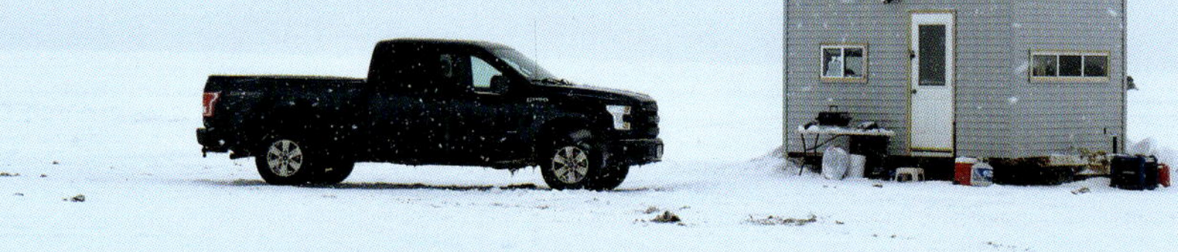

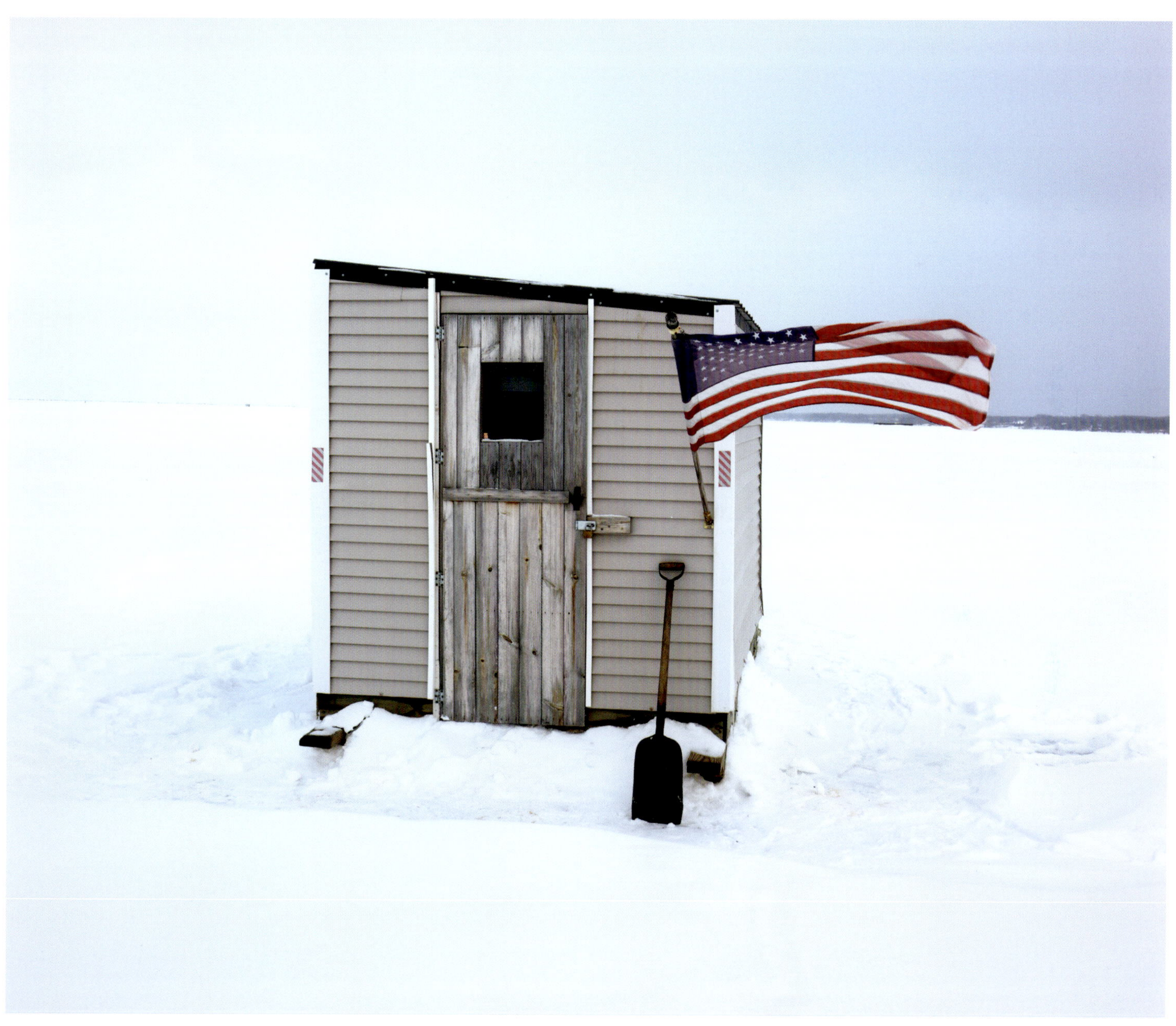

Ice fishing shanty, Chequamegon Bay, Wisconsin, 2022

Ice fishing shanty (with truck), Chequamegon Bay, Wisconsin, 2022

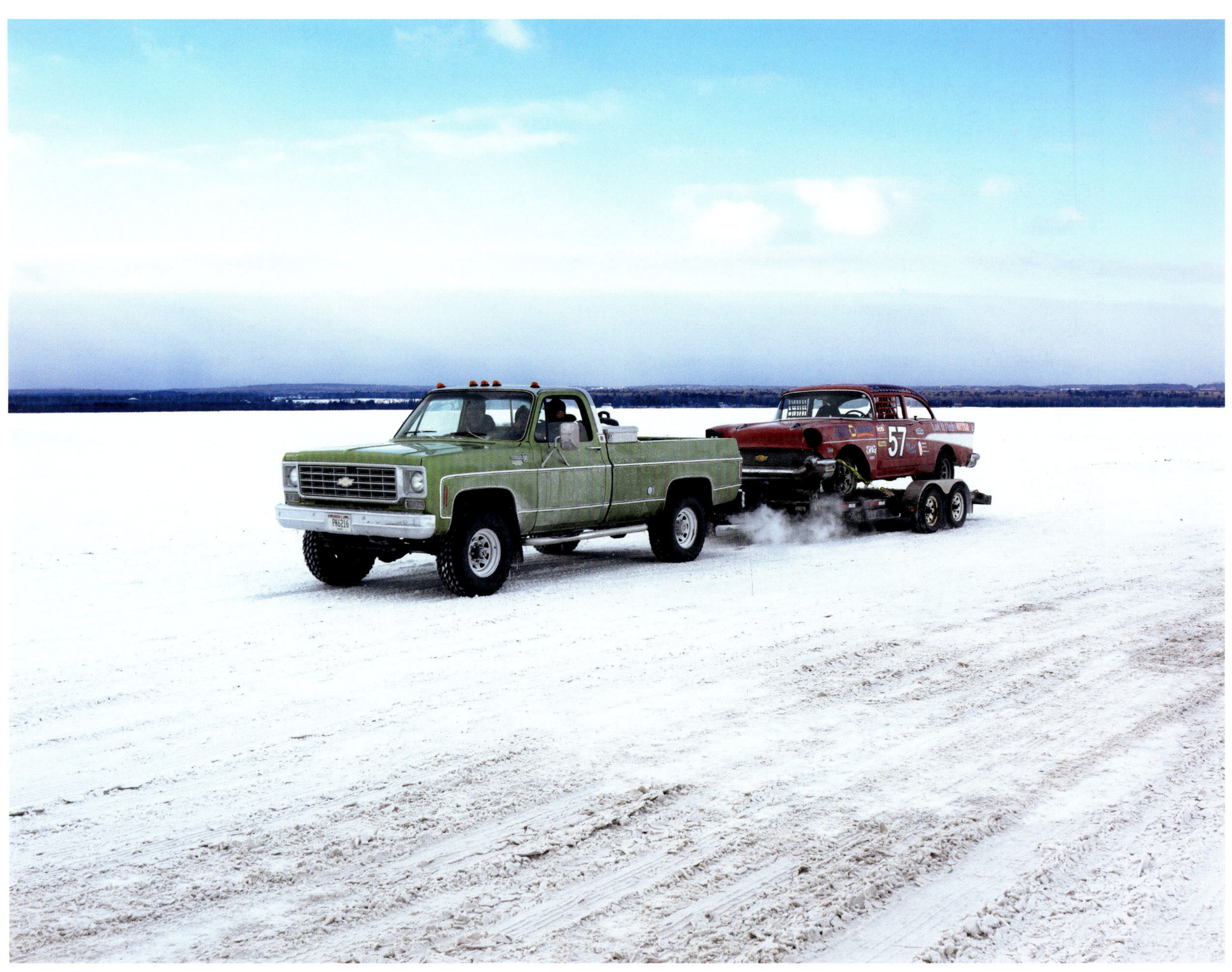

Ice races, Ashland County, Wisconsin, 2022

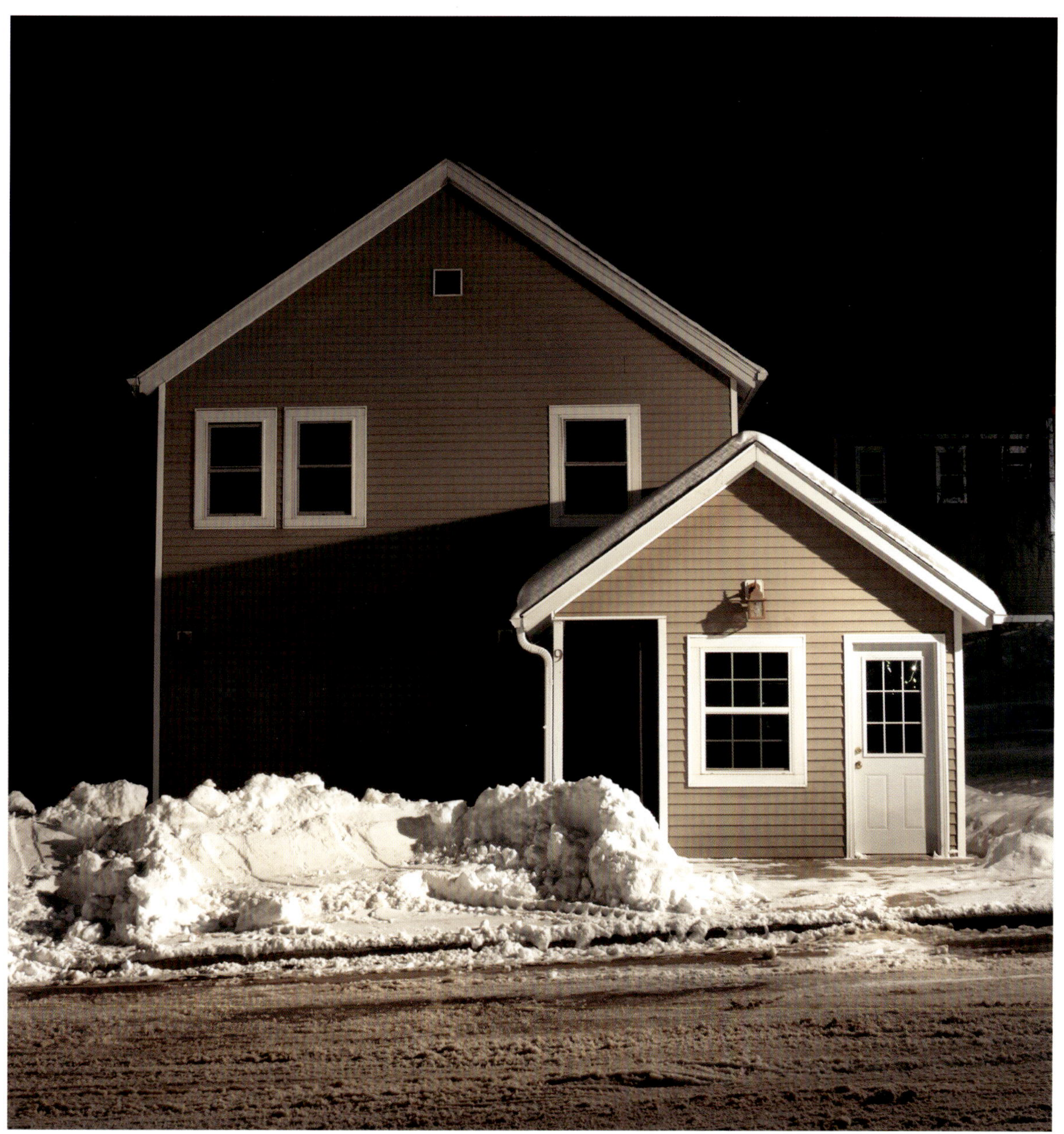

Bayfield, Wisconsin, 2022

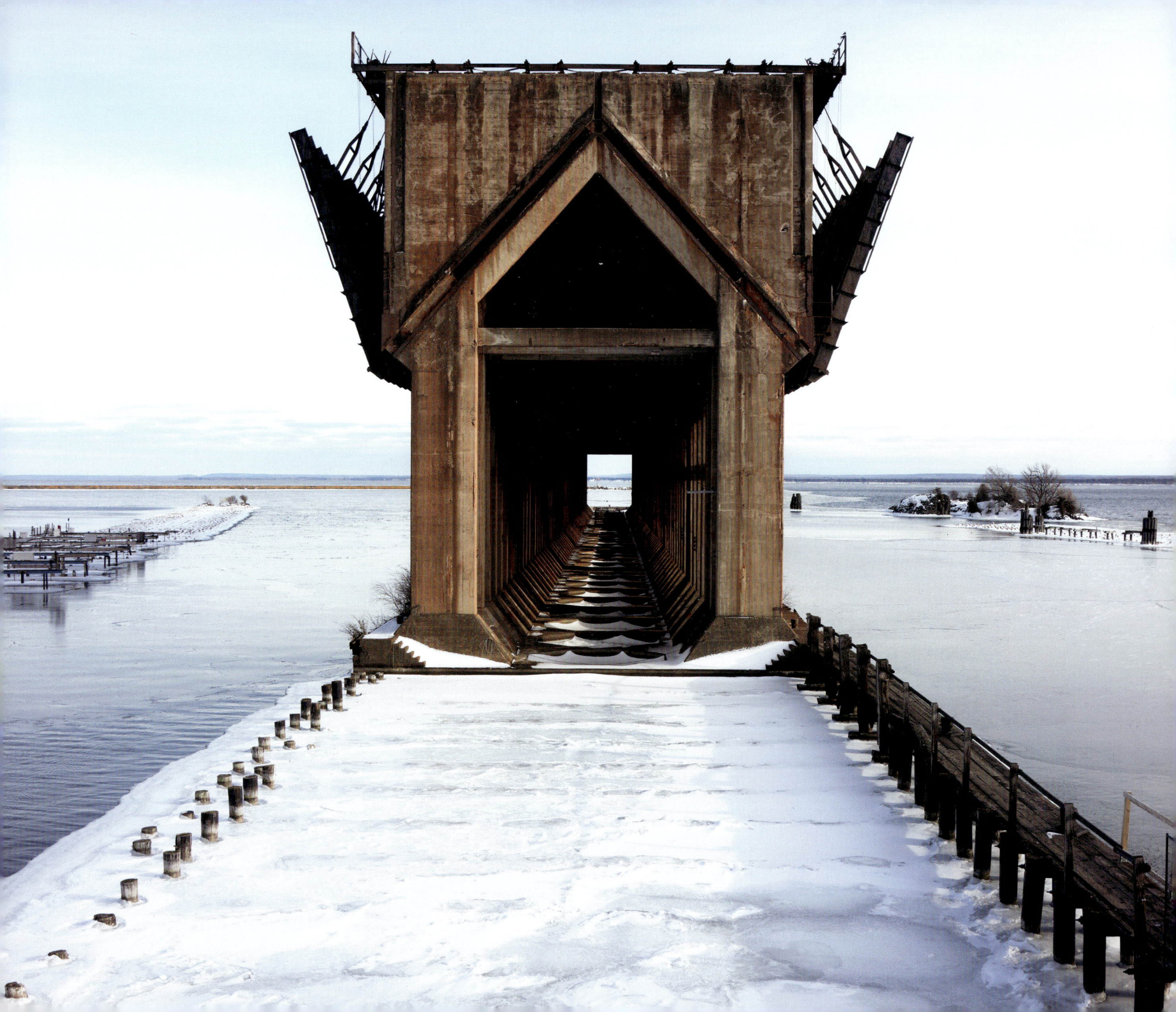

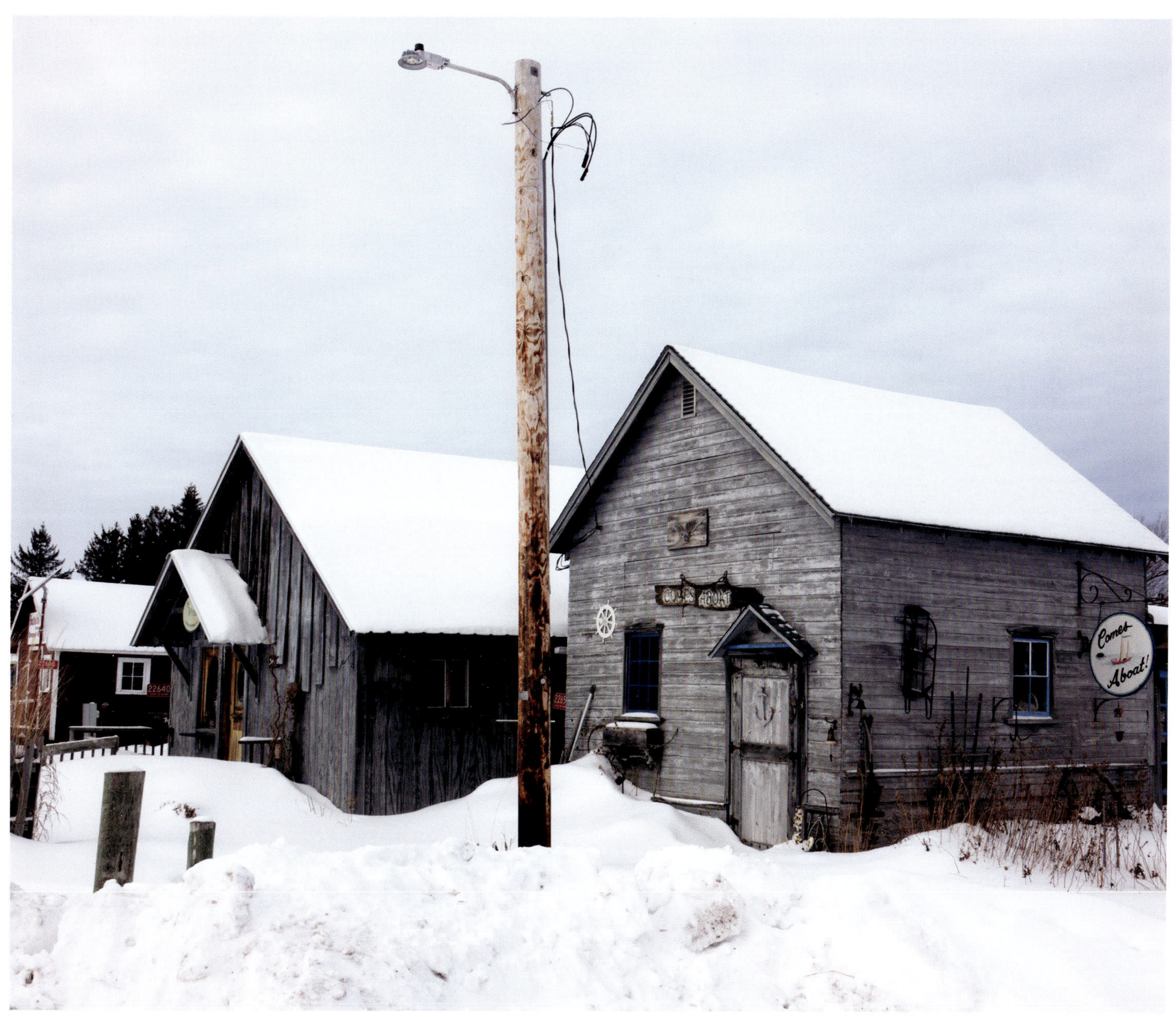

Cornucopia, Wisconsin, 2022

Iron ore dock, Marquette Bay, Michigan, 2022

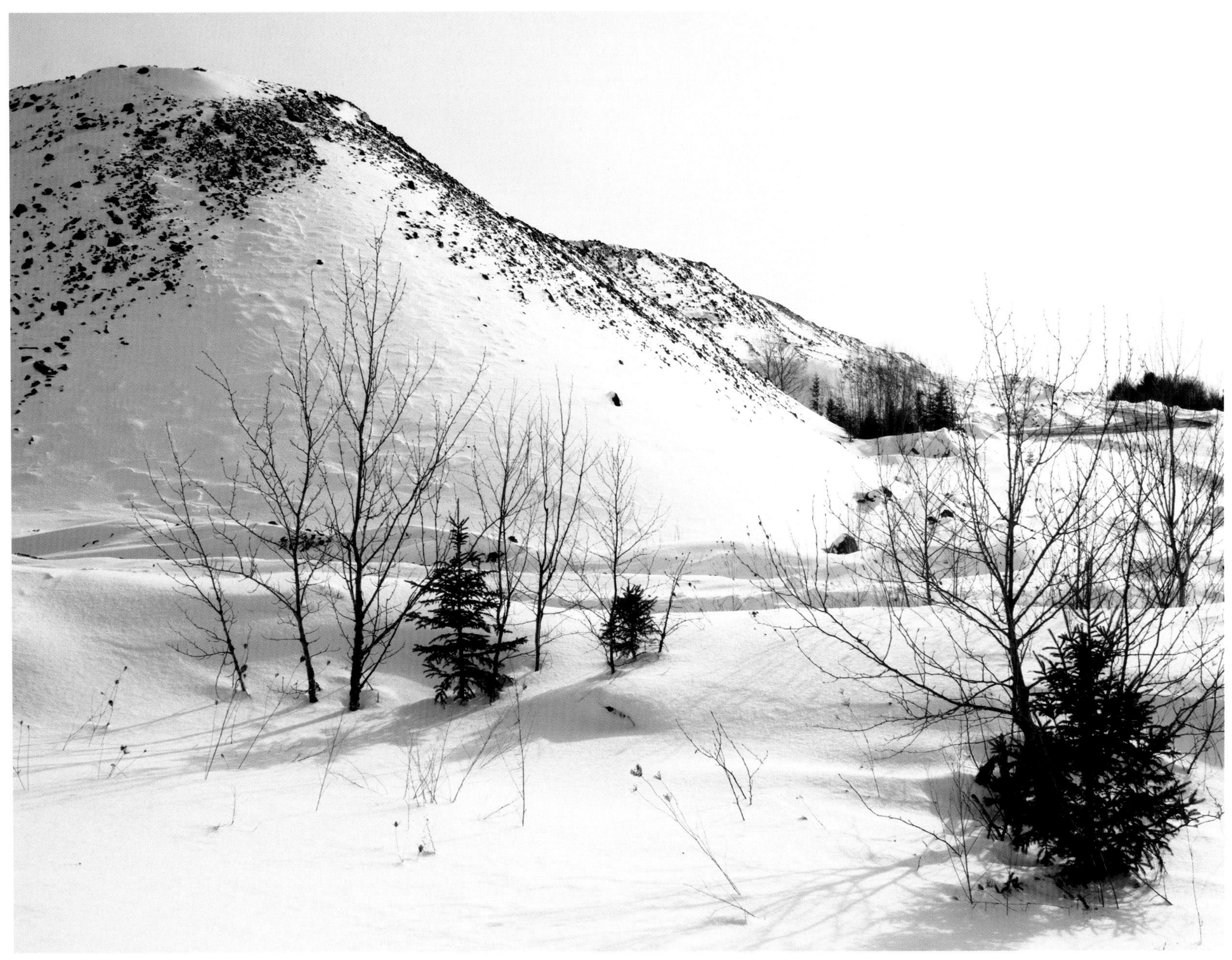

Iron ore mine tailings, Marquette County, Michigan, 2022

Hiawatha National Forest, Alger County, Michigan, 2022

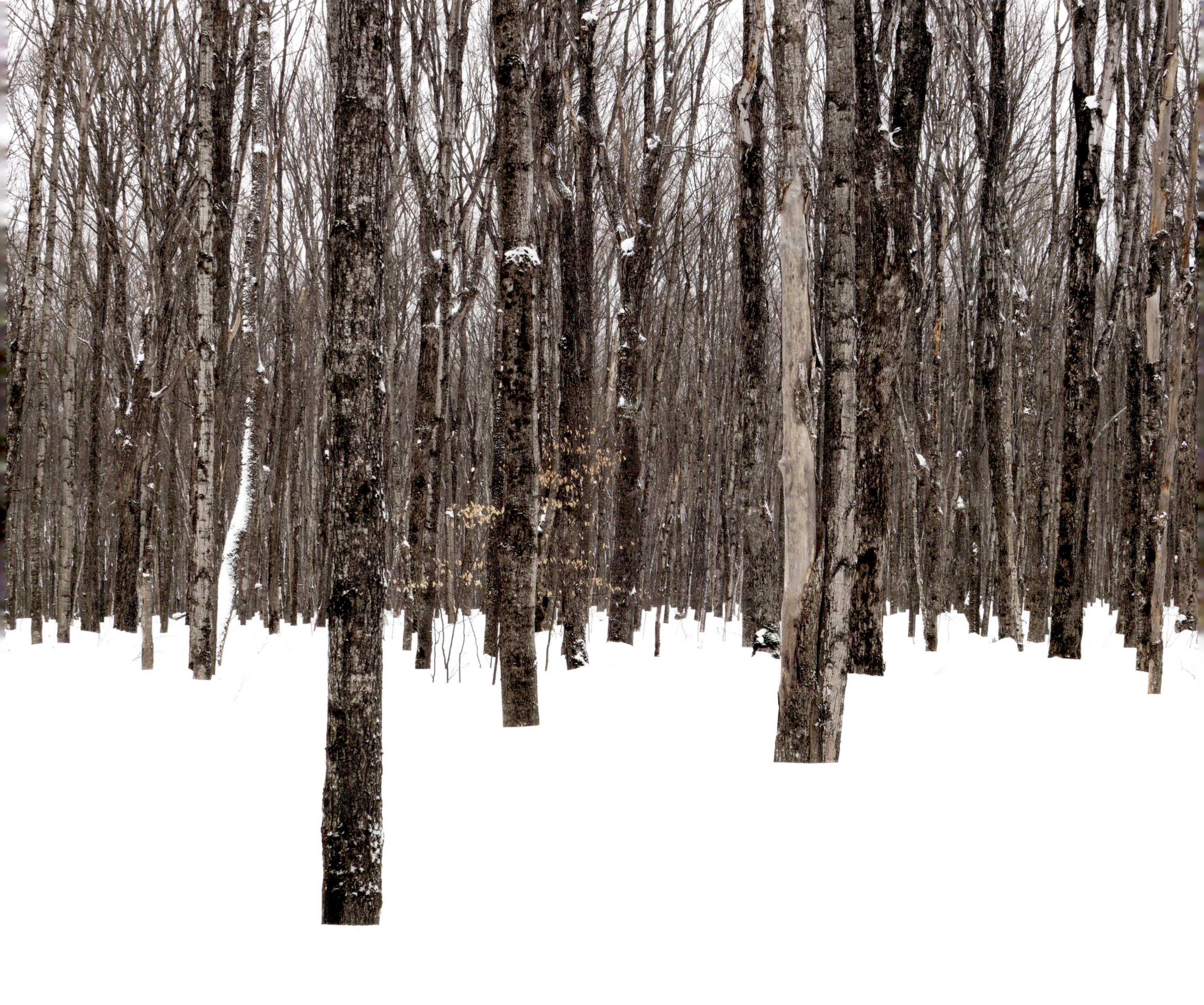

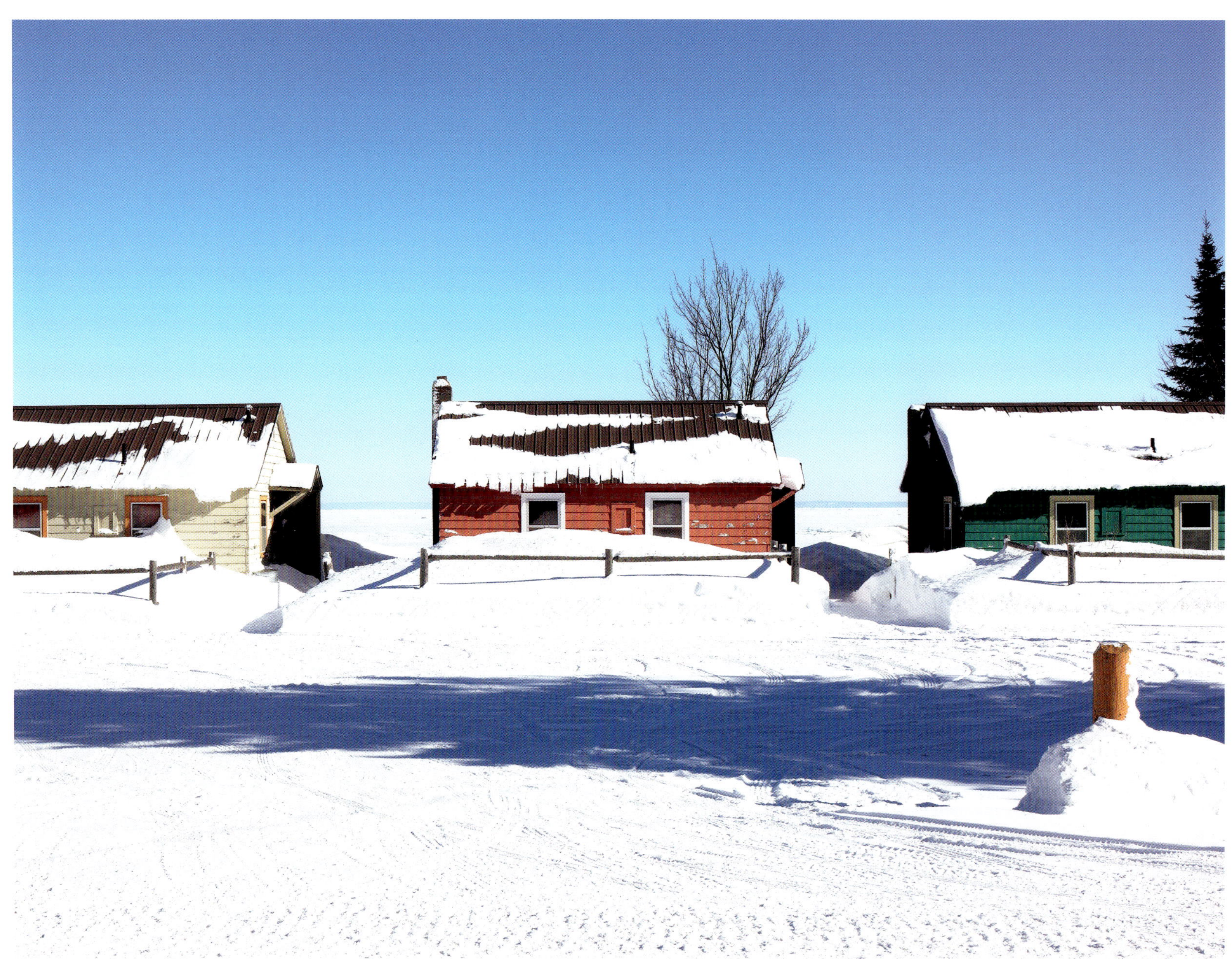

Summer cottages, Chippewa County, Michigan, 2022

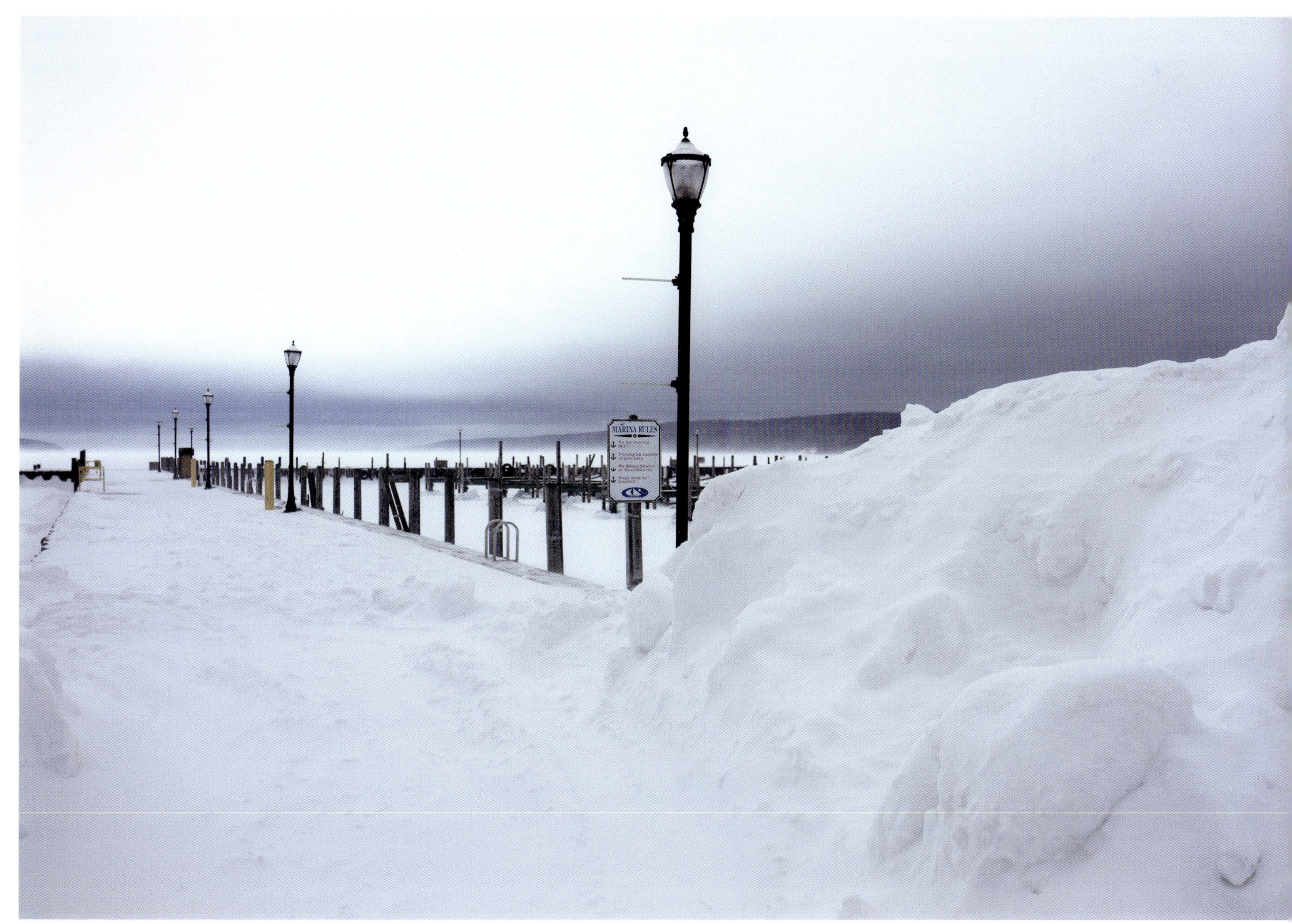

Marina, Munising, Michigan, 2022

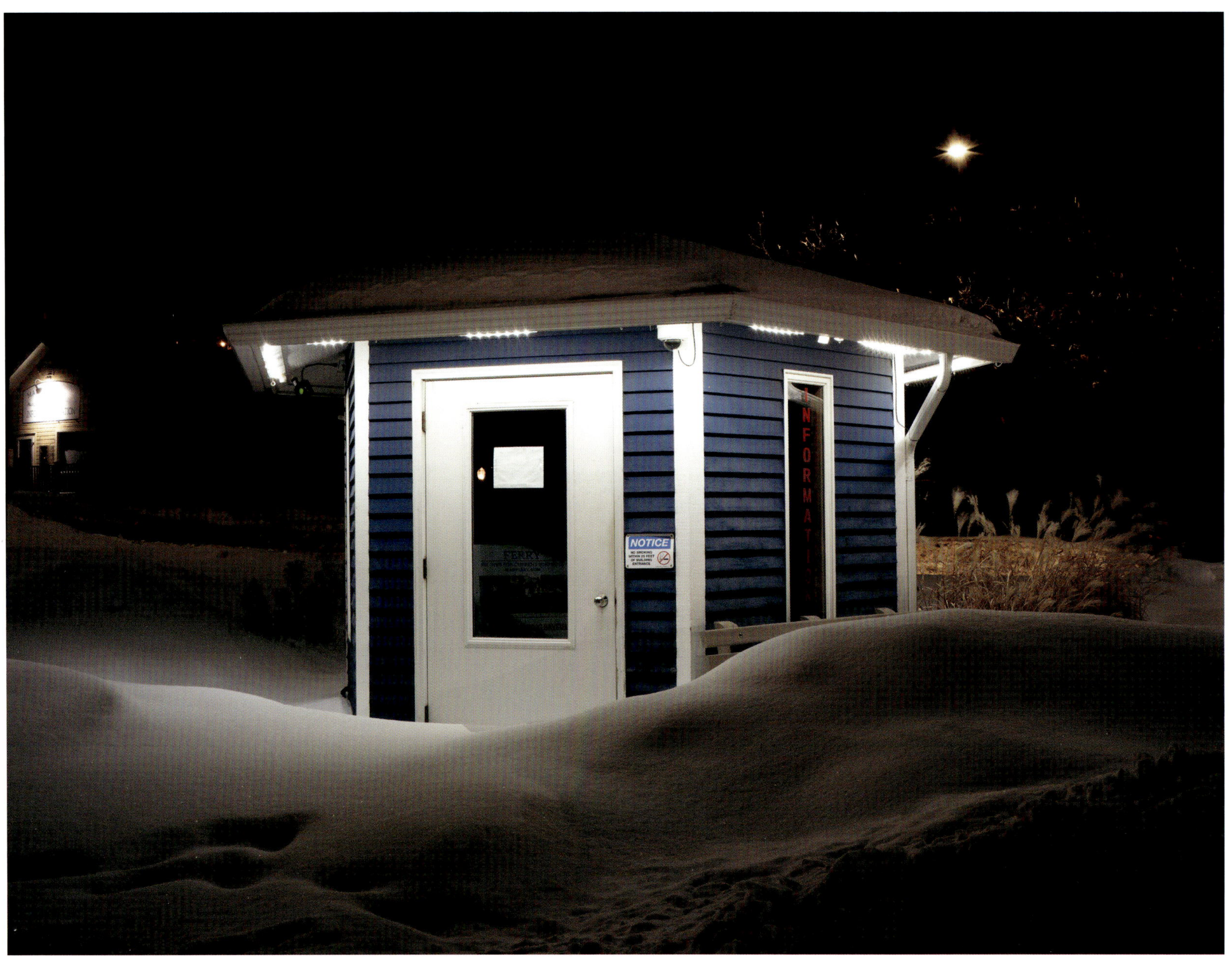

Tourist information booth, Bayfield, Wisconsin, 2022

Siskiwit Bay, Wisconsin, 2022

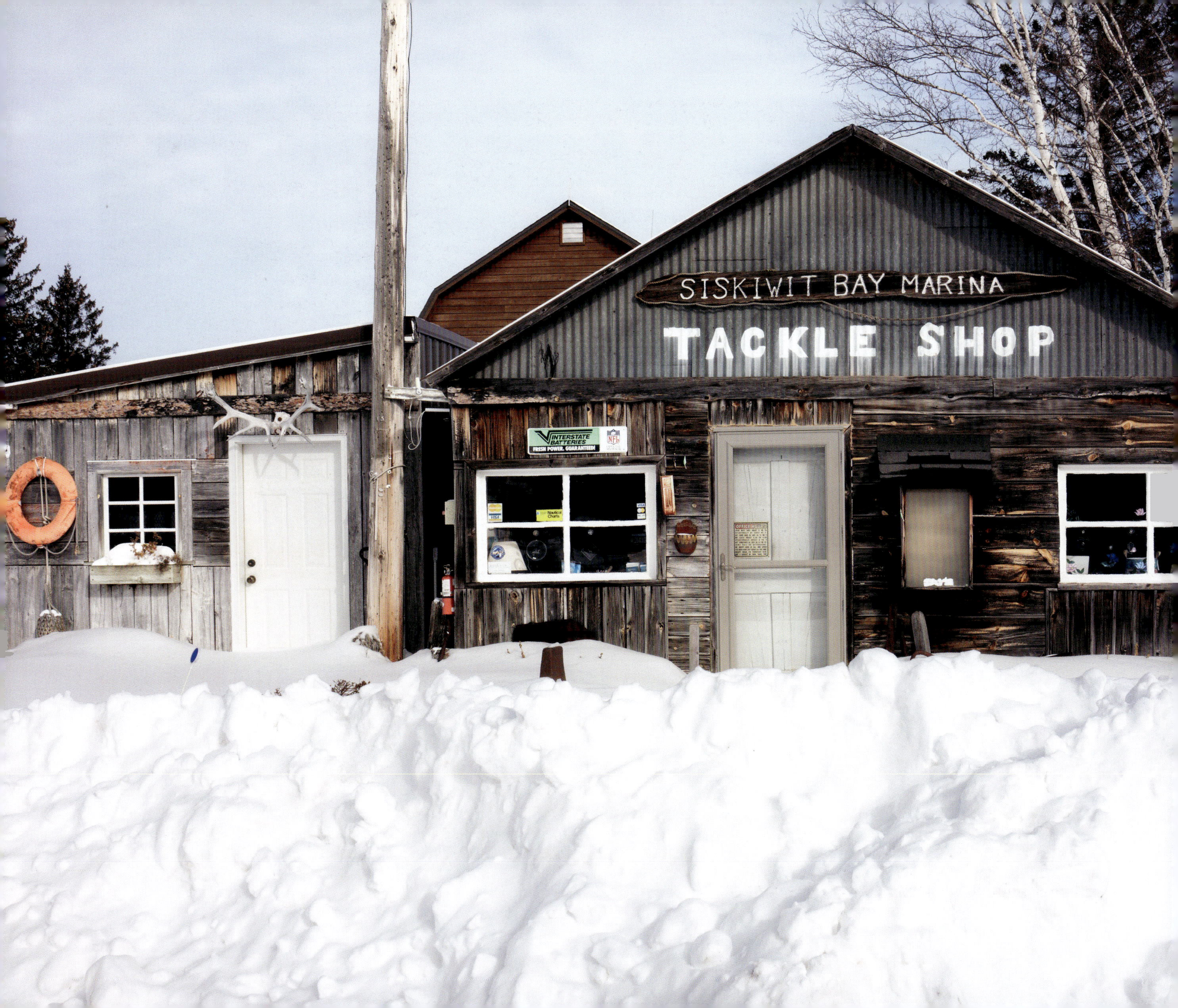
SISKIWIT BAY MARINA
TACKLE SHOP
INTERSTATE BATTERIES

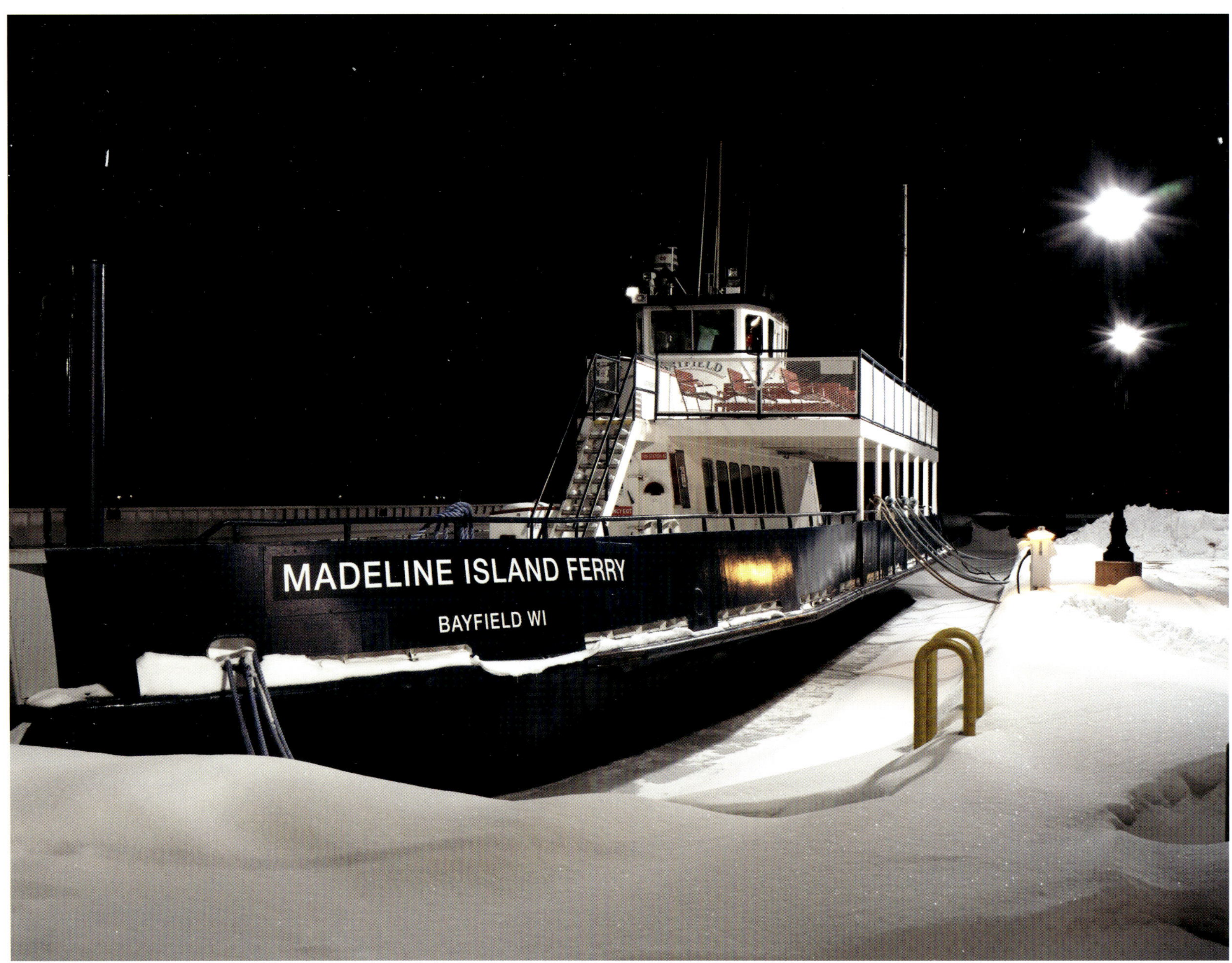

Ferryboat, Bayfield County, Wisconsin, 2022

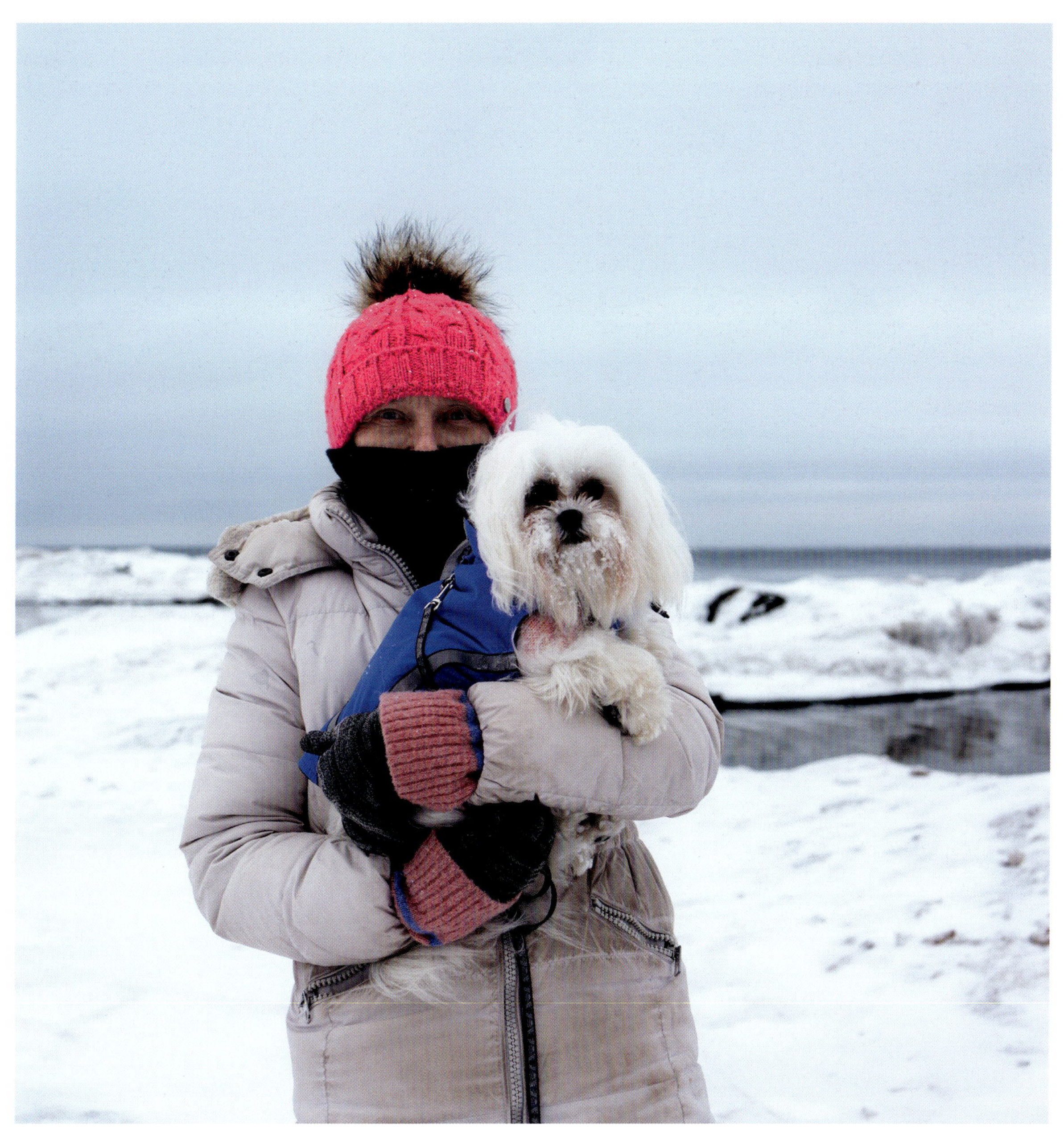

Carole and Shadow, Marquette, Michigan, 2022

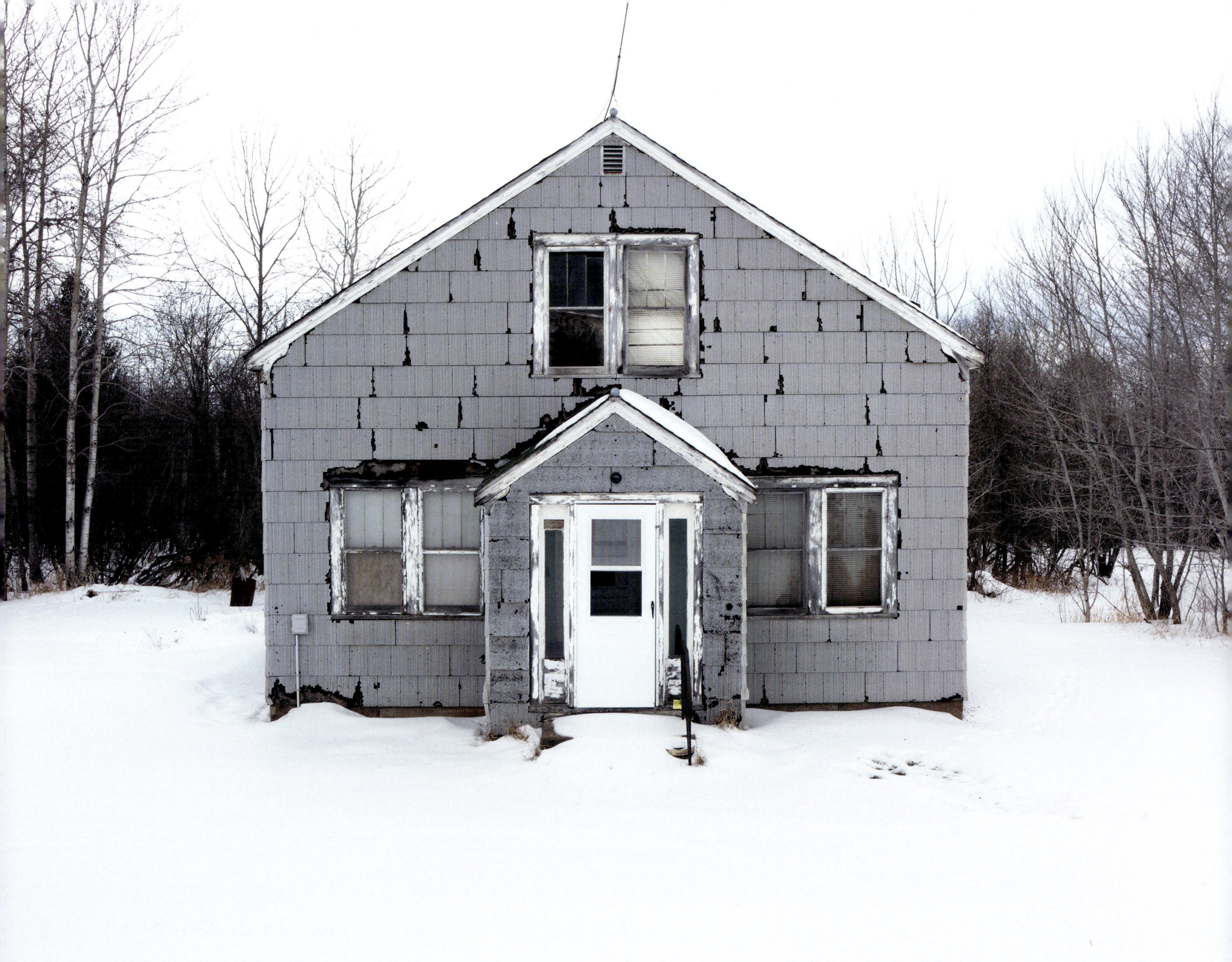

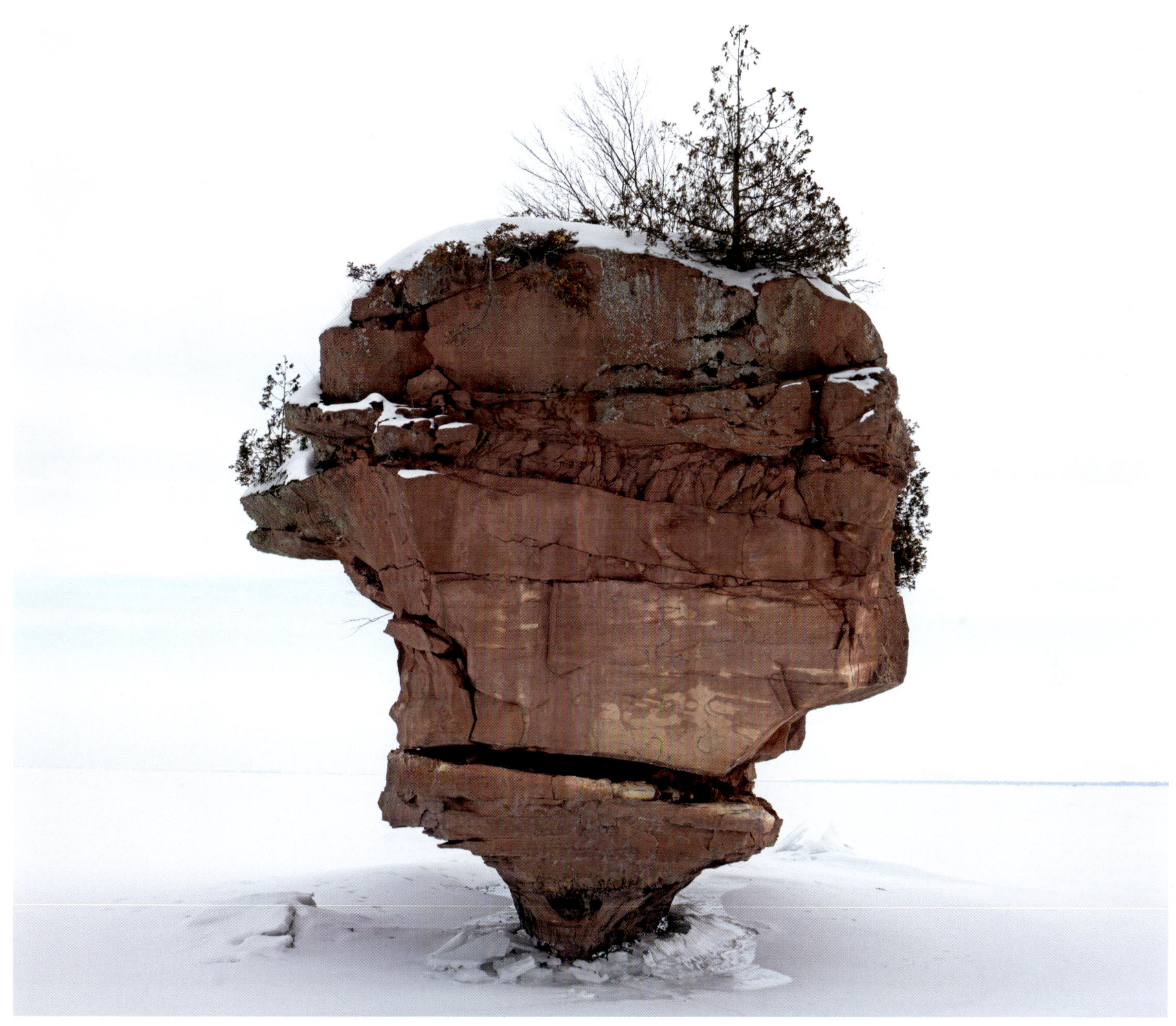

Apostle Islands, Wisconsin, 2022

Douglas County, Wisconsin, 2022

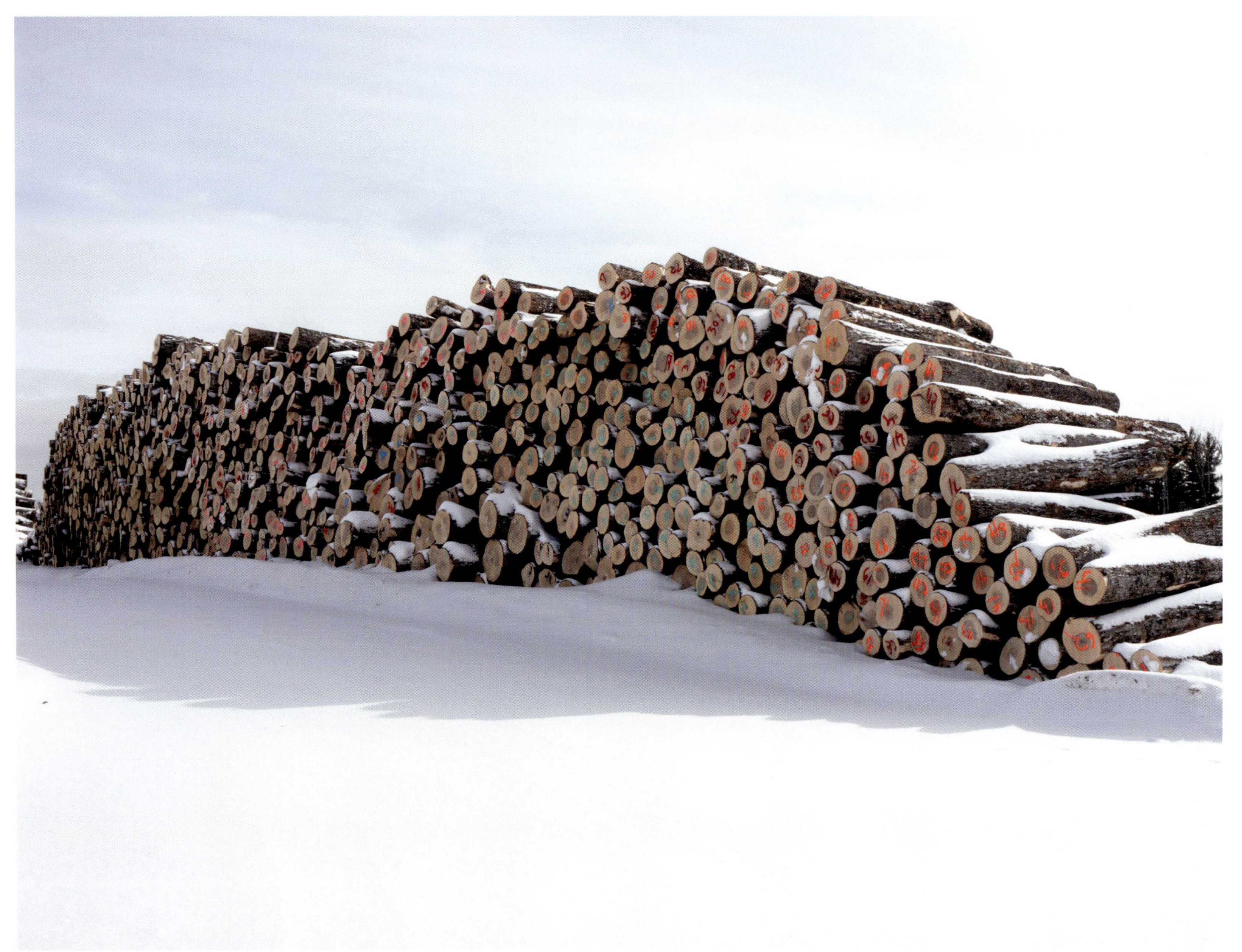

Mill logs, Alger County, Michigan, 2022

Power plant, Ashland County, Wisconsin, 2022

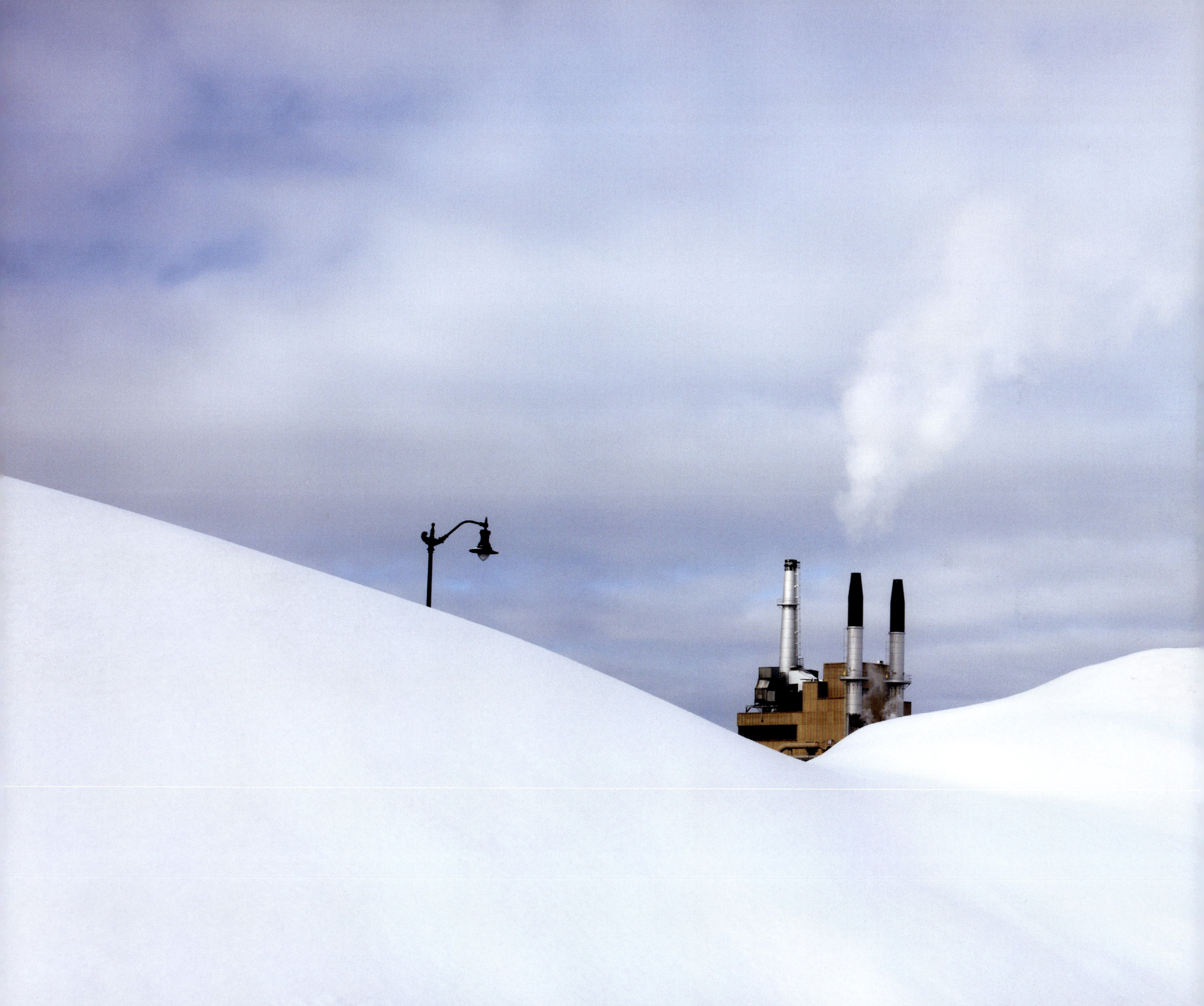

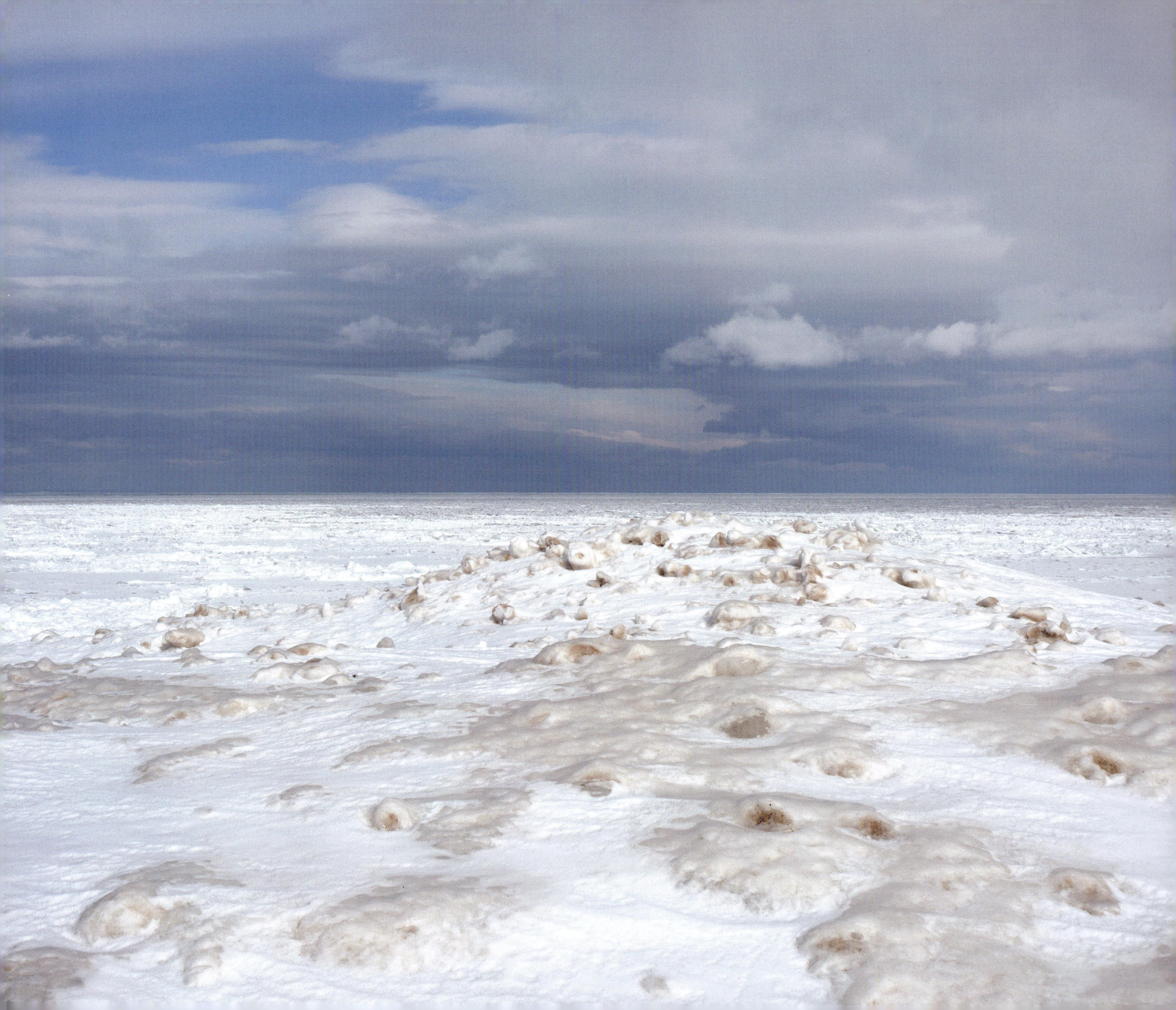

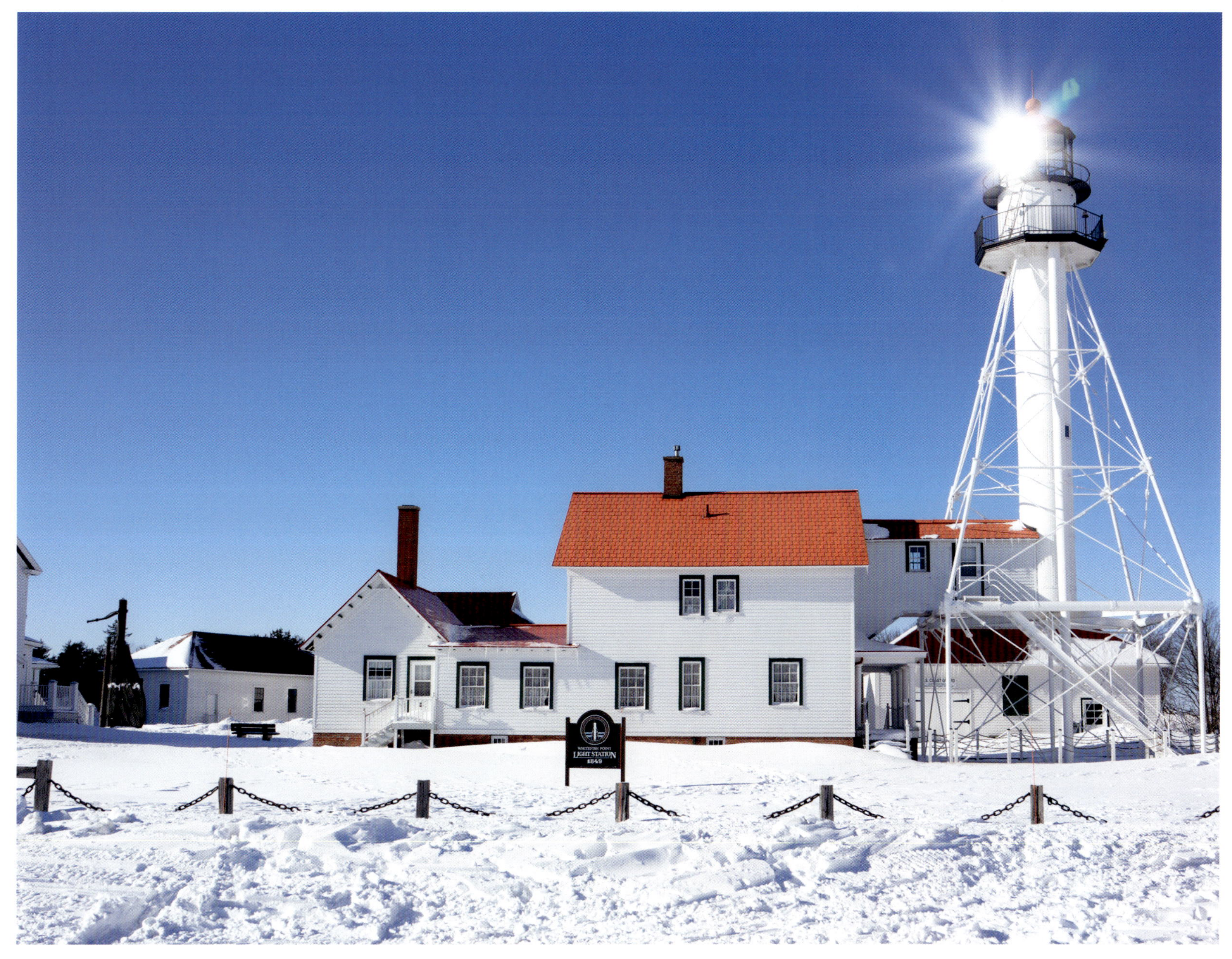

Lighthouse, Whitefish Point, Michigan, 2022

Port Wing, Wisconsin, 2022

SPRING

LAKE MICHIGAN

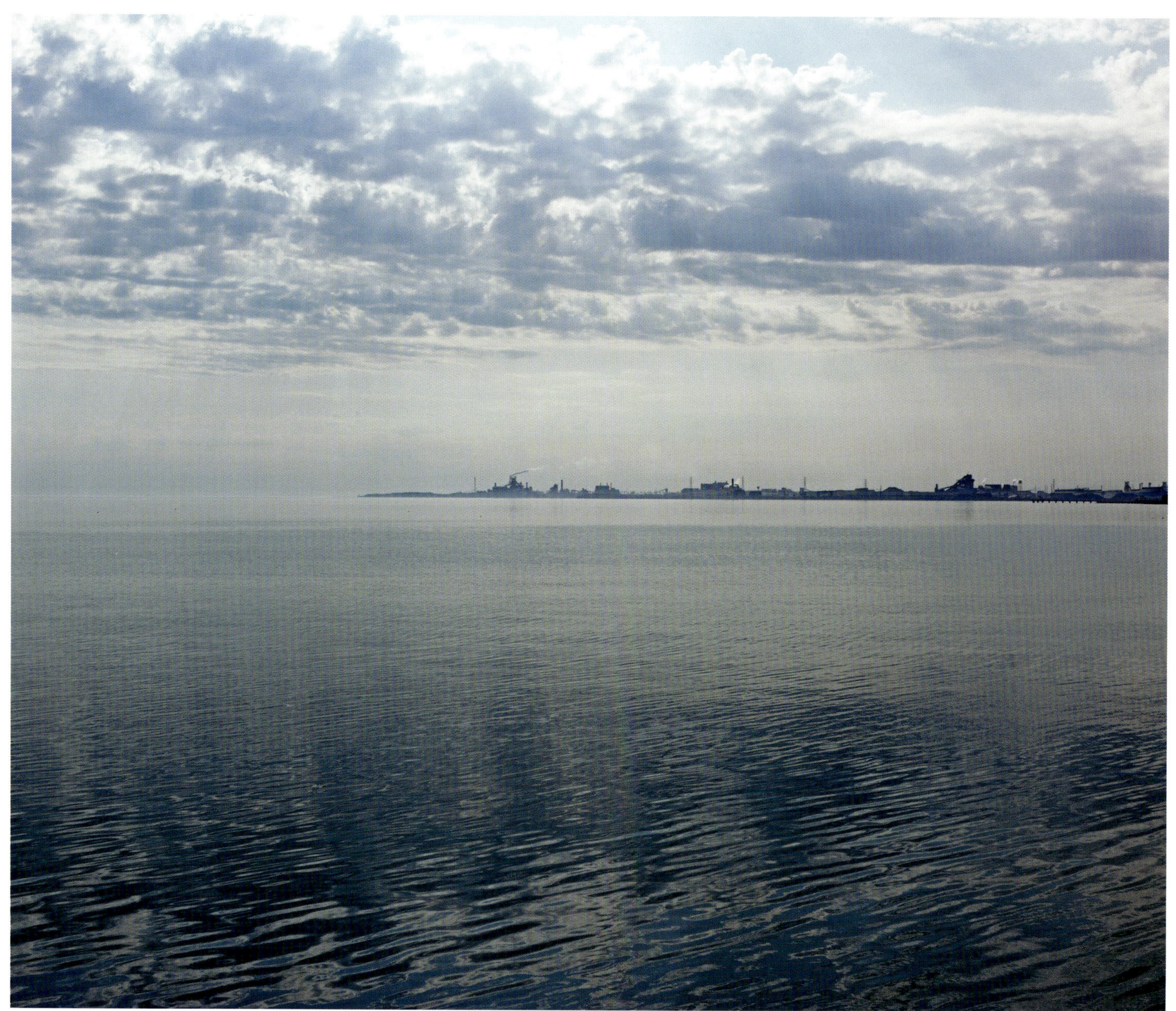
Industrial lagoon, Hammond, Indiana, 2022

City park, Petoskey, Michigan, 2023

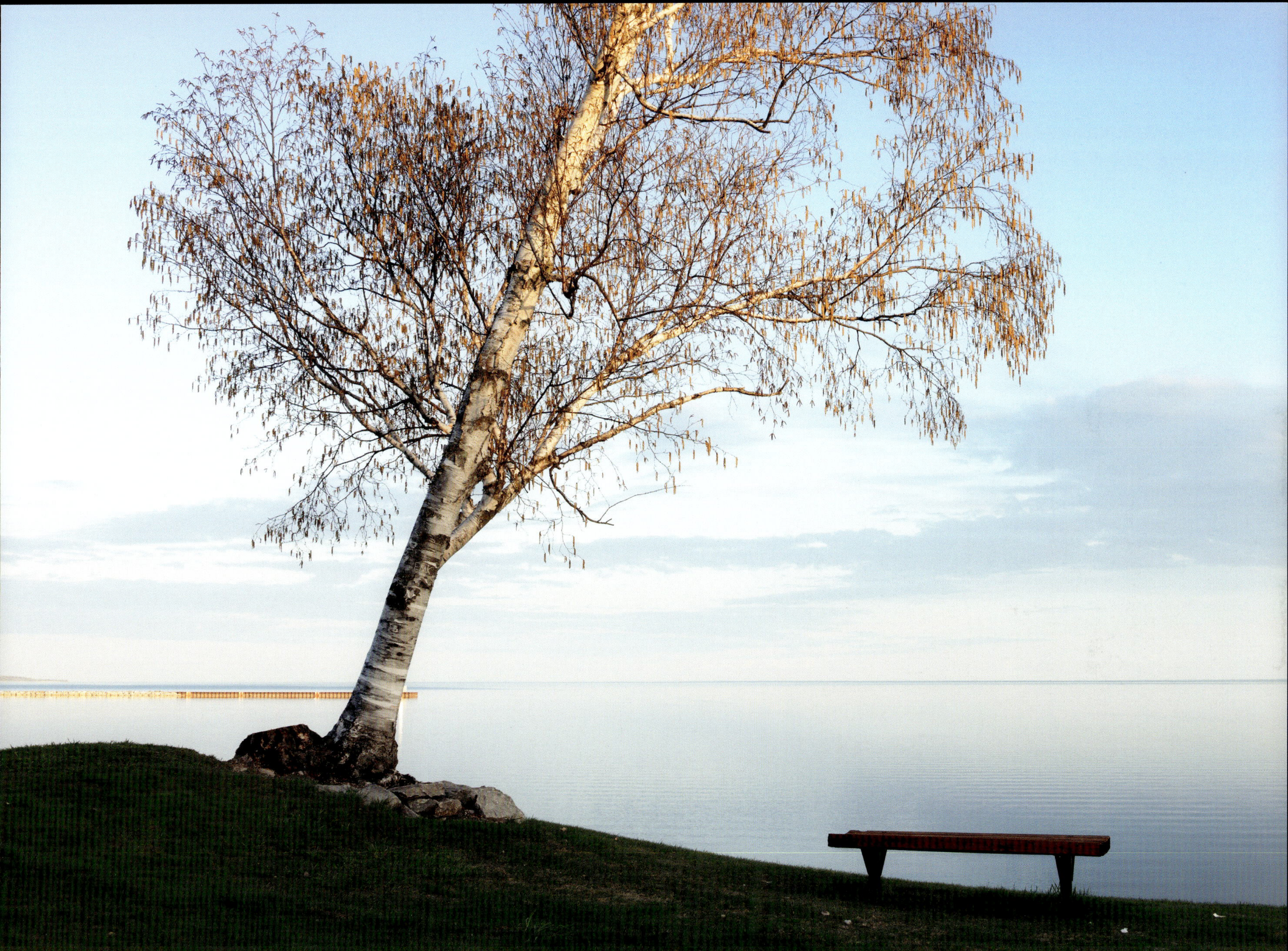

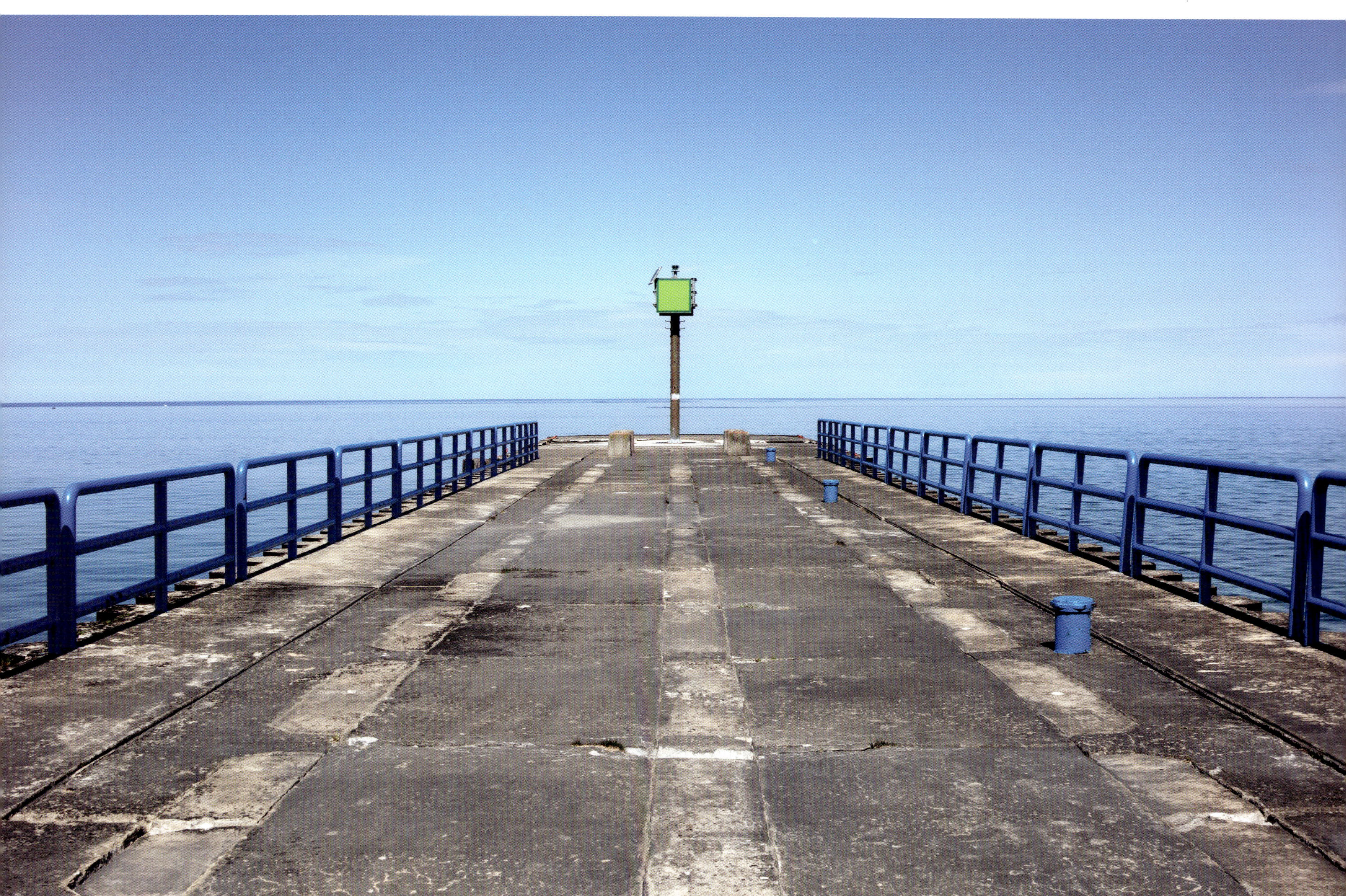

Pier, Charlevoix, Michigan, 2023

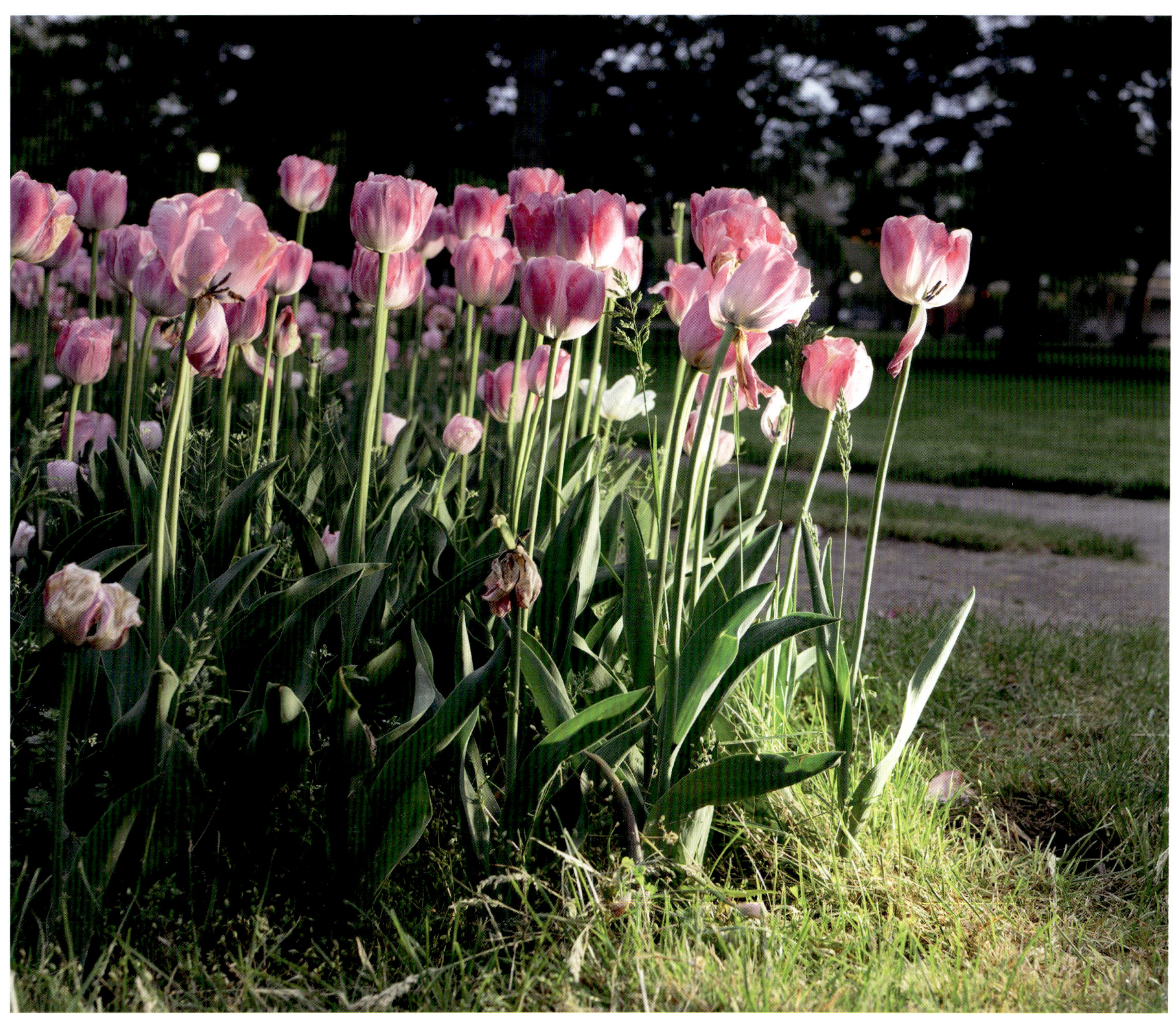

Tulip festival, Holland, Michigan, 2023

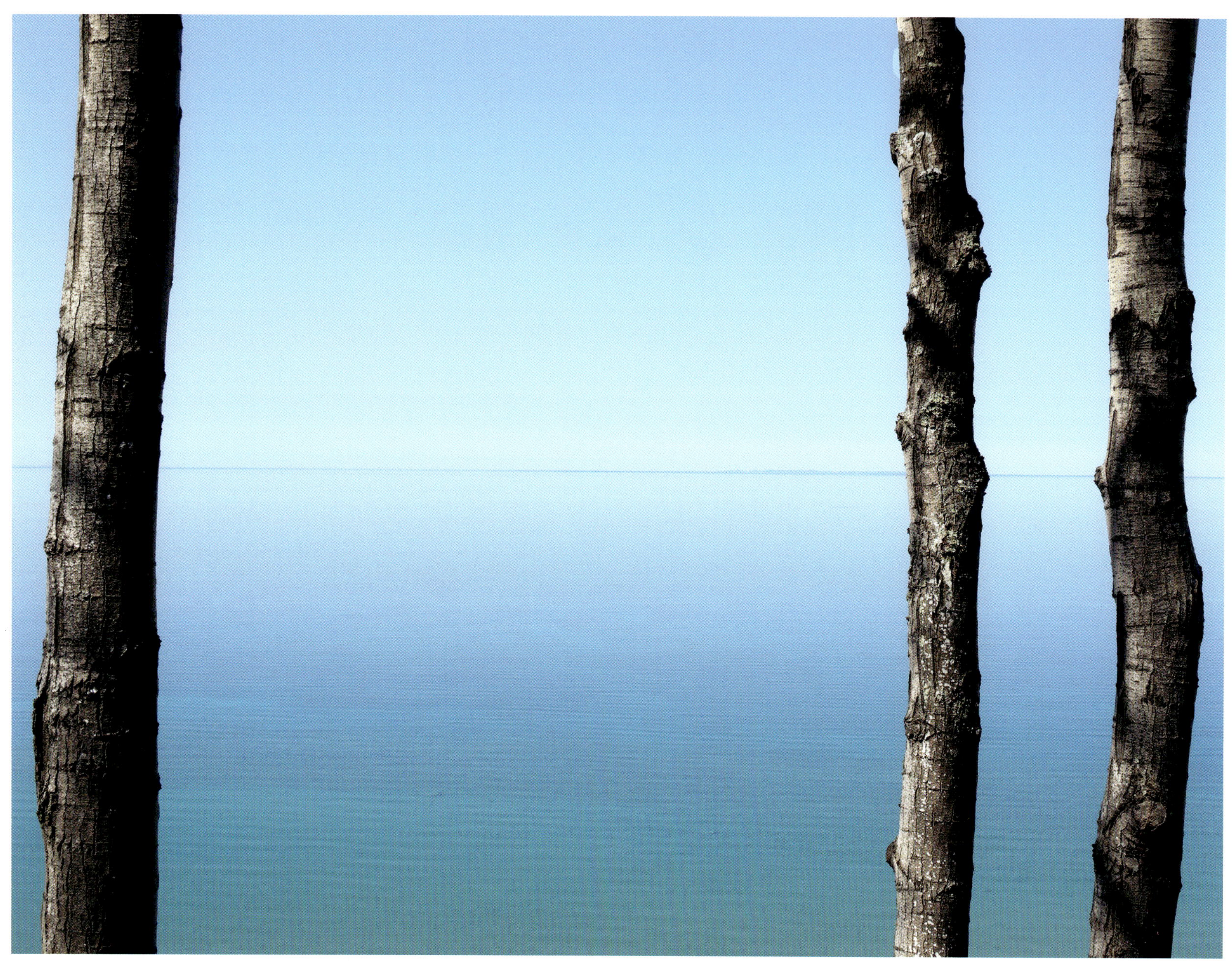

Silver birch, Harbor Springs, Michigan, 2023

City park, Chicago, Illinois, 2022

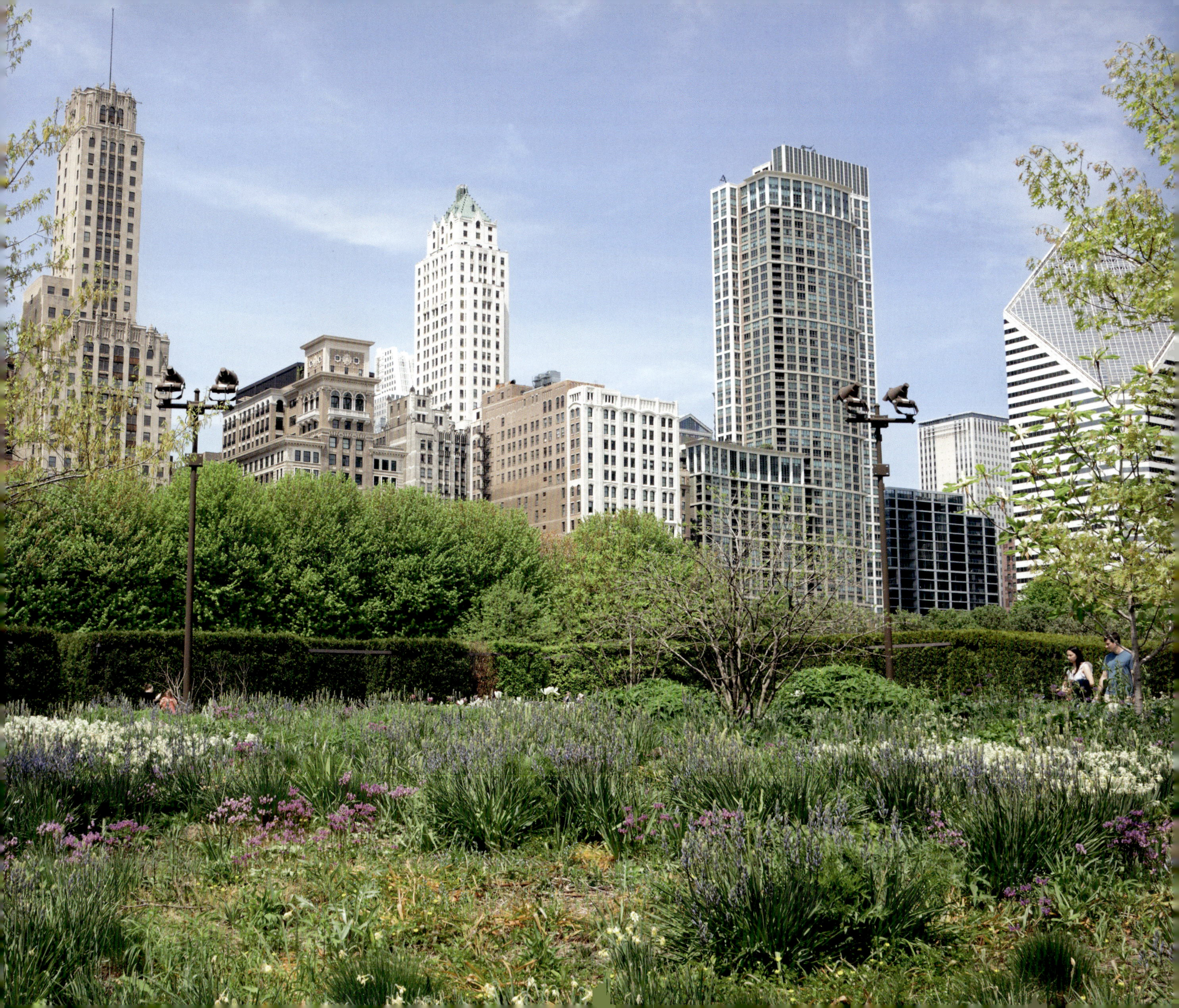

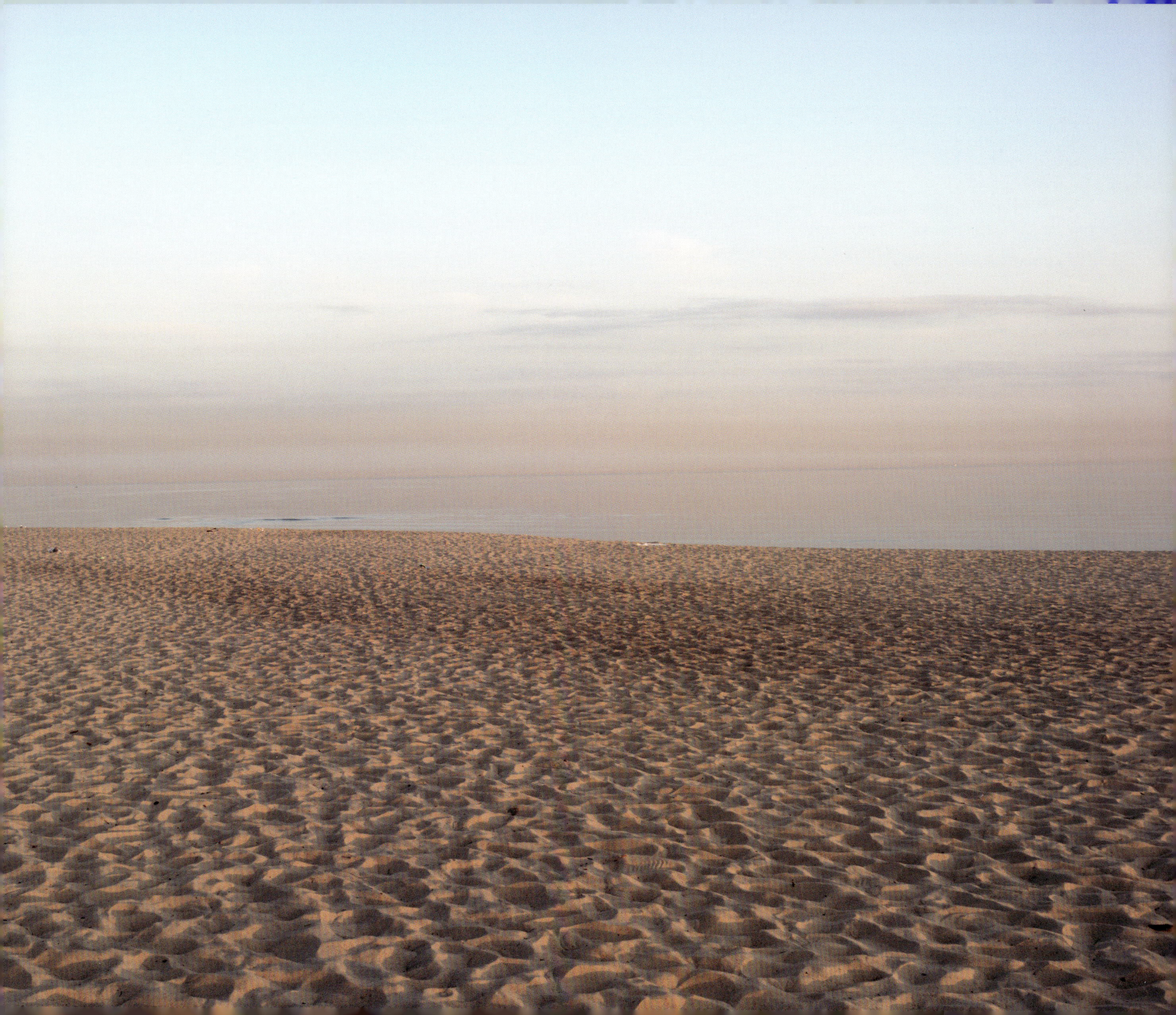

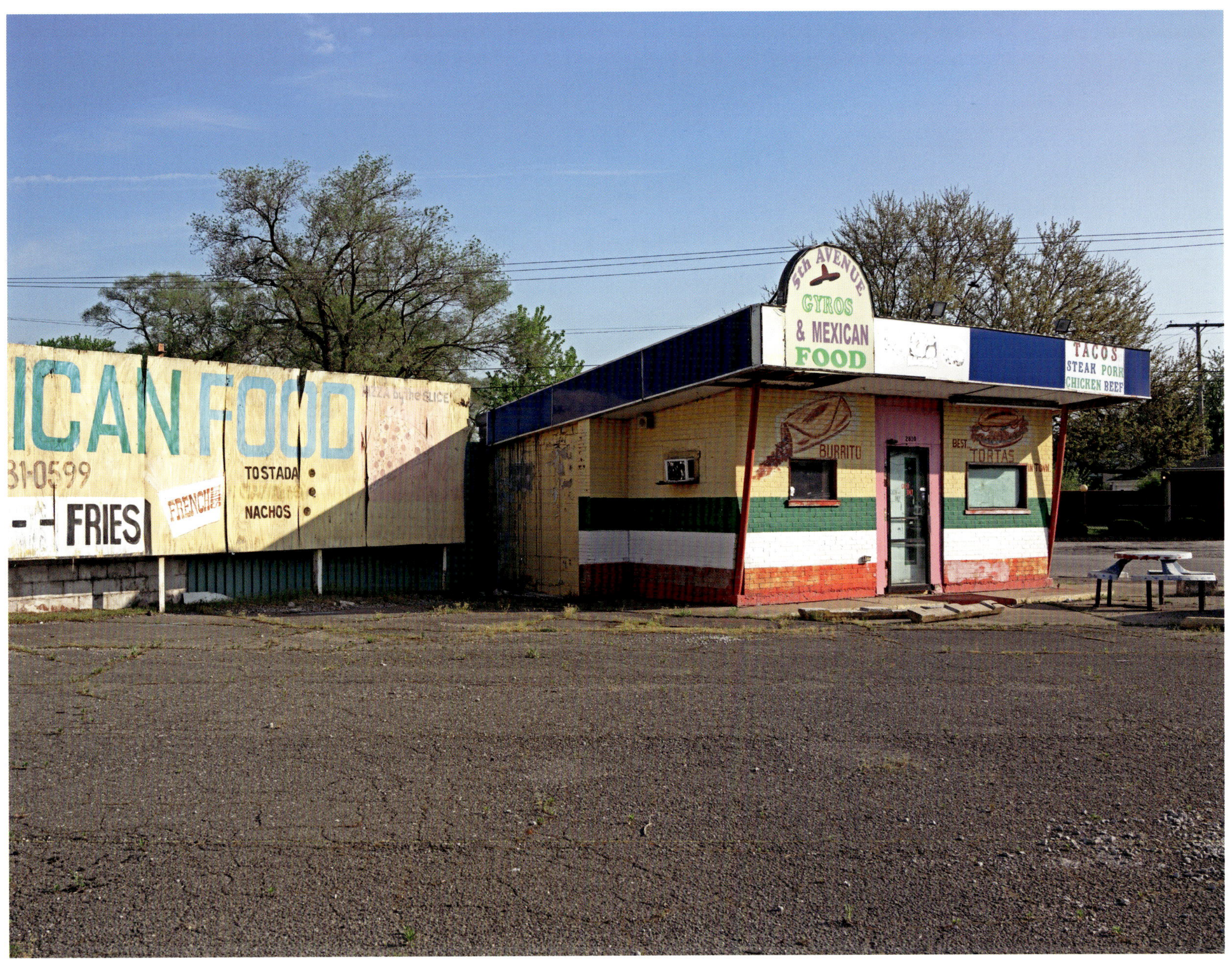

East Chicago, Indiana, 2023

Smog layer, Lake County, Indiana, 2022

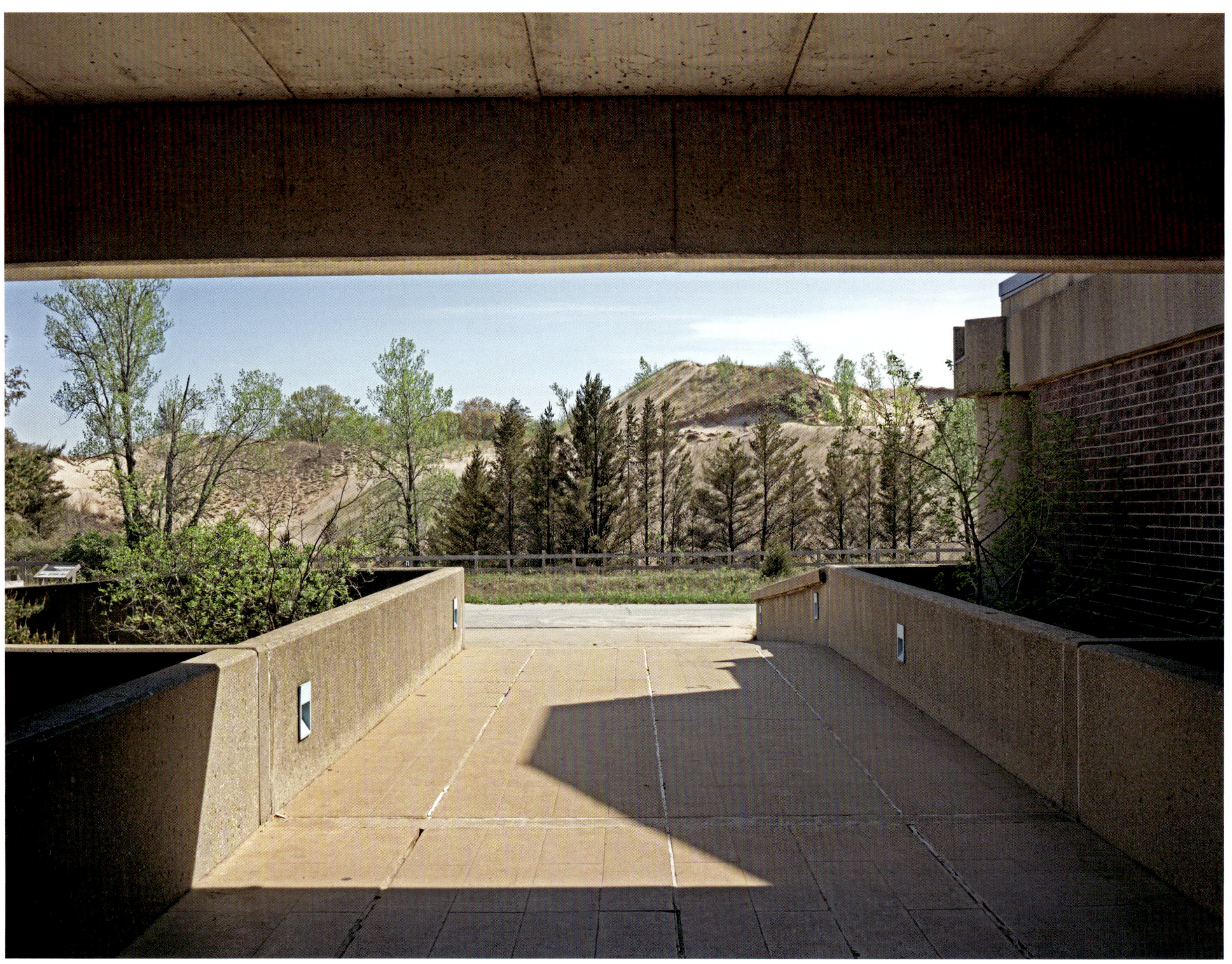

Visitors' center, Indiana Dunes, Indiana, 2022

Big Rock Point, Michigan, 2023

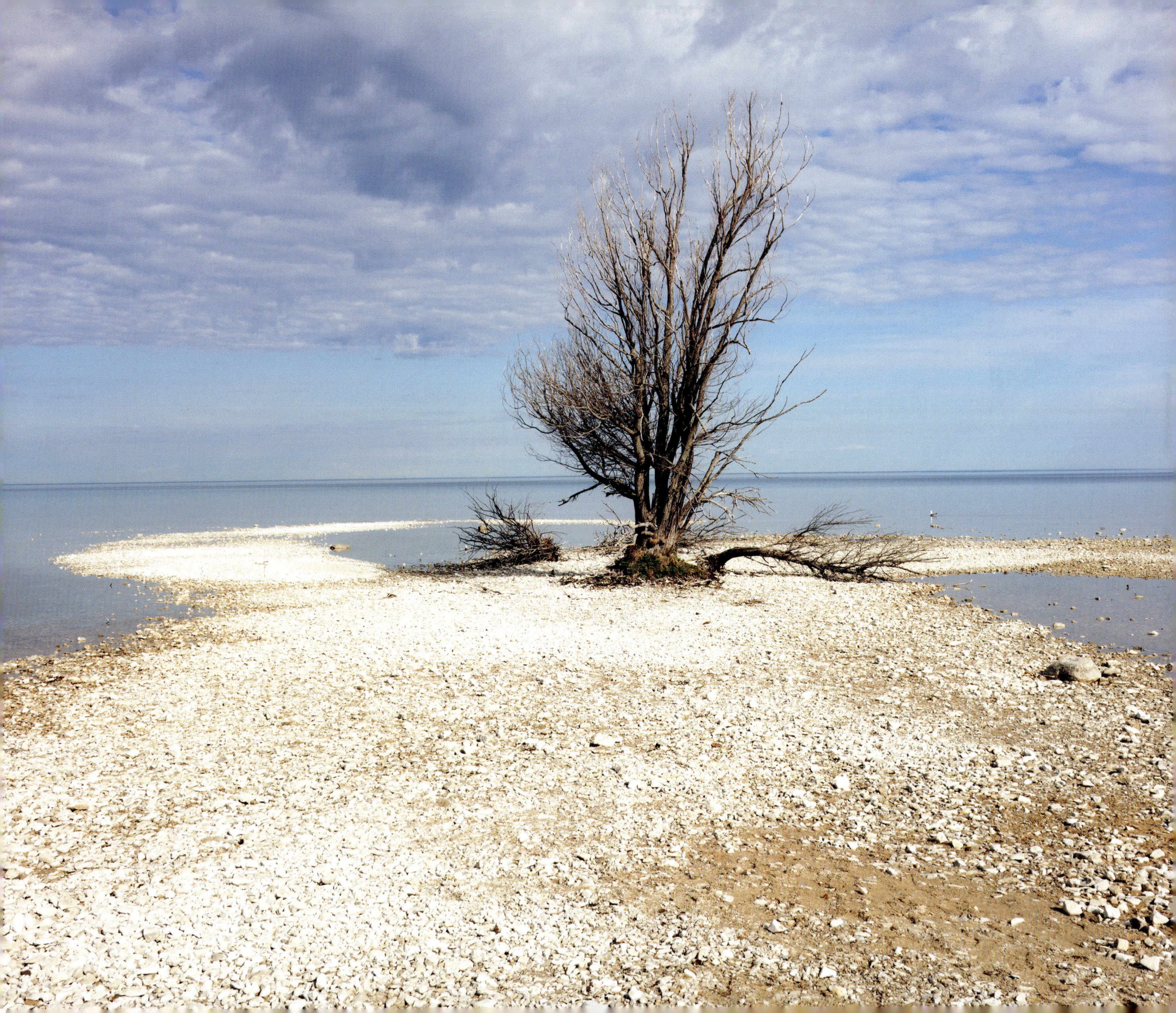

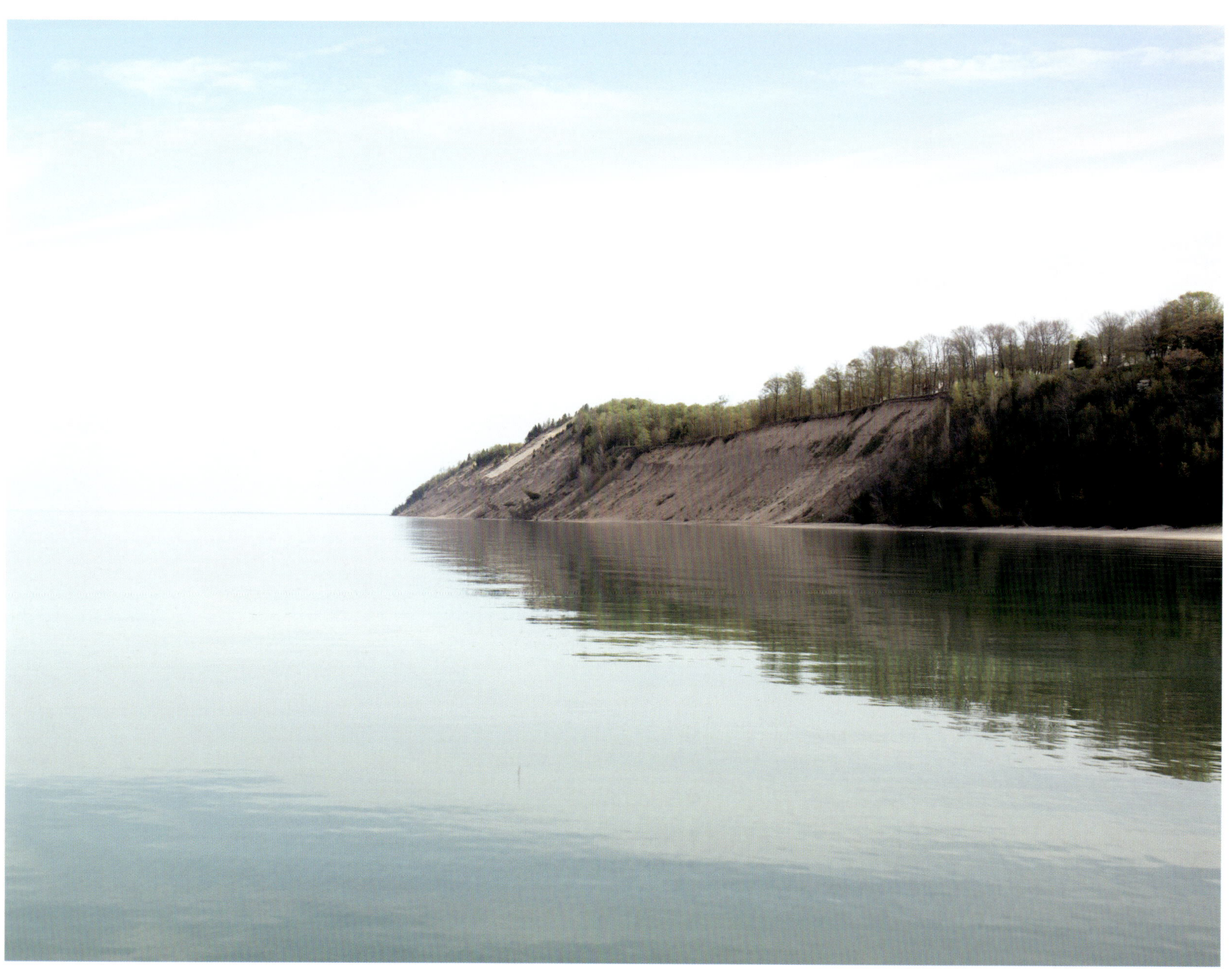

Sand dune, Benzie County, Michigan, 2023

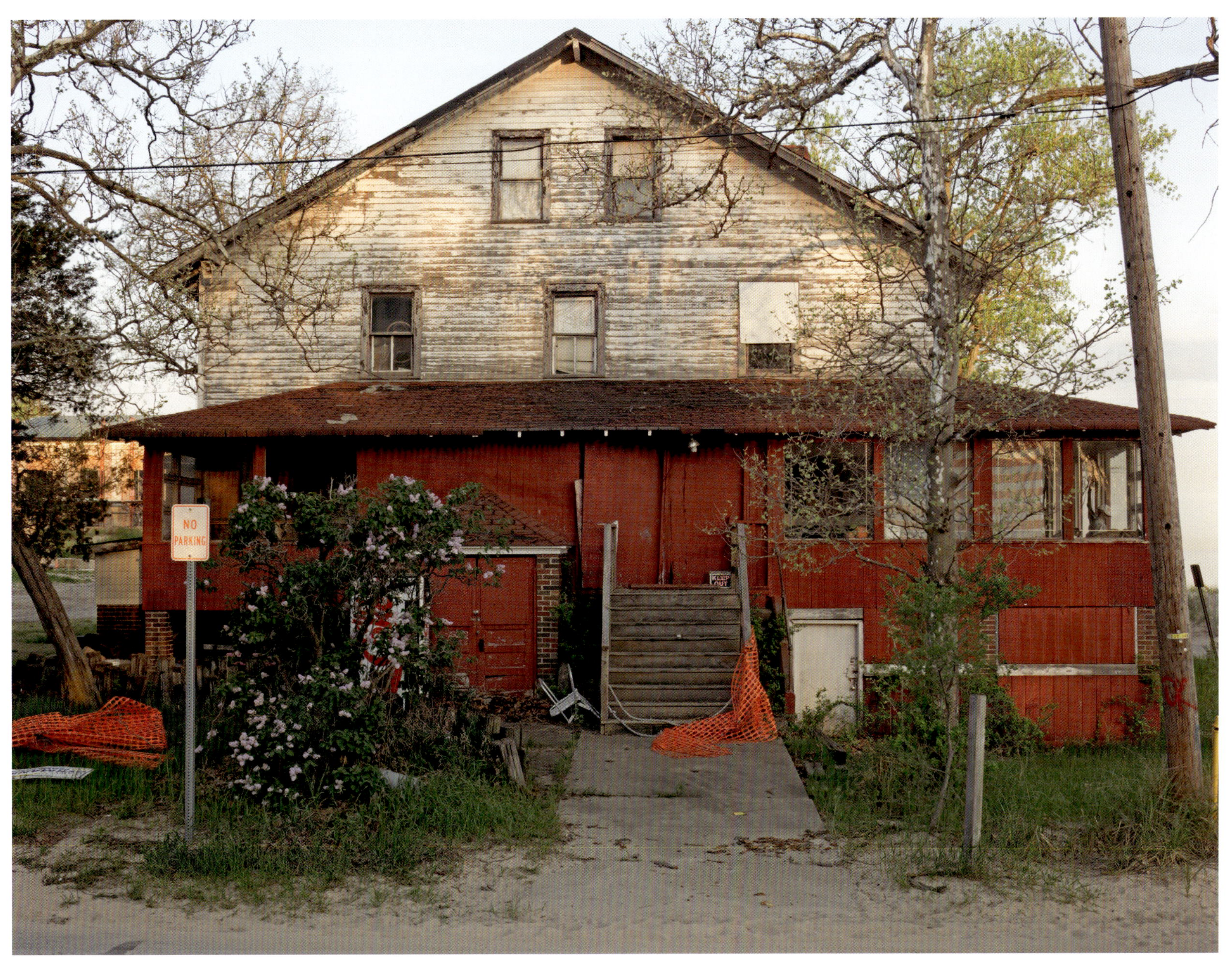

Abandoned beach house, Lake County, Indiana, 2023

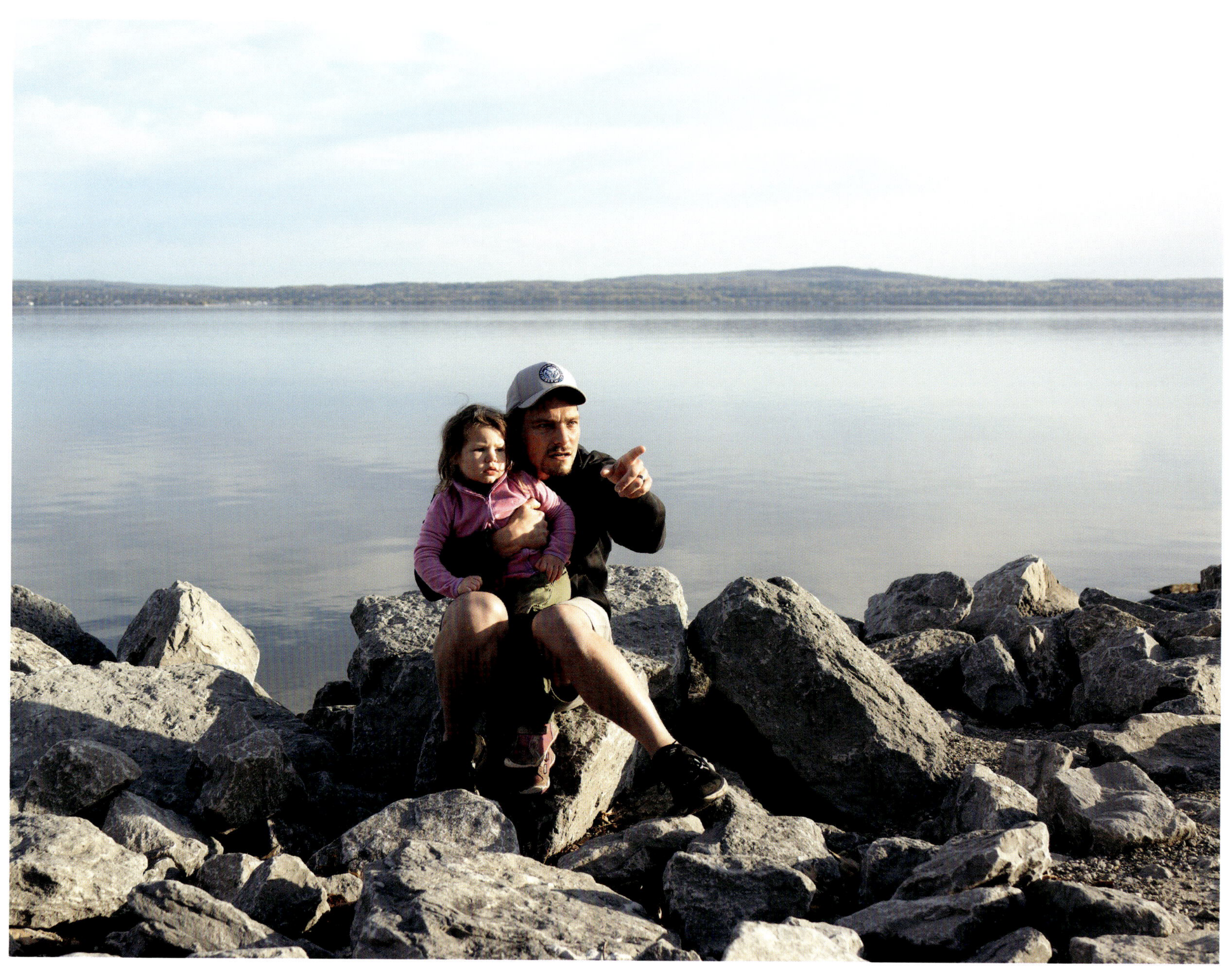

Laura and Colin, Little Traverse Bay, Michigan, 2023

Point Betsie Lighthouse, Benzie County, Michigan, 2023

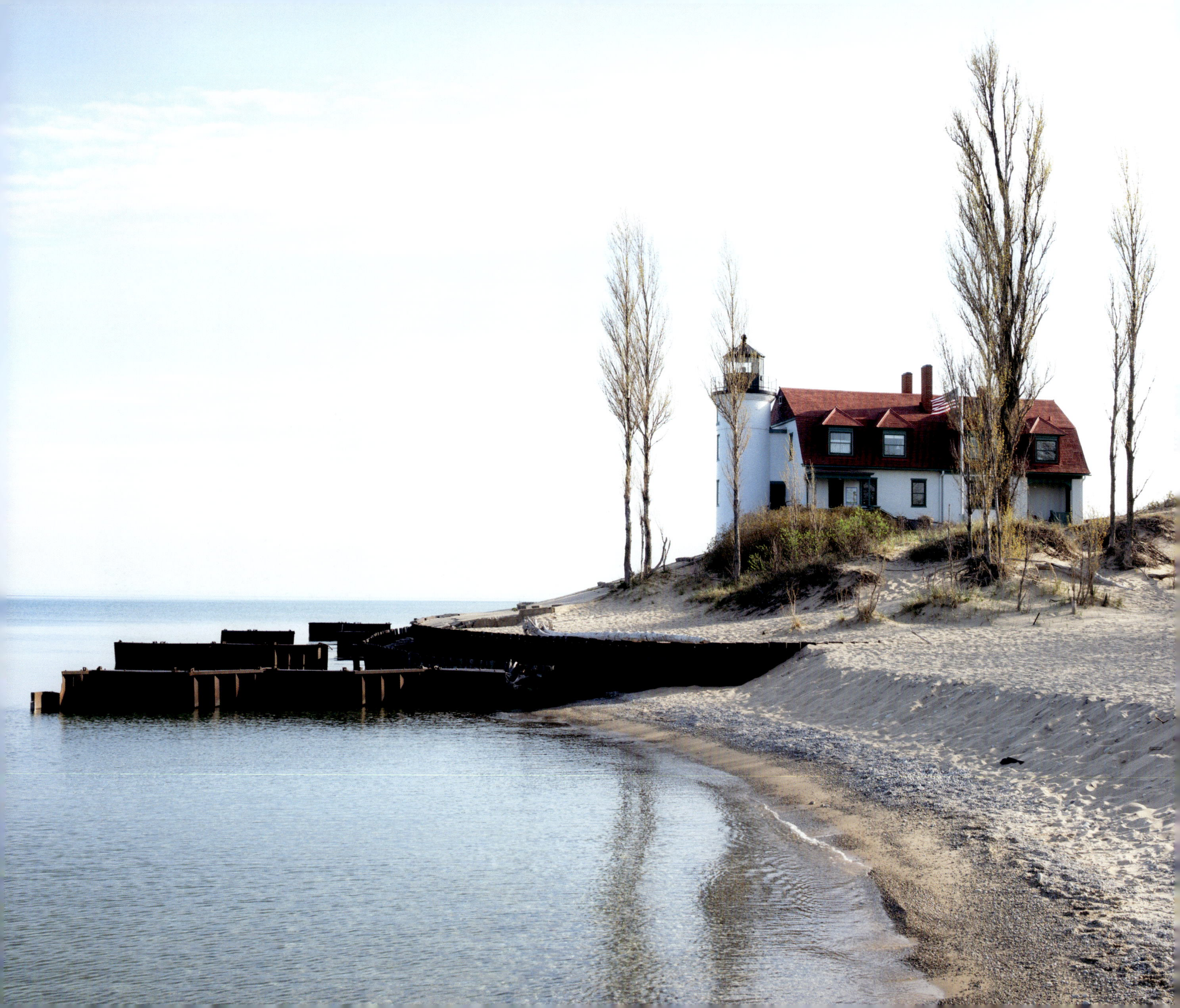

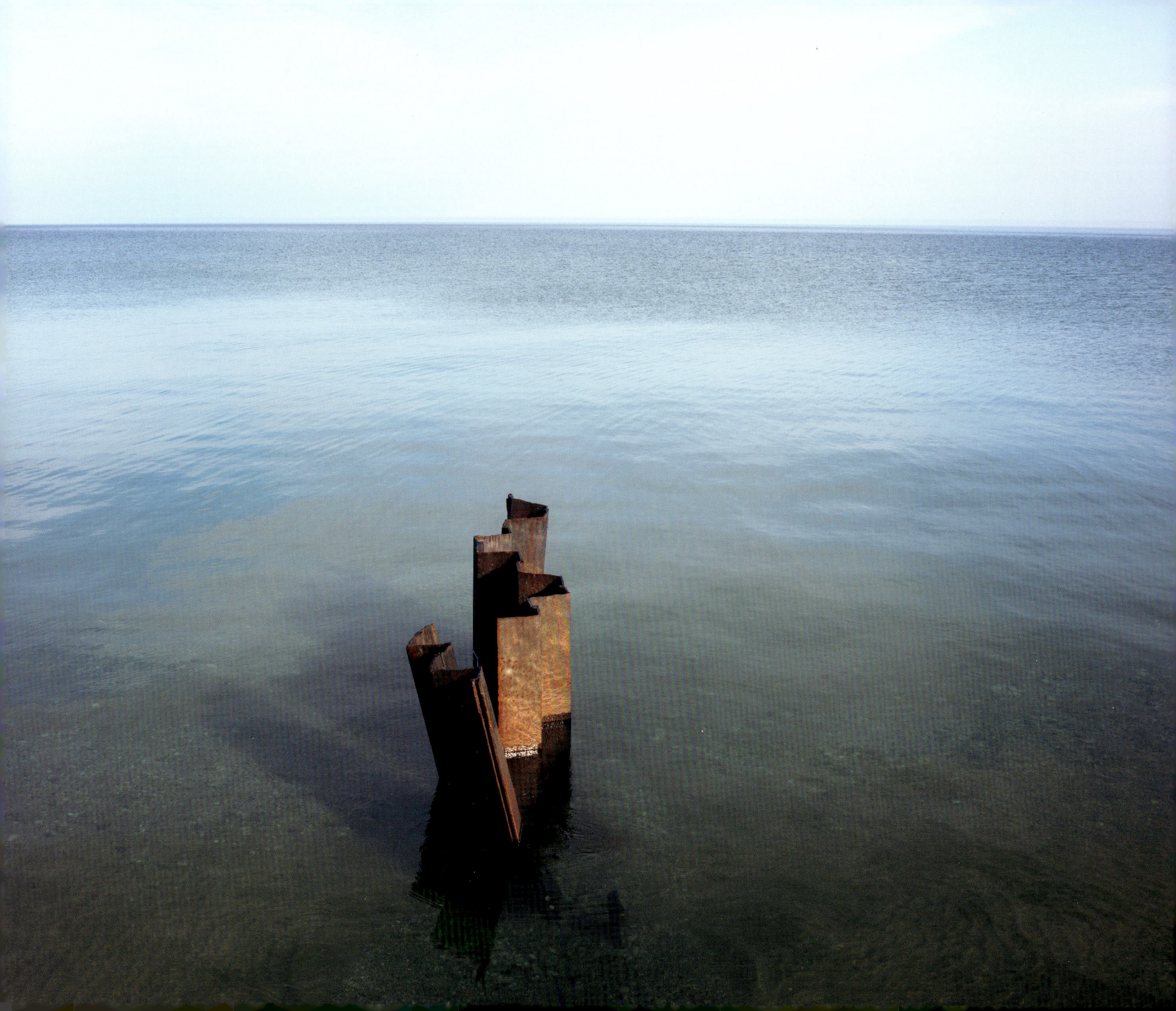

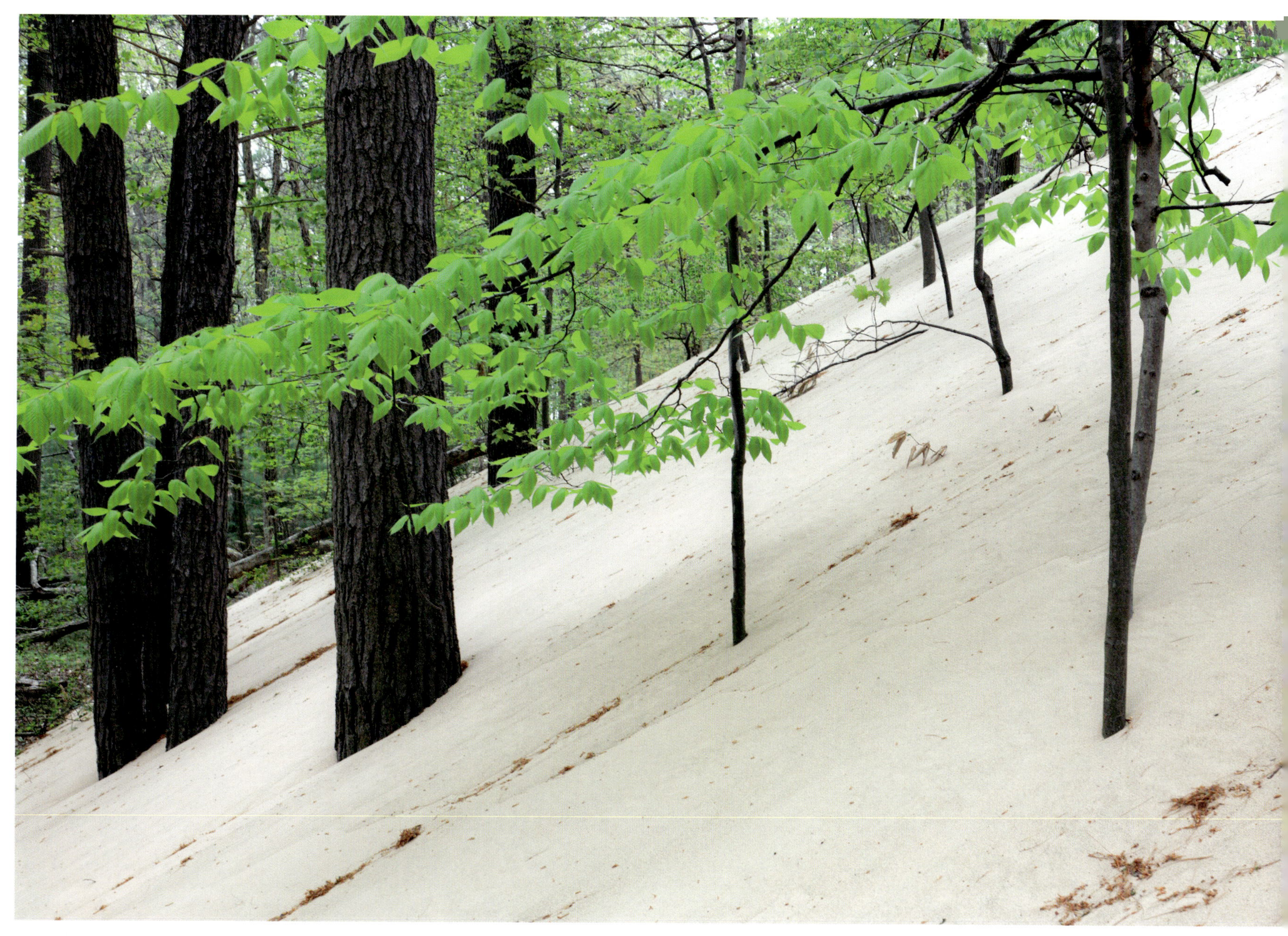

Dune migration, Oceana County, Michigan, 2023

Abandoned pier, Benzie County, Michigan, 2023

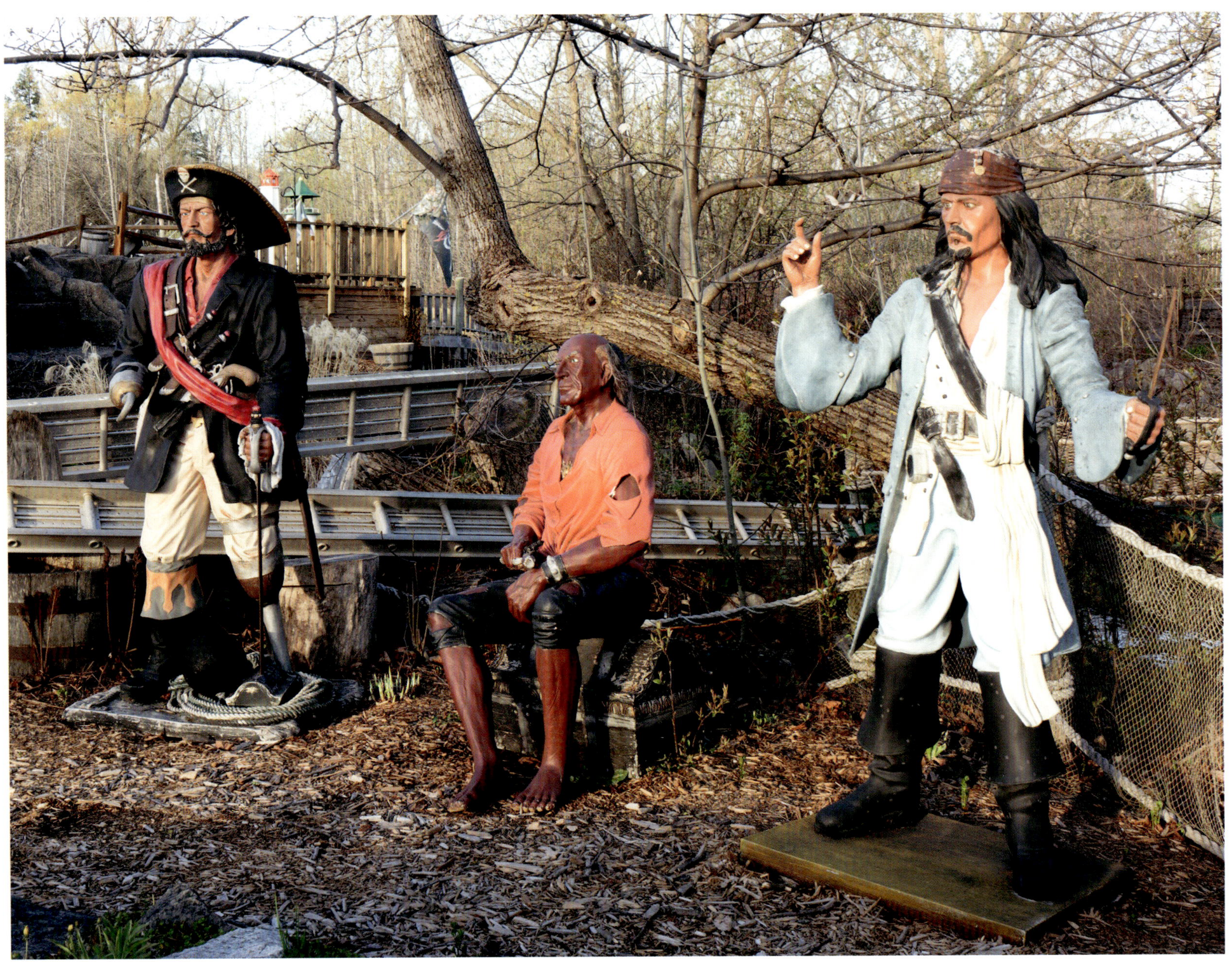

Pirate's Cove (miniature golf), Emmet County, Michigan, 2023

Jolene (Miss Uniroyal), Northport, Michigan, 2023

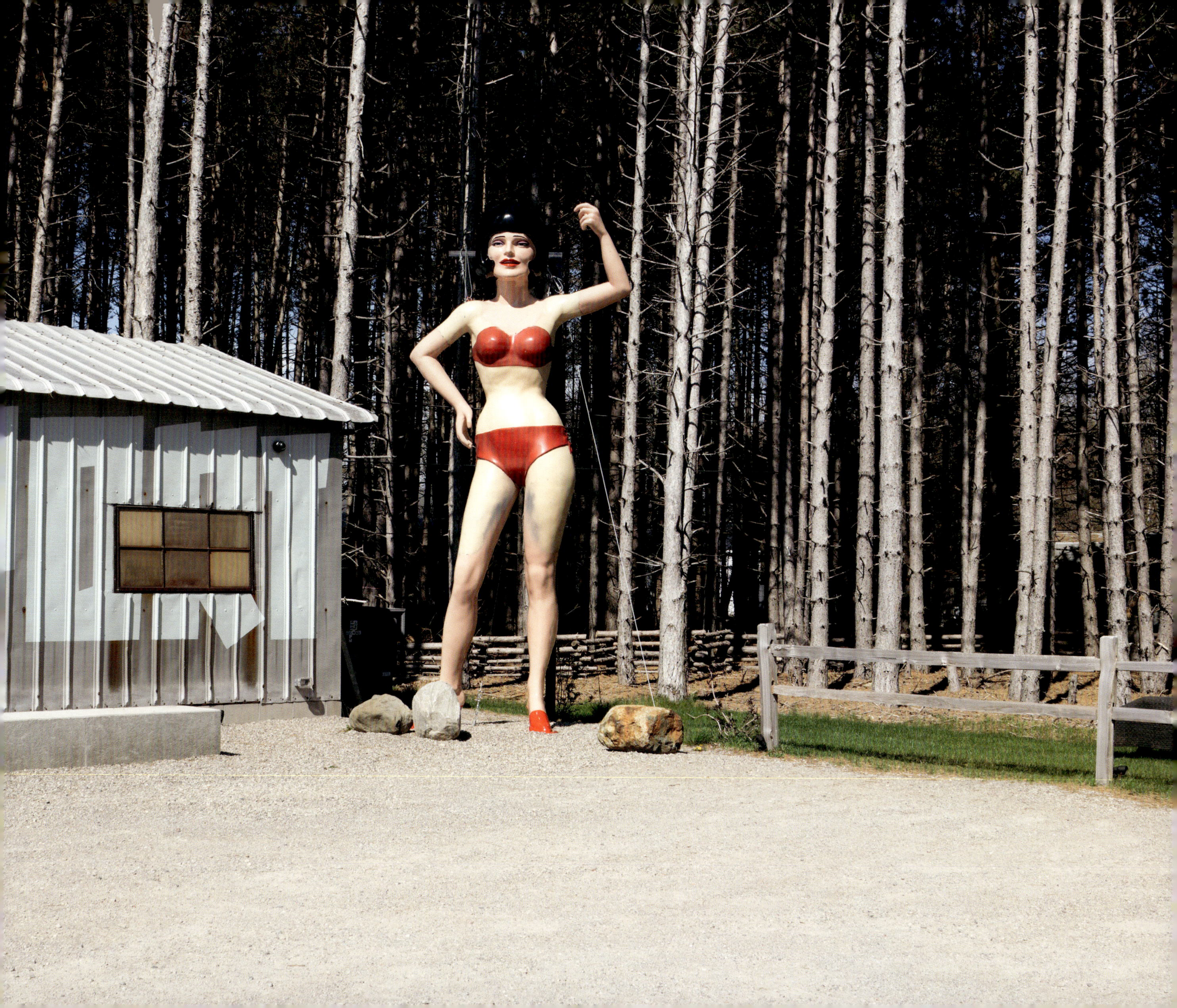

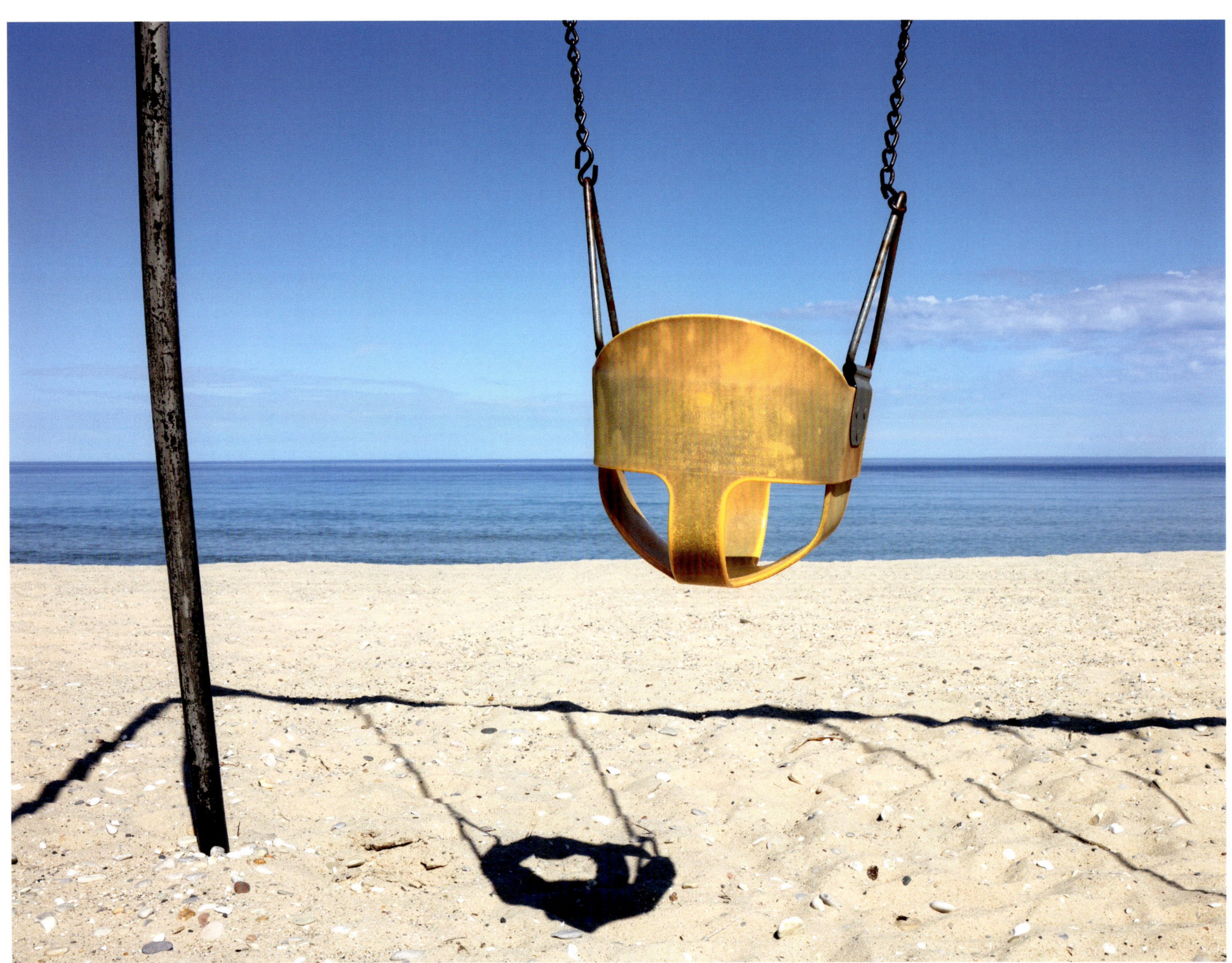

Child's swing, Charlevoix, Michigan, 2023

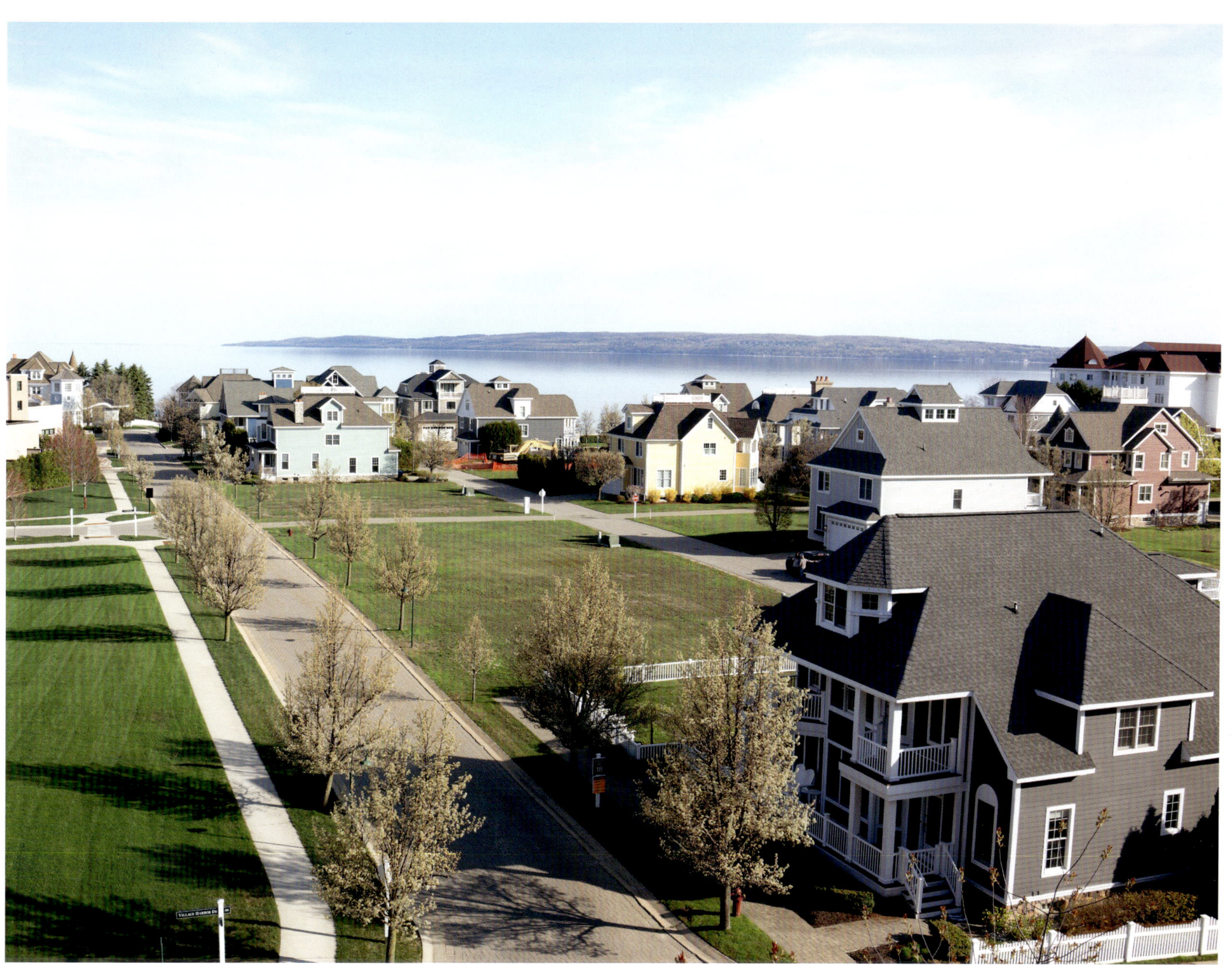

Waterfront development, Charlevoix, Michigan, 2023

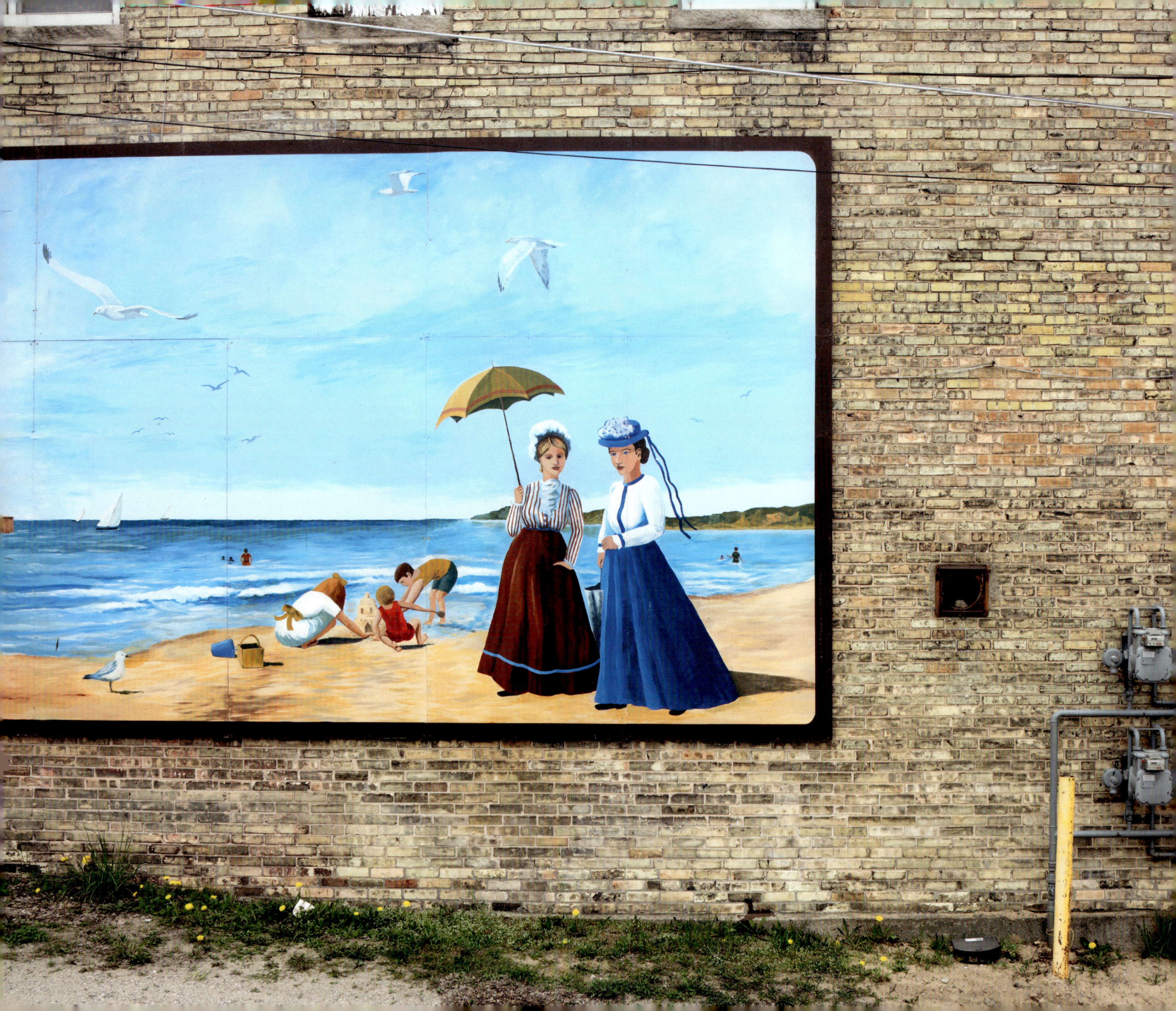

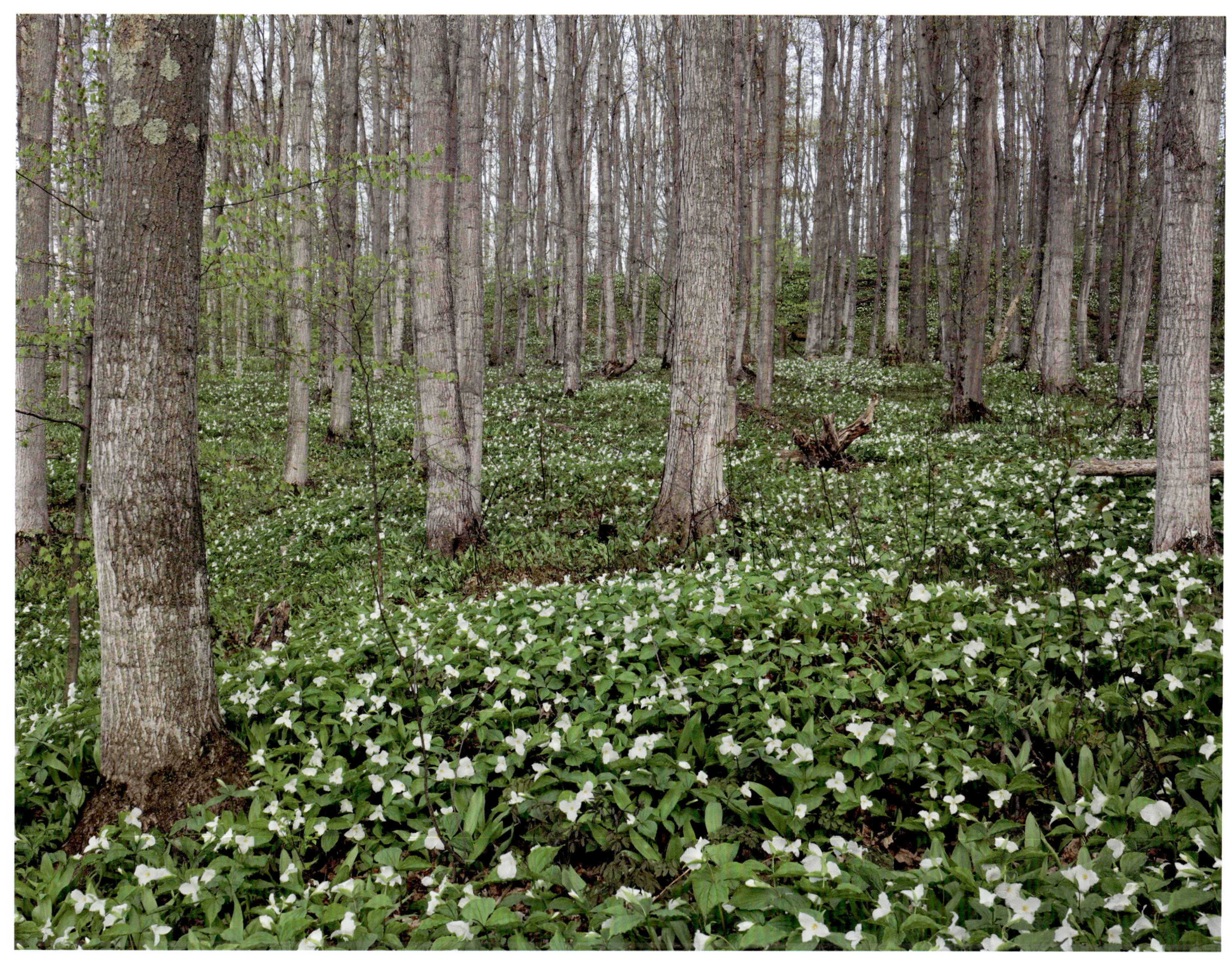

Trilliums, Leelanau Peninsula, Michigan, 2023

Ludington, Michigan, 2023

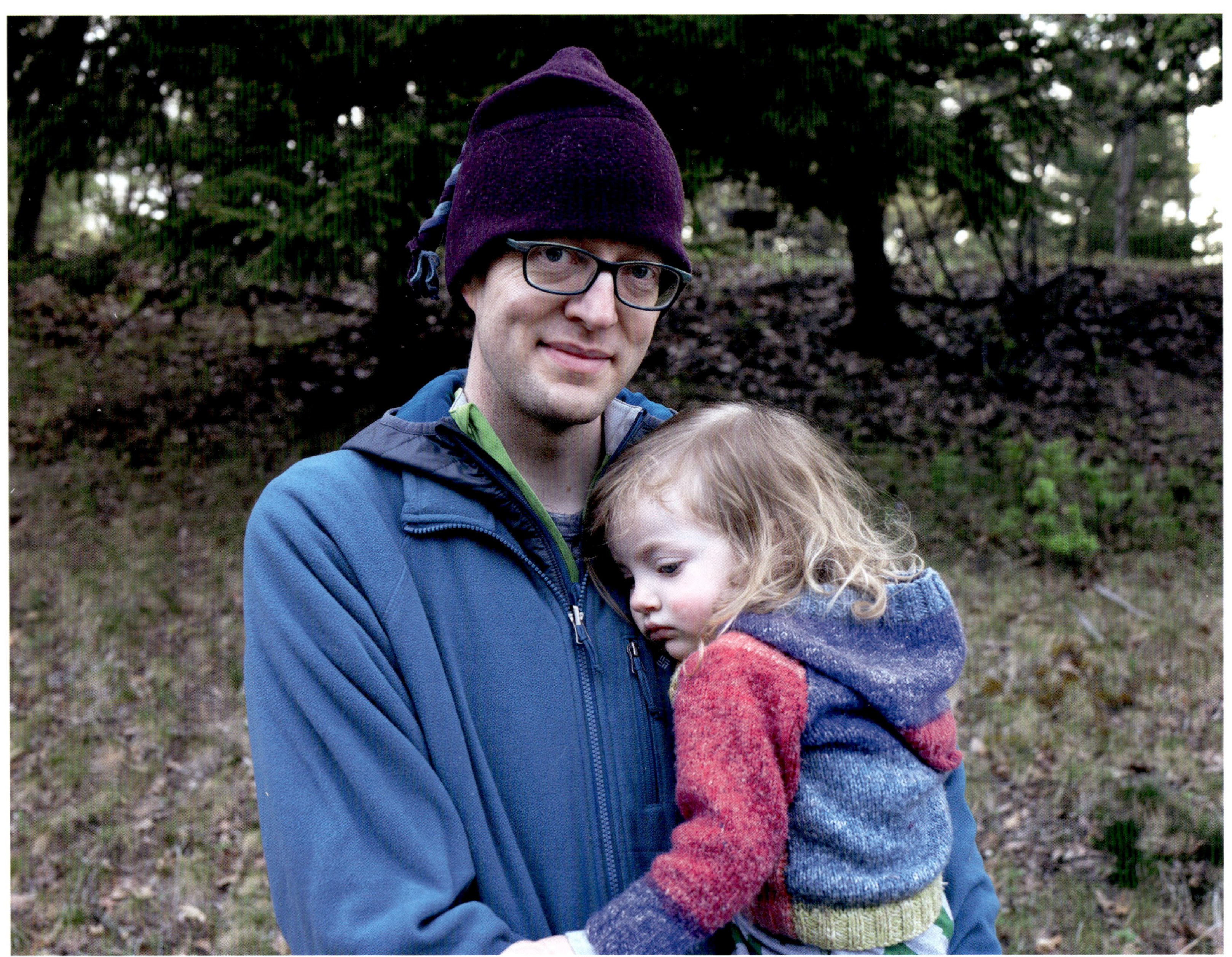

Paul and Elsa, Platte River Campground, Michigan, 2023

Spring floodwaters, Emmet County, Michigan, 2023

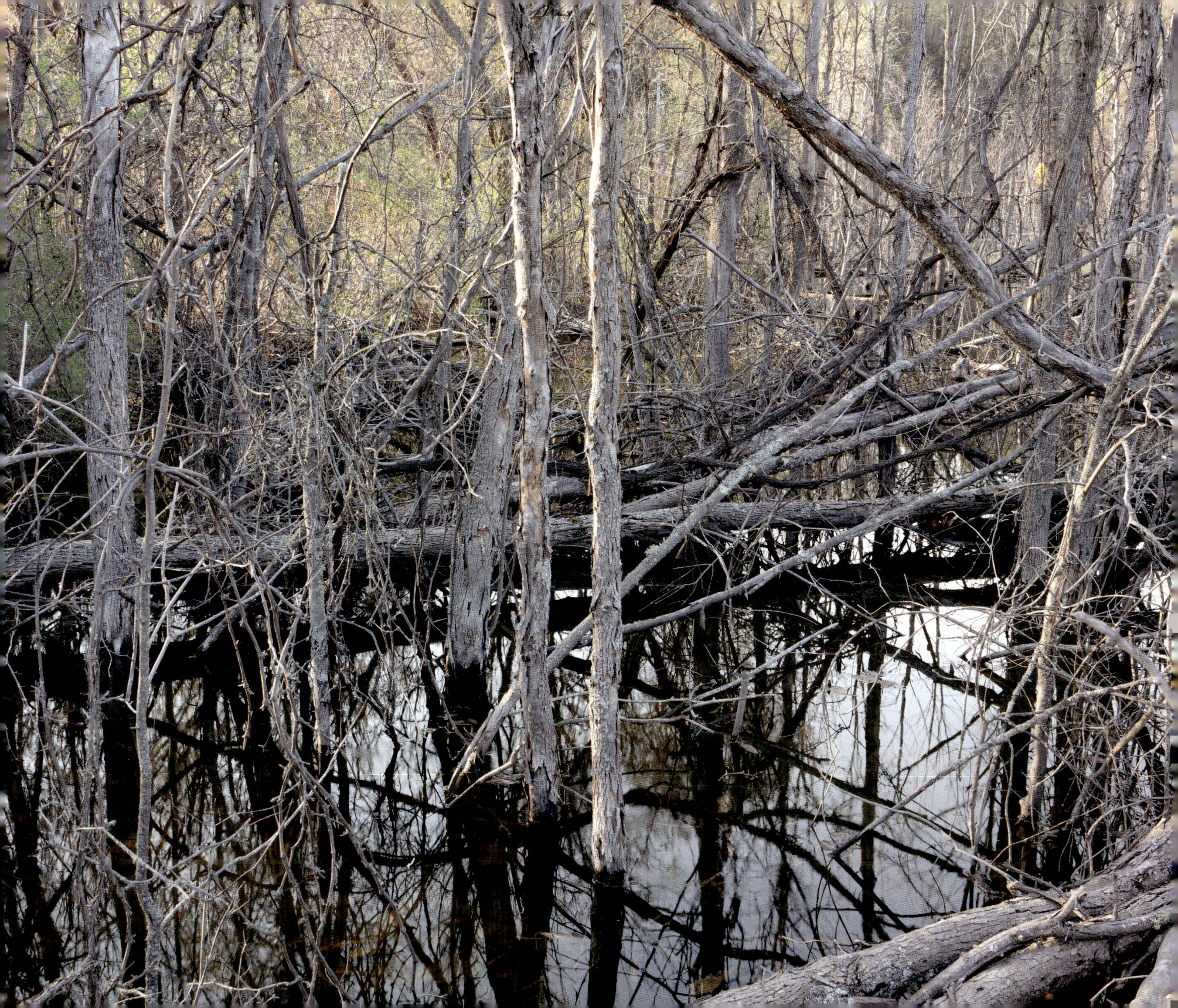

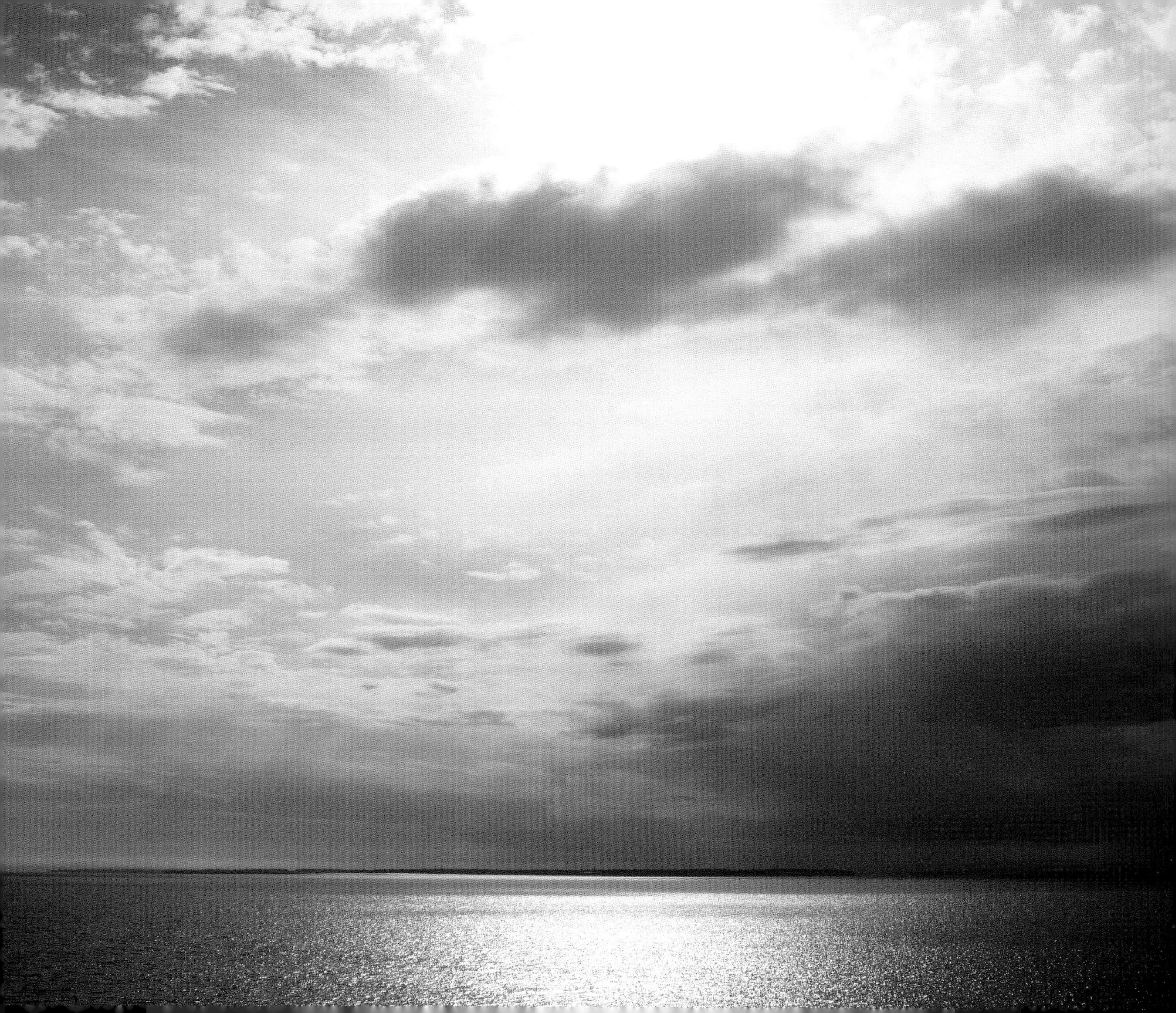

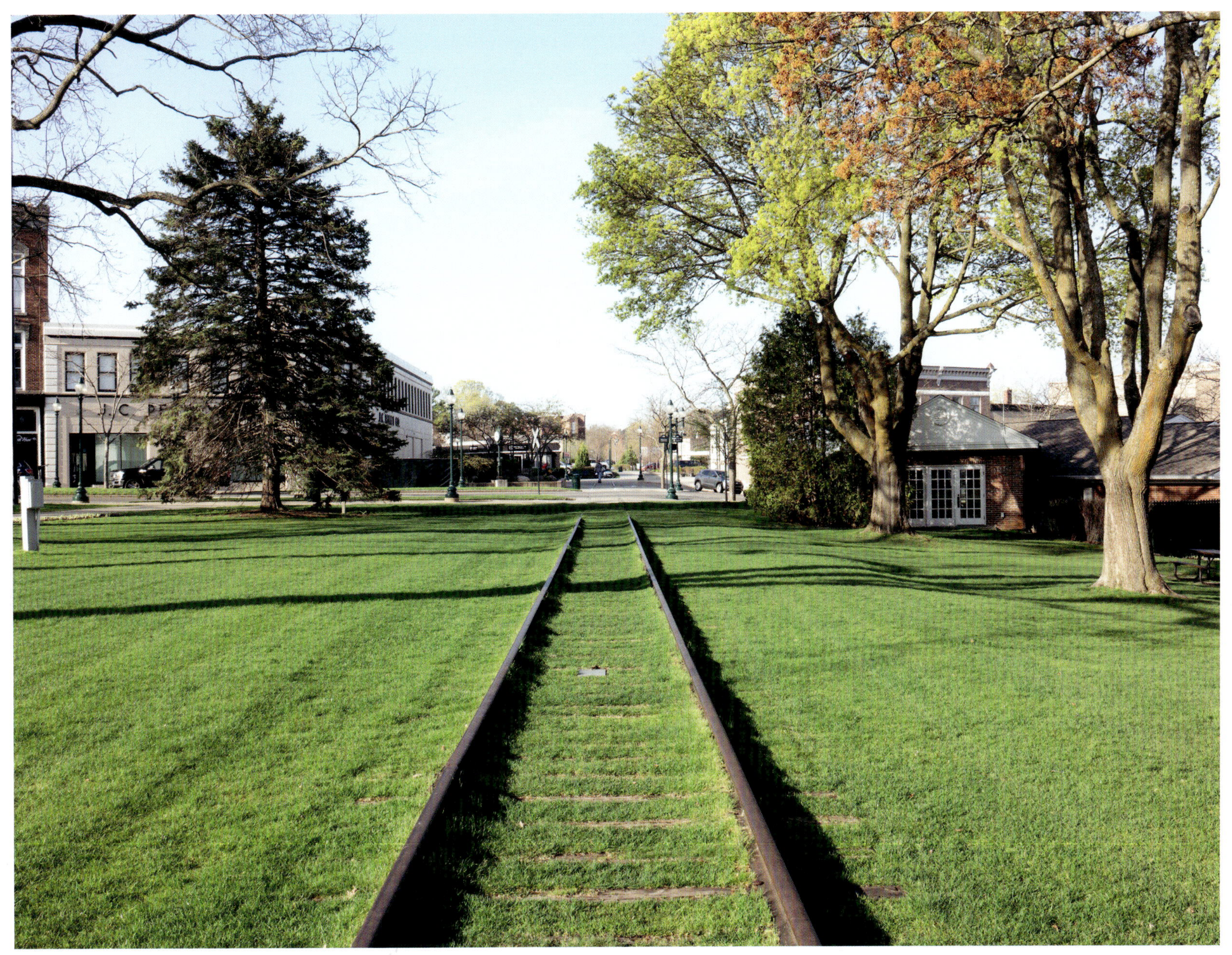

Charlevoix (downtown), Michigan, 2023

North Manitou Island, Michigan, 2023

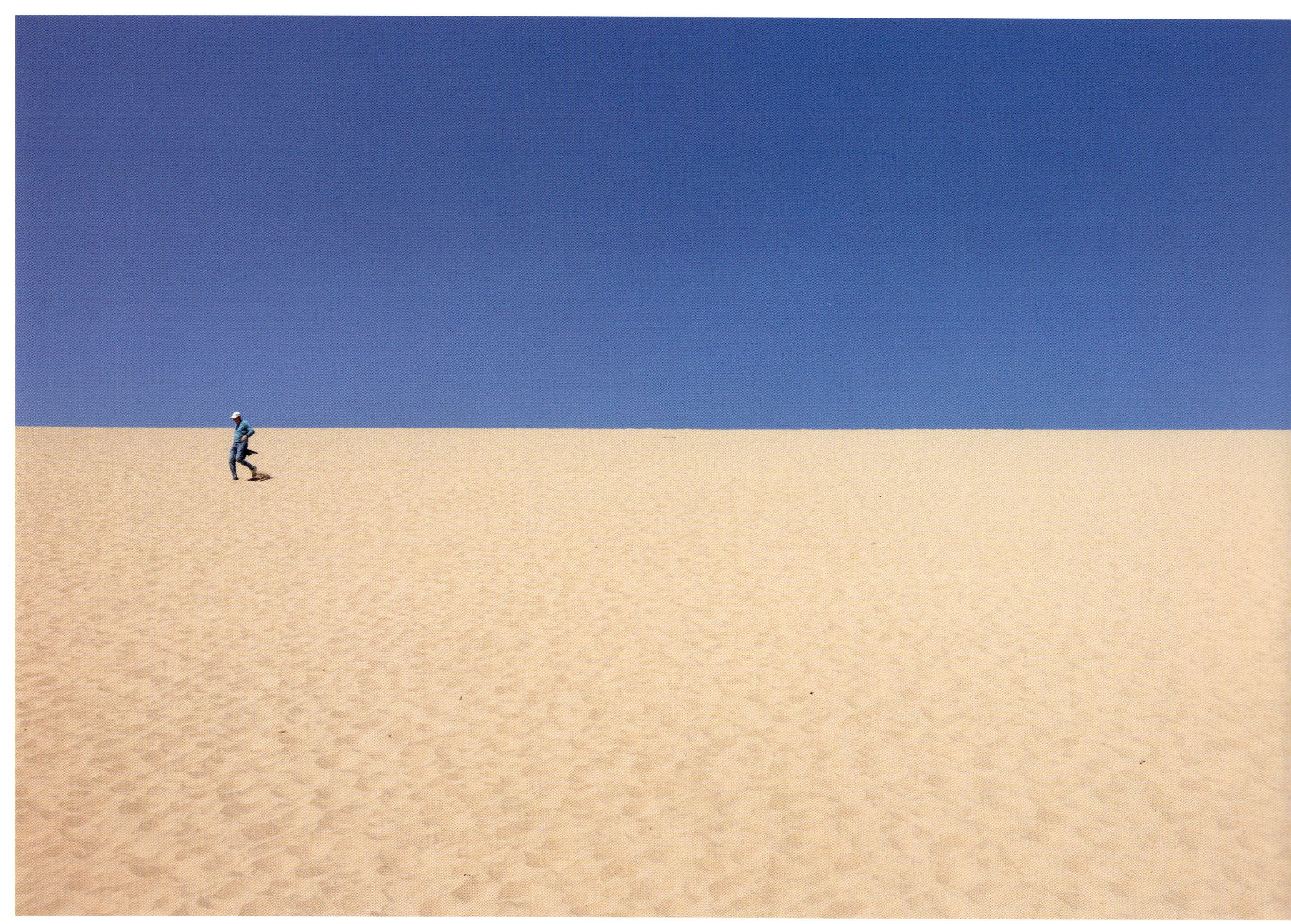

Sleeping Bear Dunes, Michigan, 2023

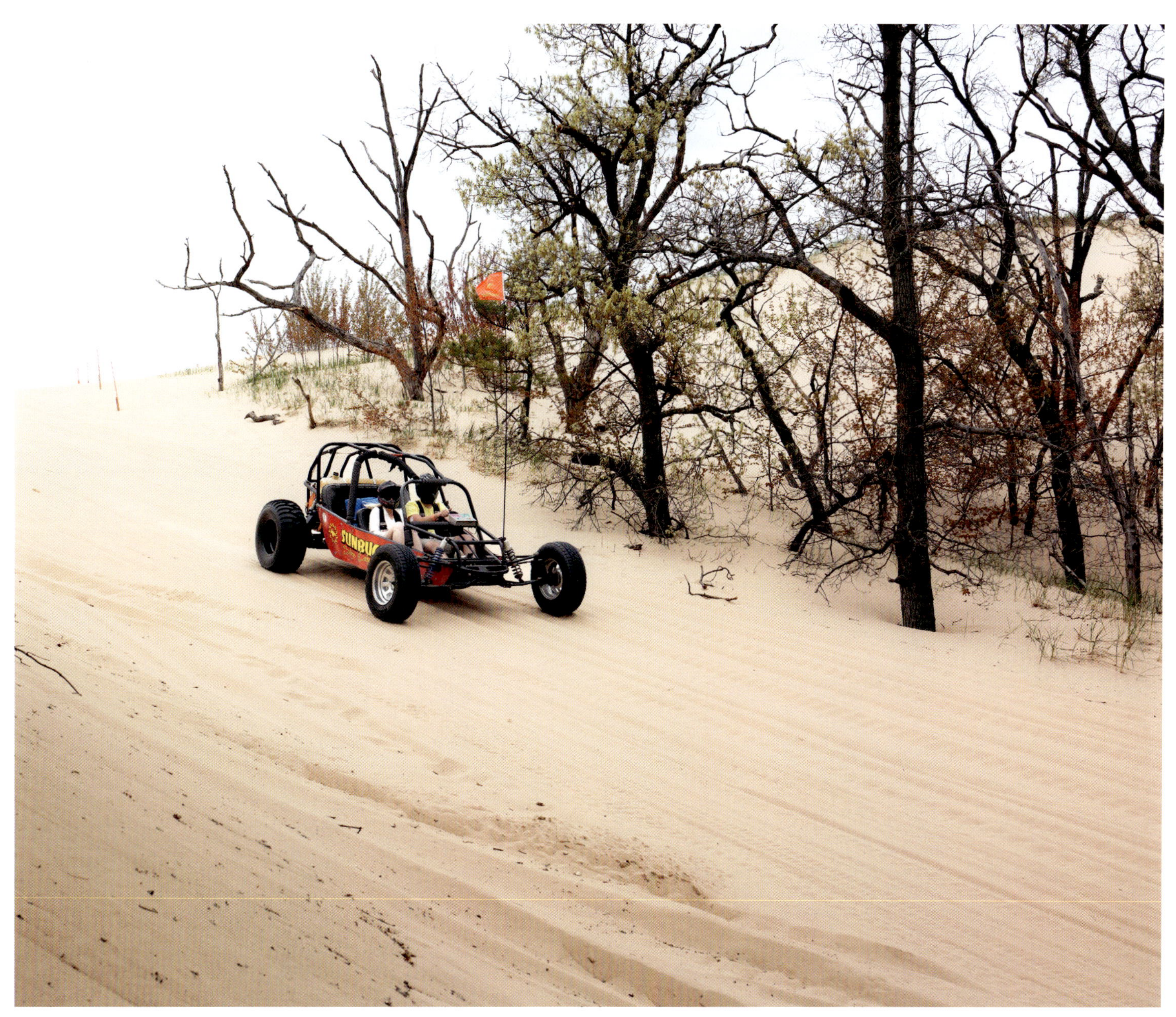

Dune buggy track, Silver Lake, Michigan, 2023

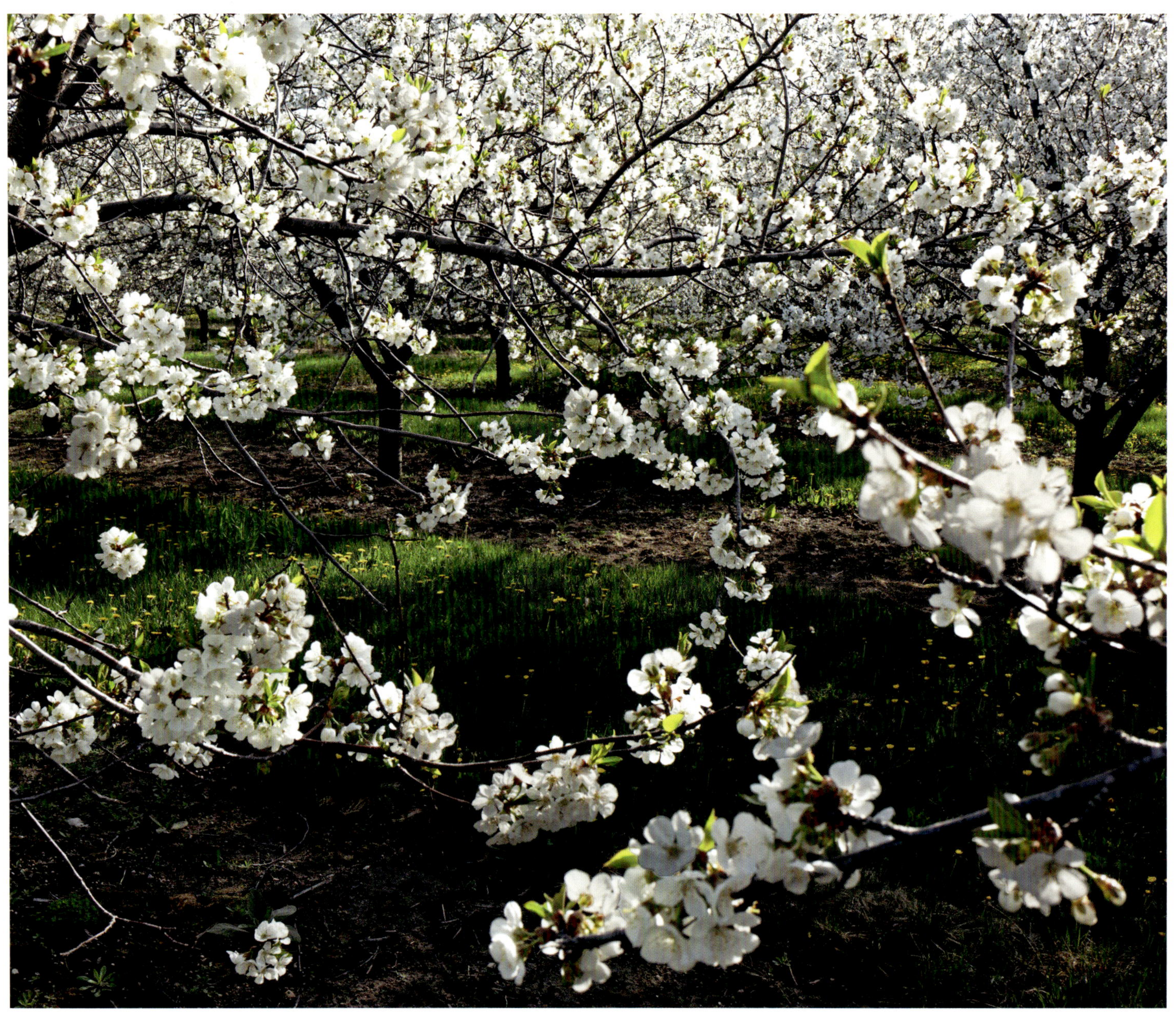

Cherry blossoms, Leelanau Peninsula, Michigan, 2023

Posy swimming, Frankfort, Michigan, 2023

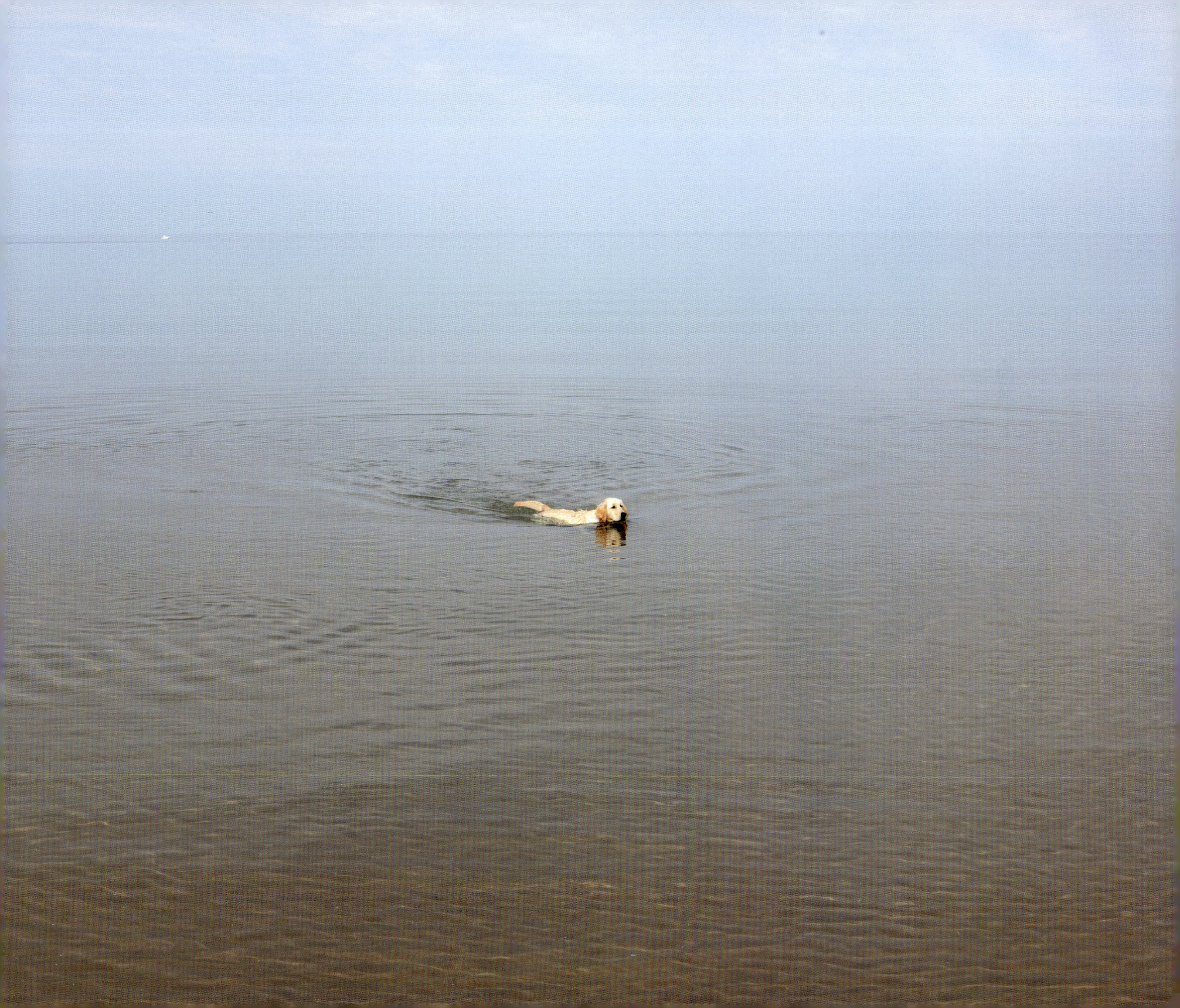

SUMMER

LAKE ERIE AND LAKE ONTARIO

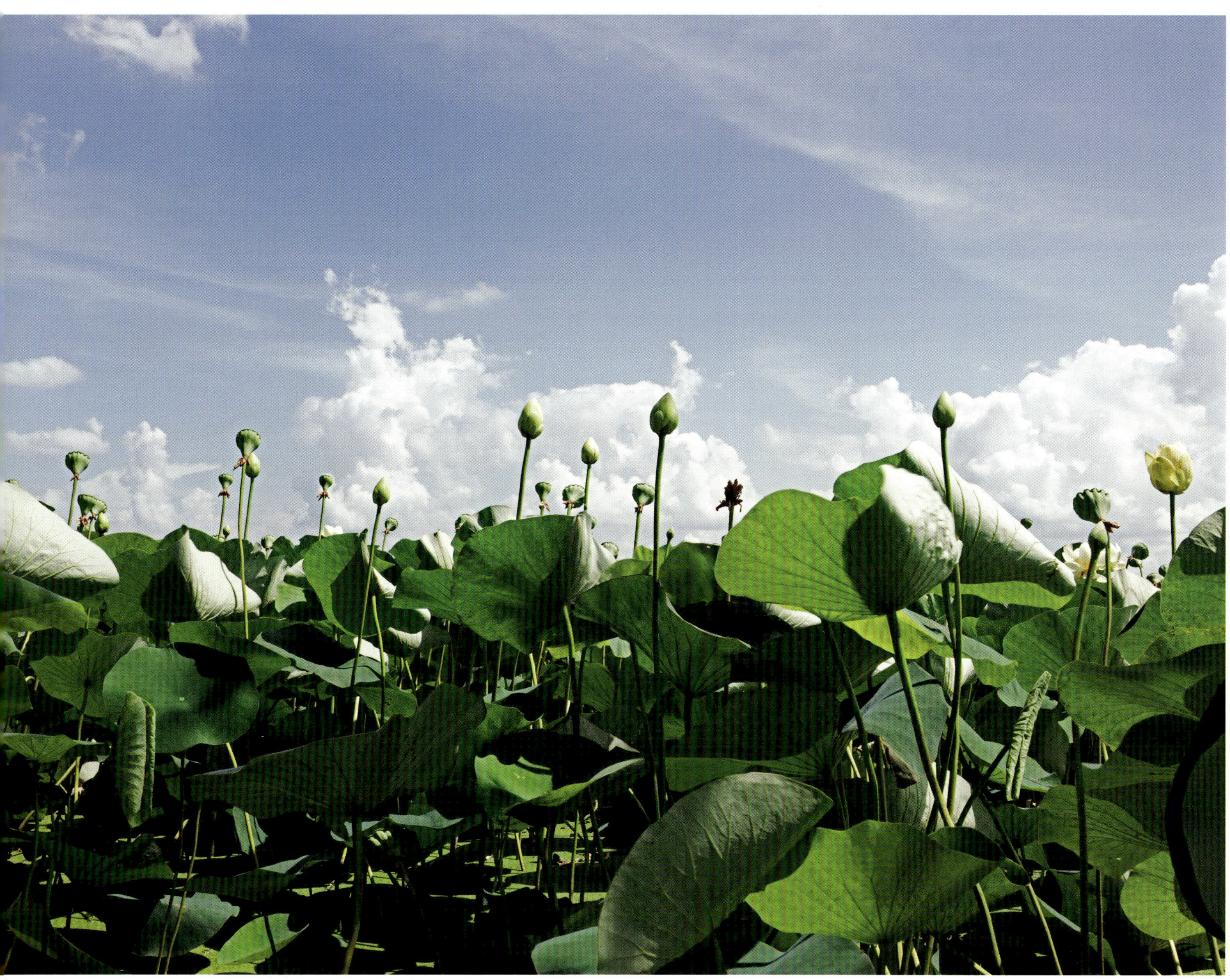

Lotus infestation, Ottawa County, Ohio, 2022

Sailboat (and Toronto skyline, just visible), Wilson, New York, 2022

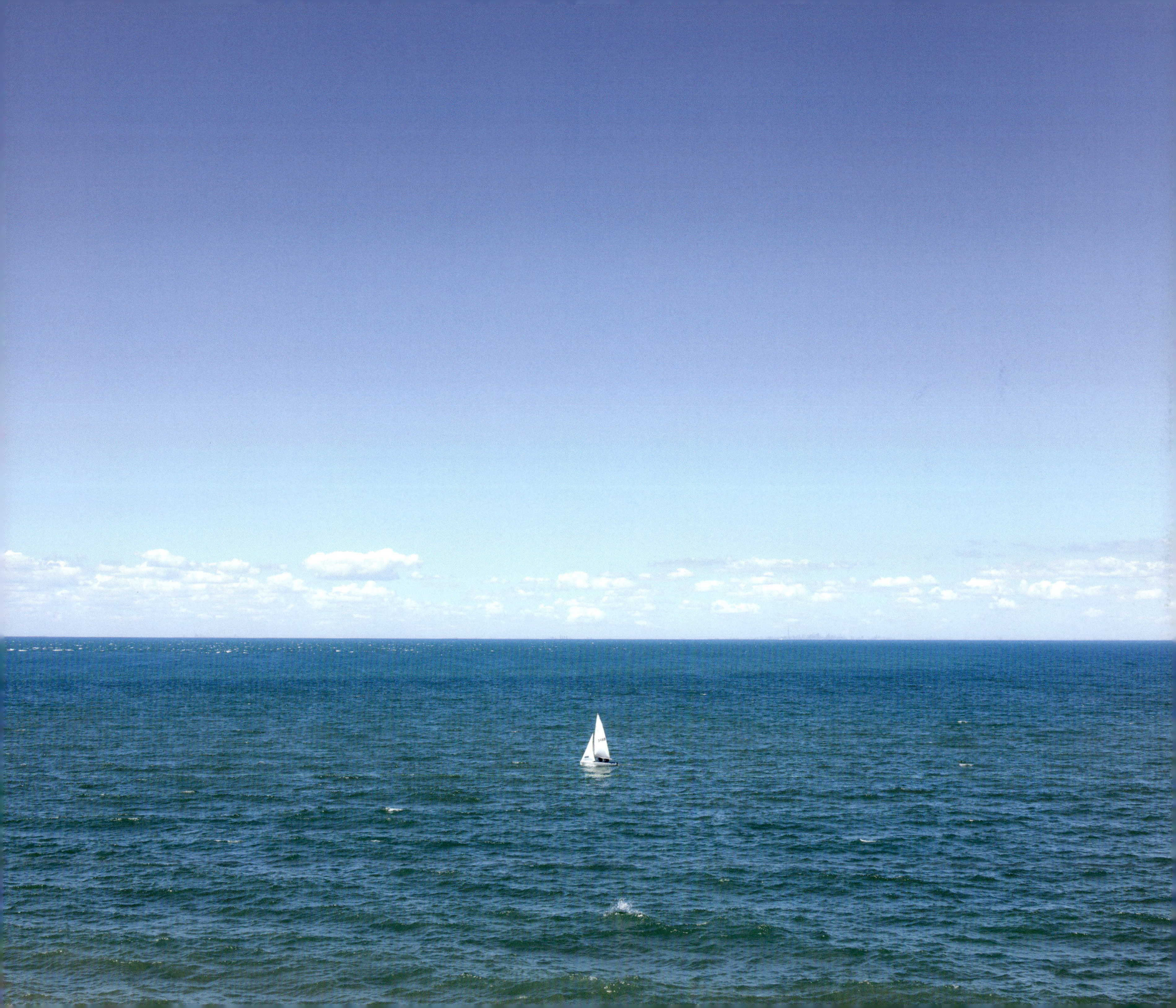

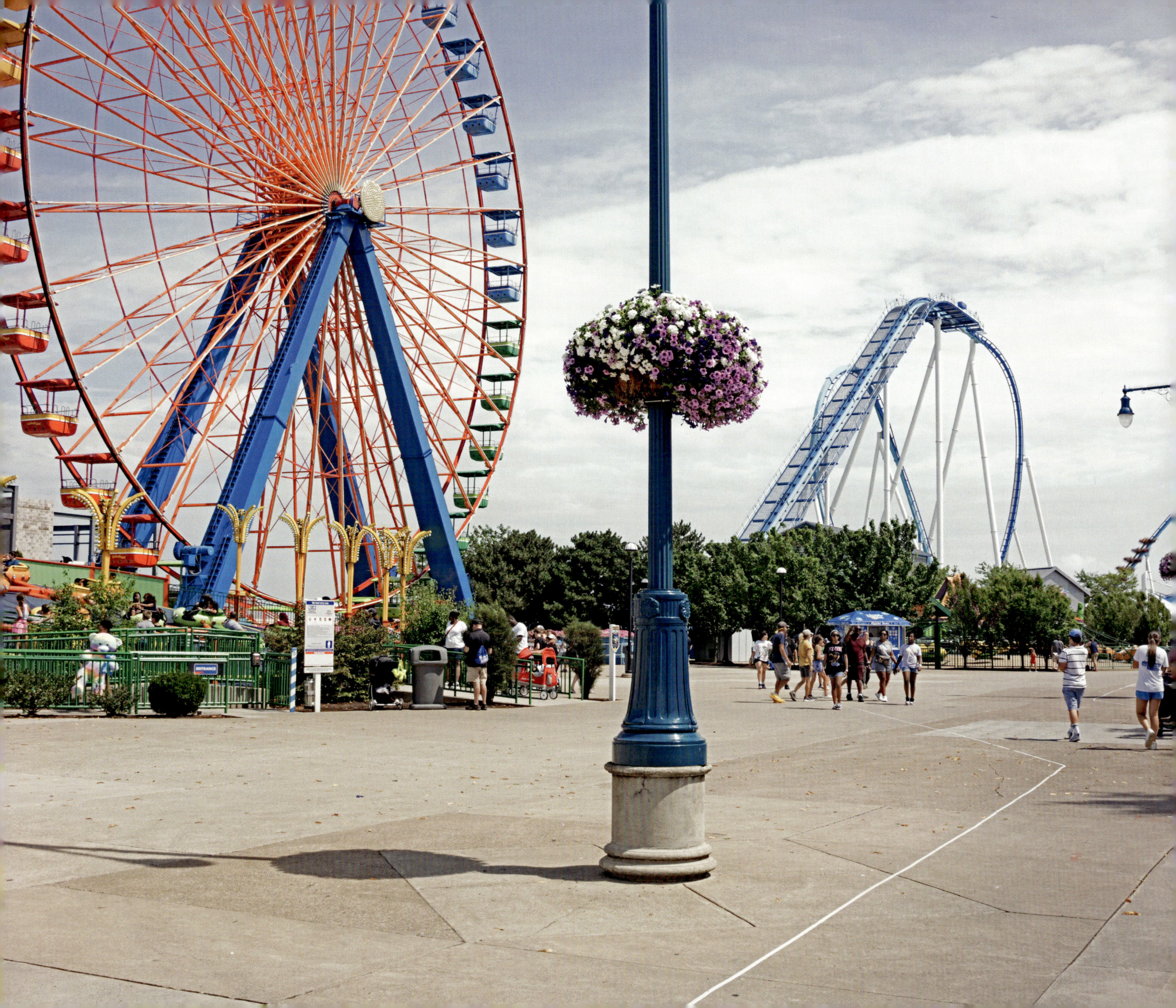
ENTRANCE

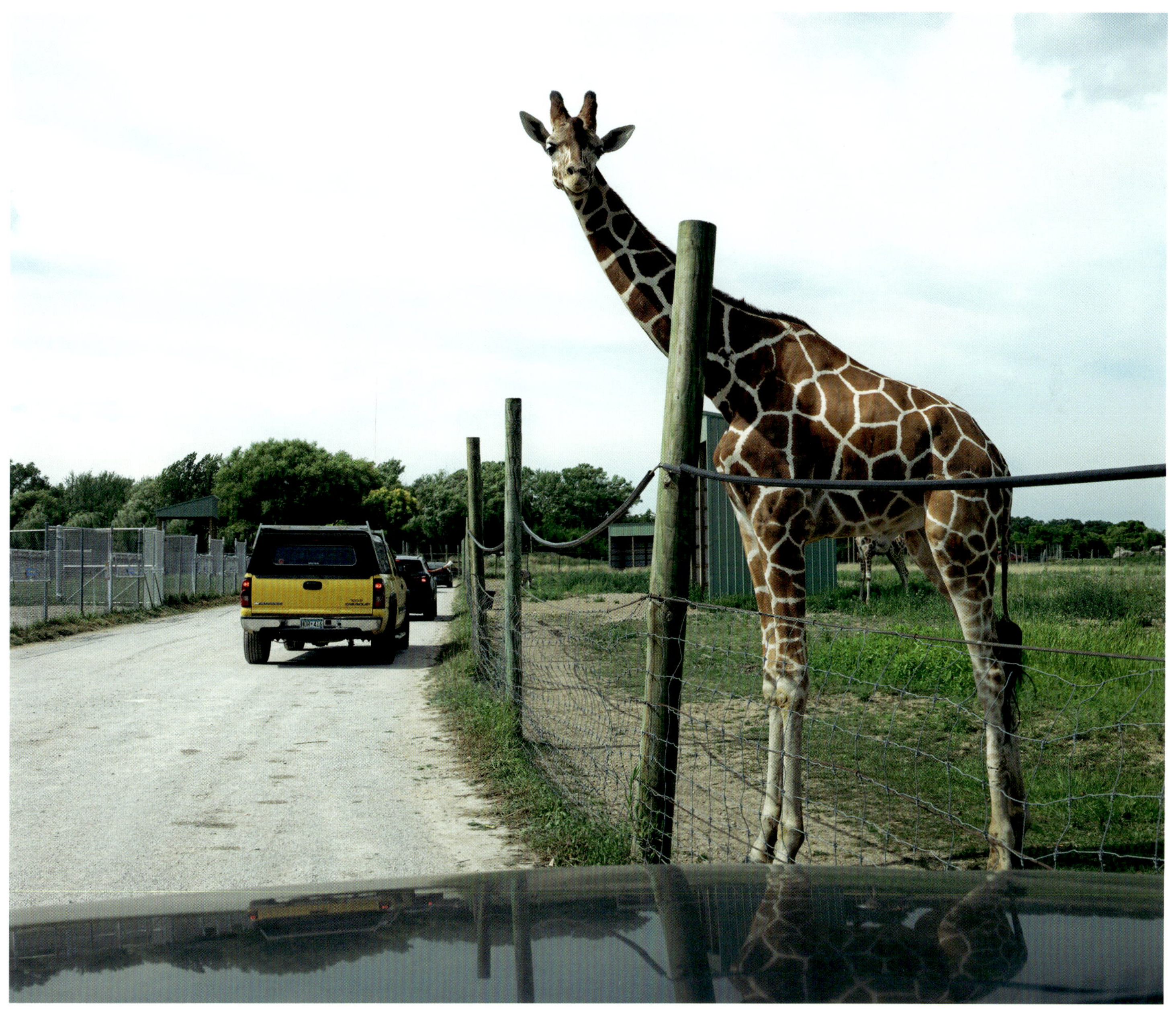

African safari, Ottawa County, Ohio, 2022

Amusement park, Cedar Point, Ohio, 2022

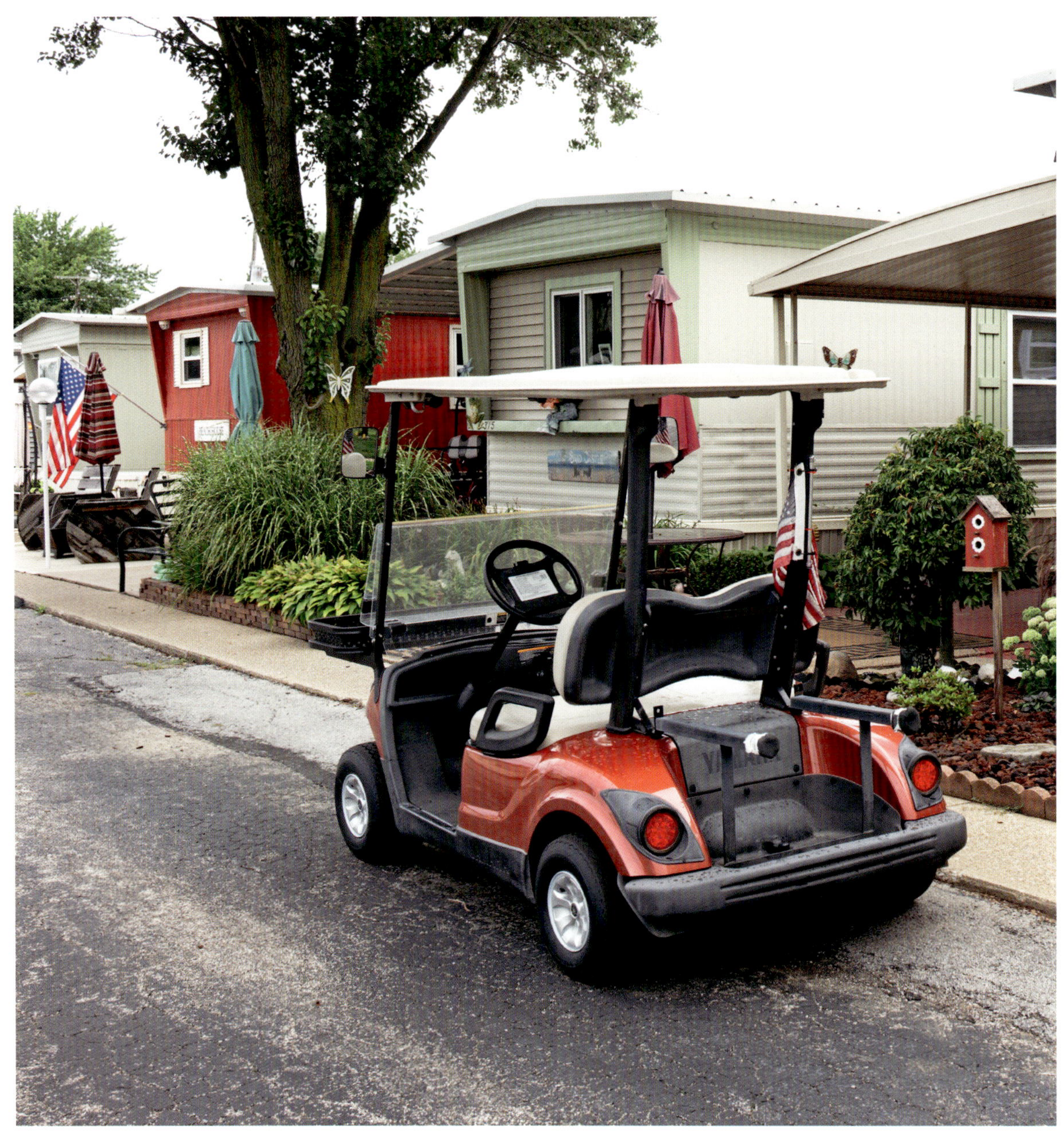

Mobile home park, Ruggles Beach, Ohio, 2022

Presque Isle Beach, Pennsylvania, 2022

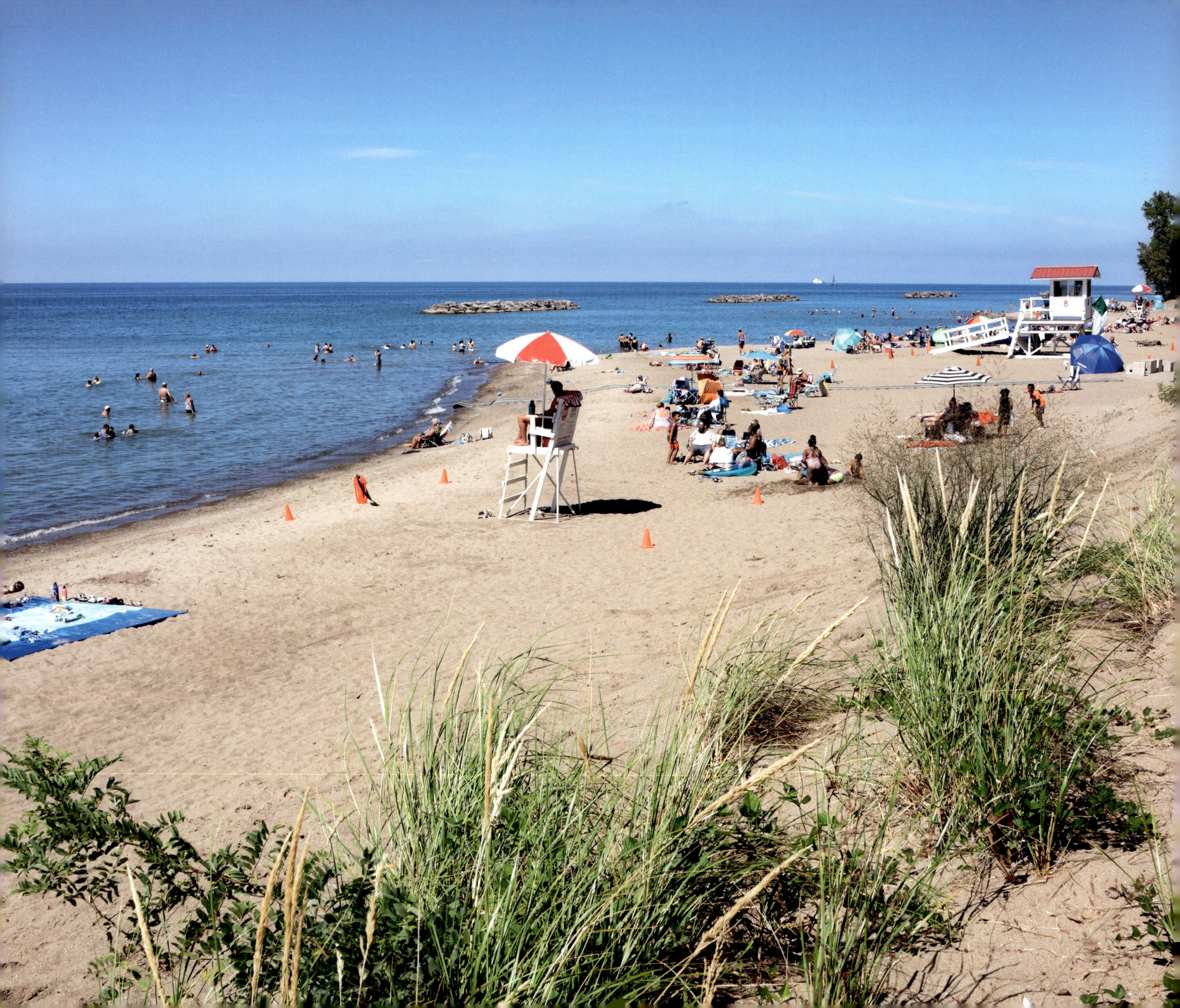

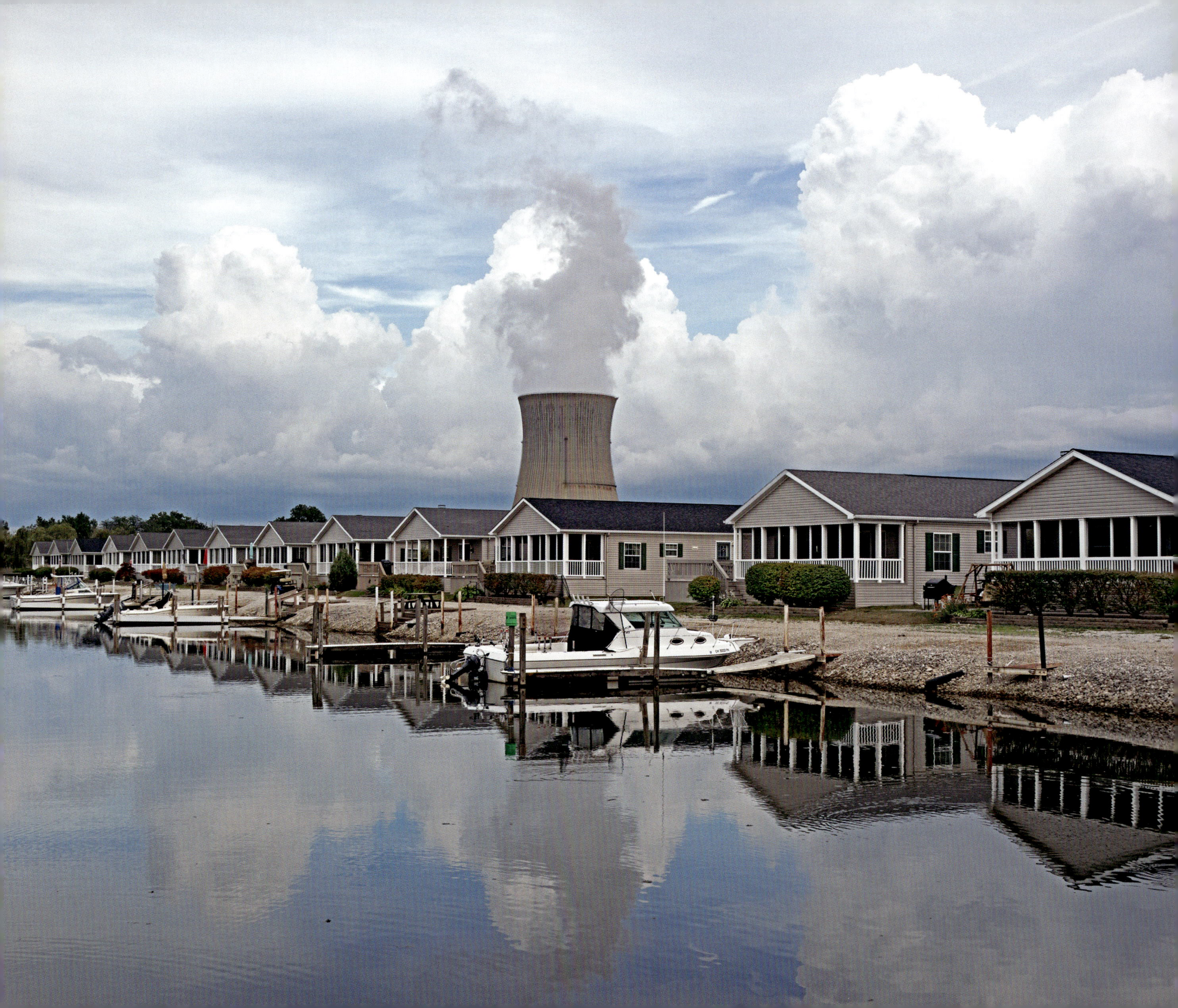

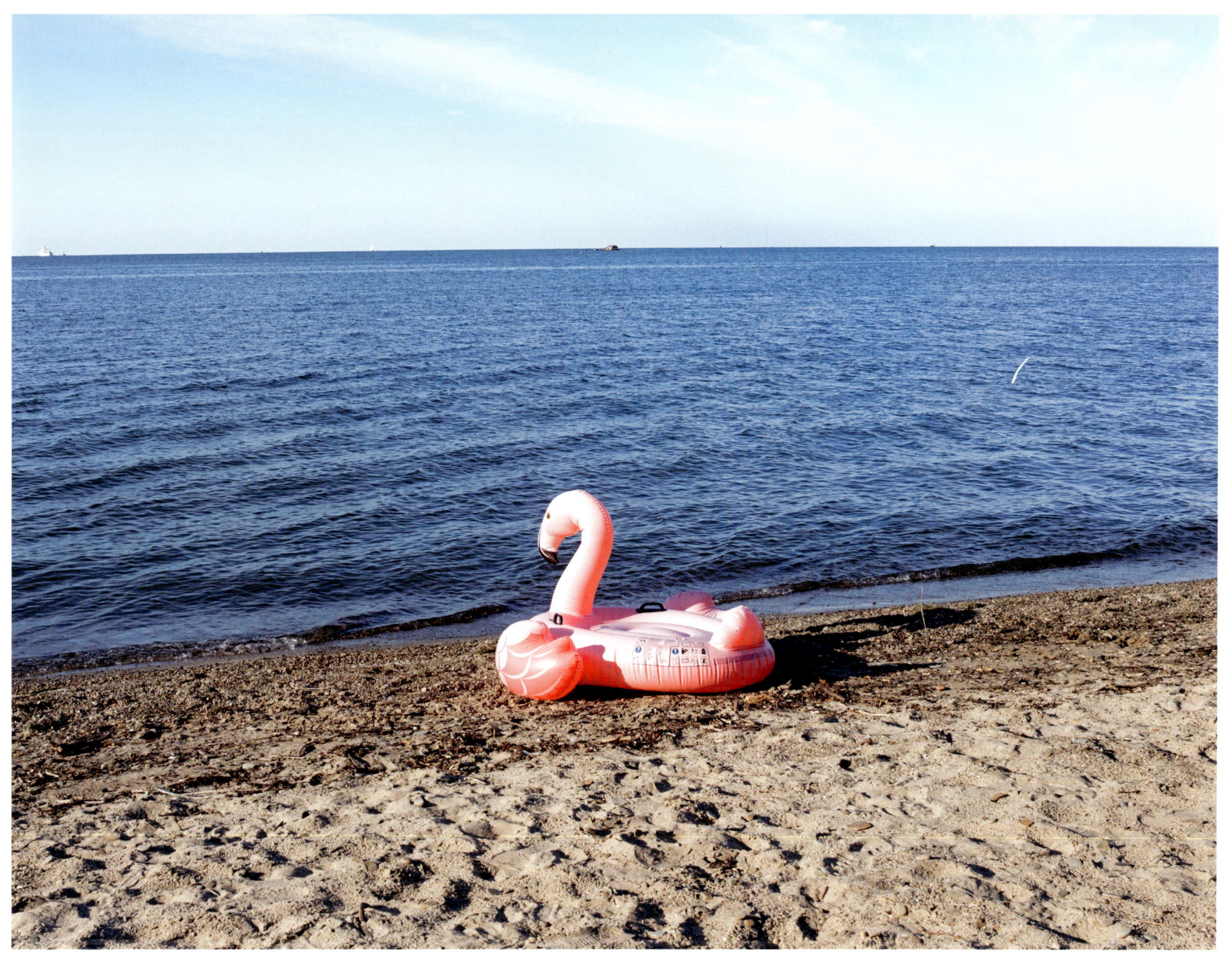

Pink flamingo, Freeport Beach, Pennsylvania, 2022

Nuclear power plant, Port Clinton, Ohio, 2022

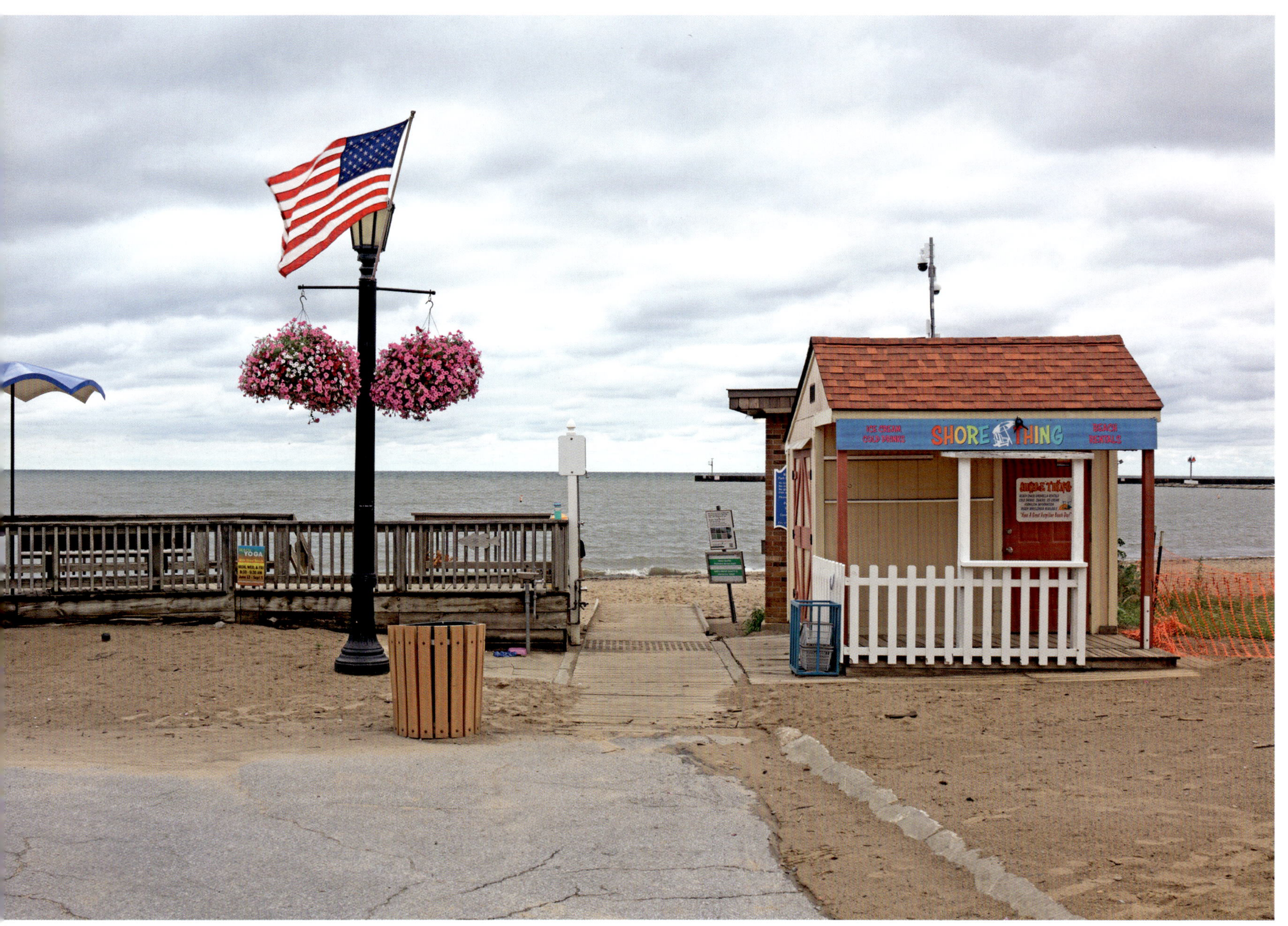

Vermilion Beach, Ohio, 2022

Boat storage, Port Clinton, Ohio, 2022

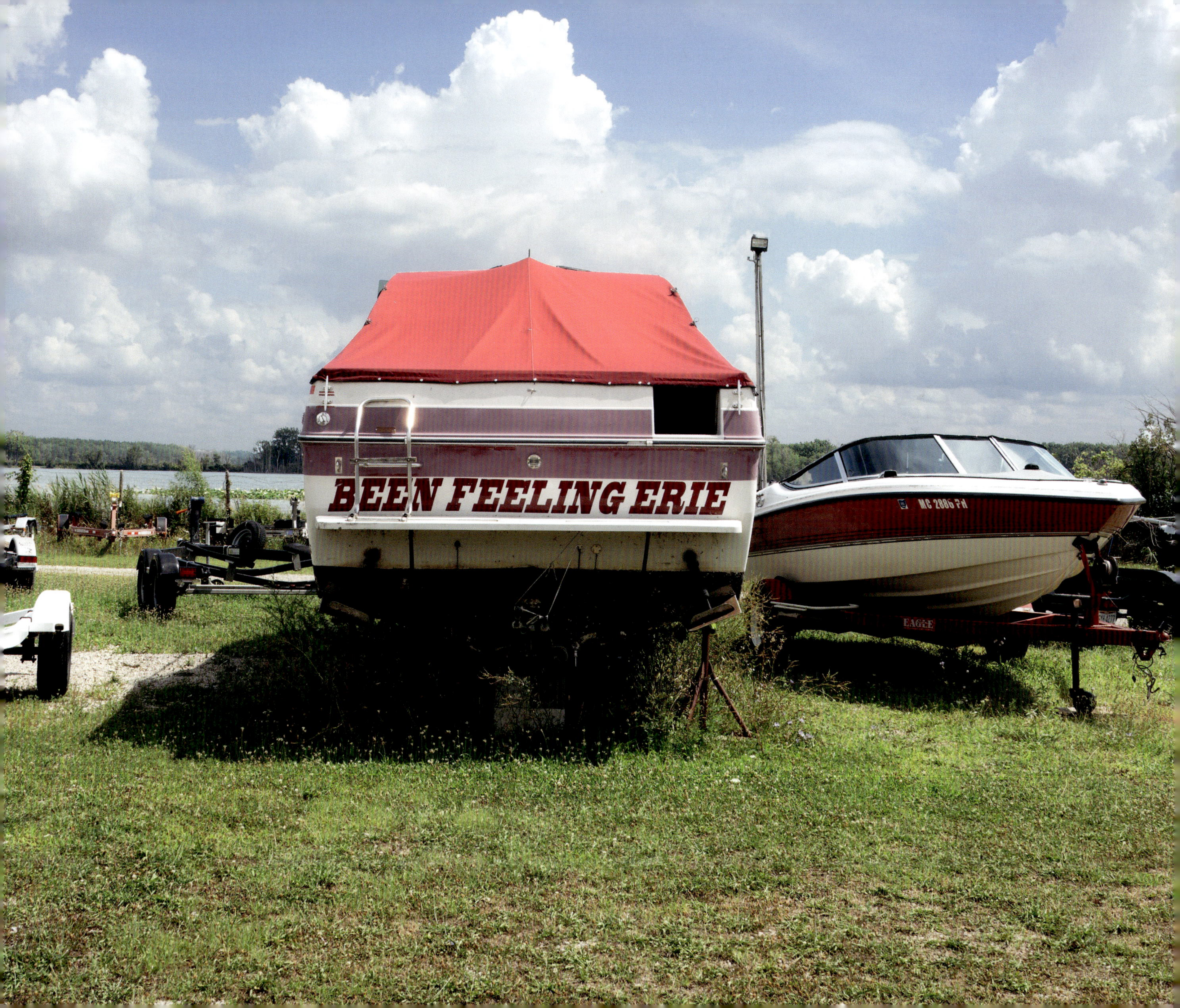
BEEN FEELING ERIE
EAGLE

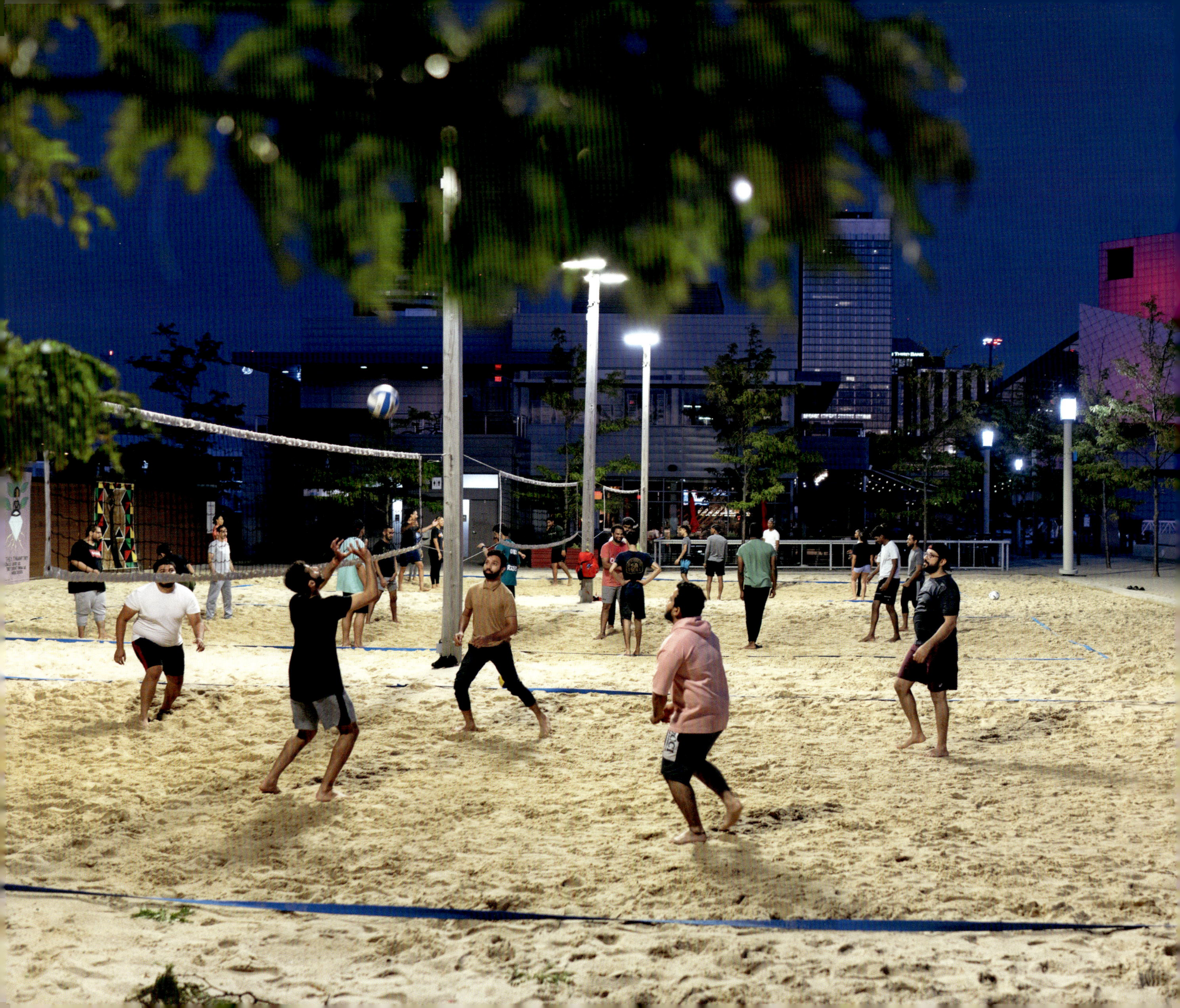

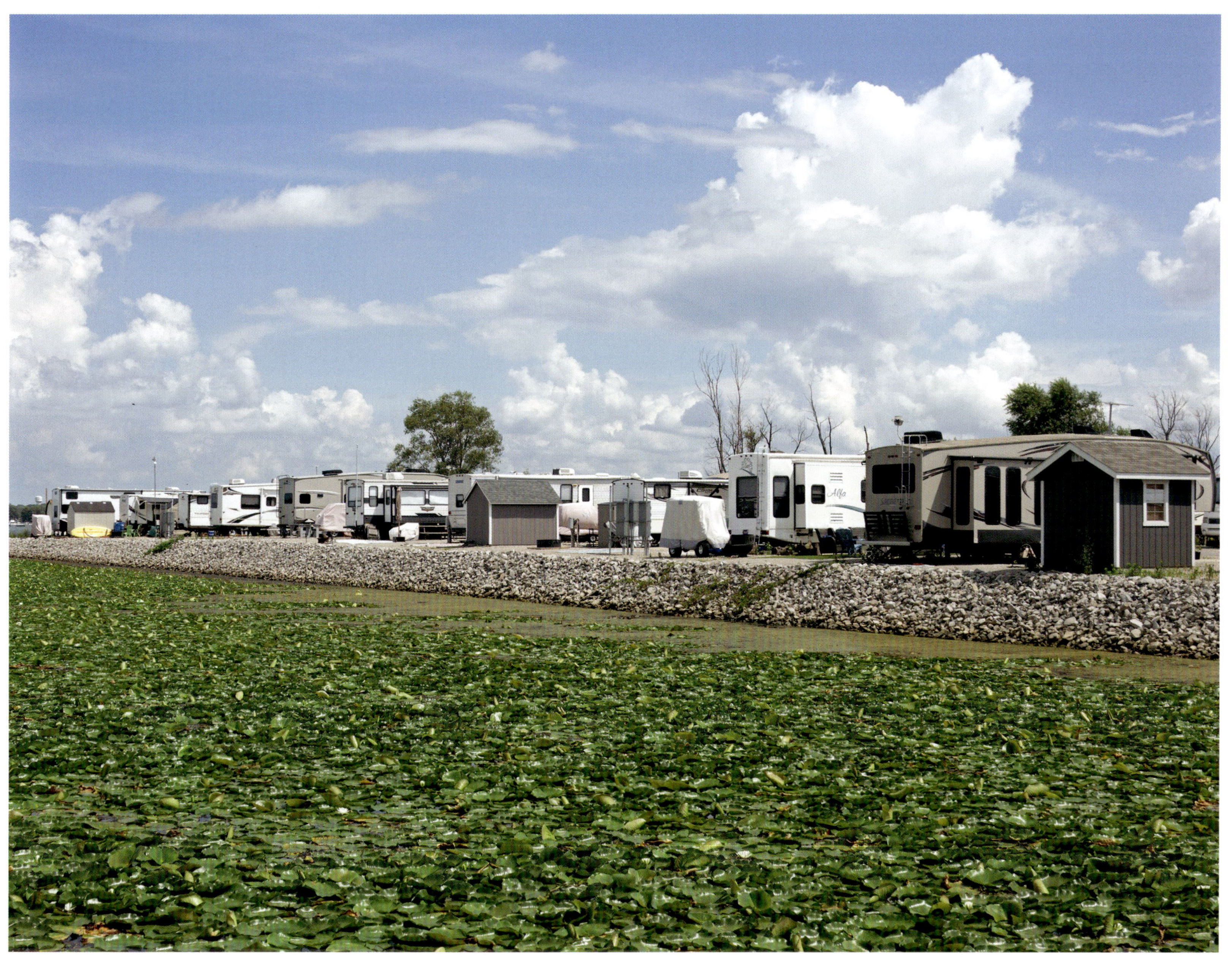

RV park, Ottawa County, Ohio, 2022

Beach volleyball, Cleveland, Ohio, 2022

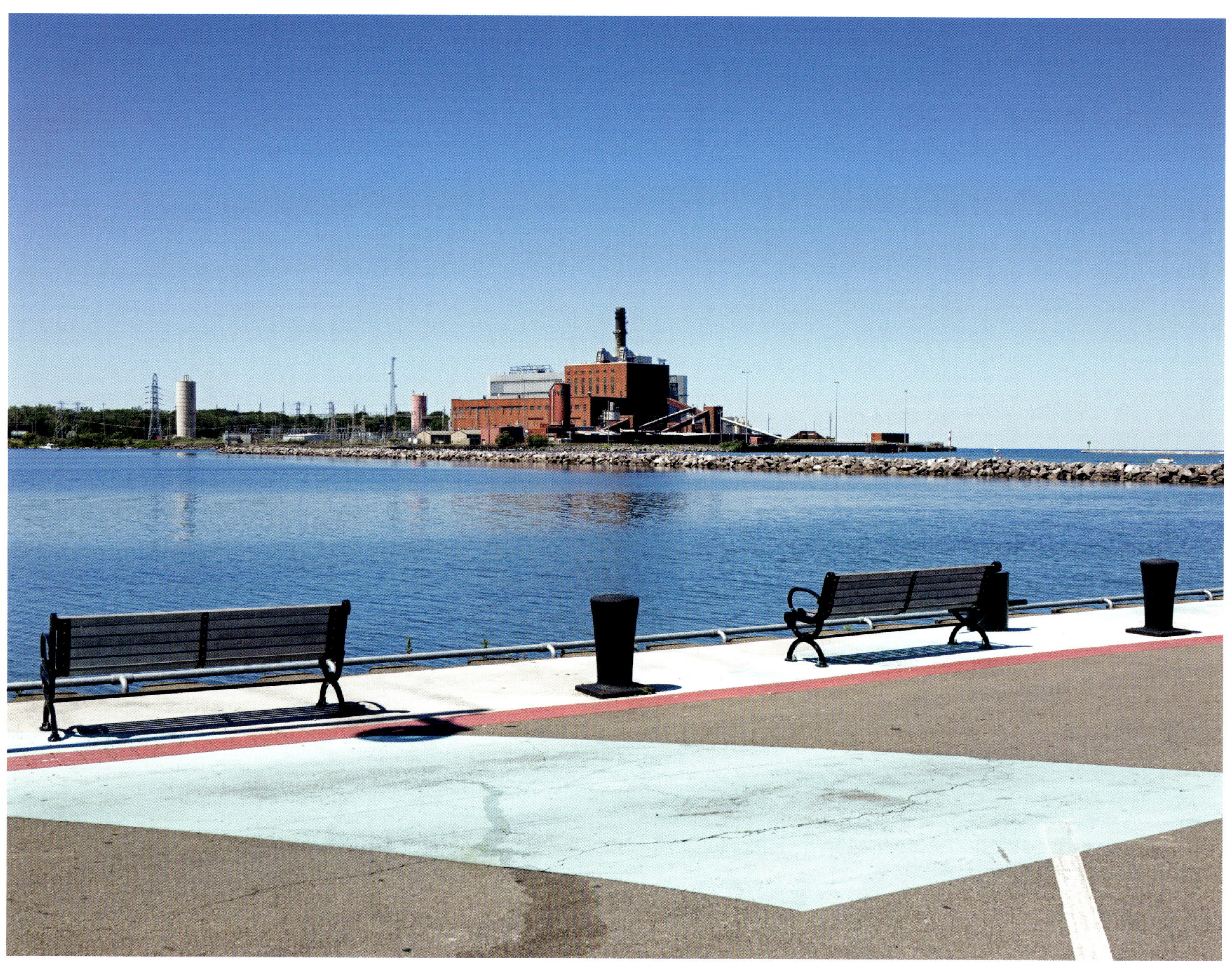

Scenic view, Dunkirk, New York, 2022

Here Comes the Sun, Olcott Beach, New York, 2022

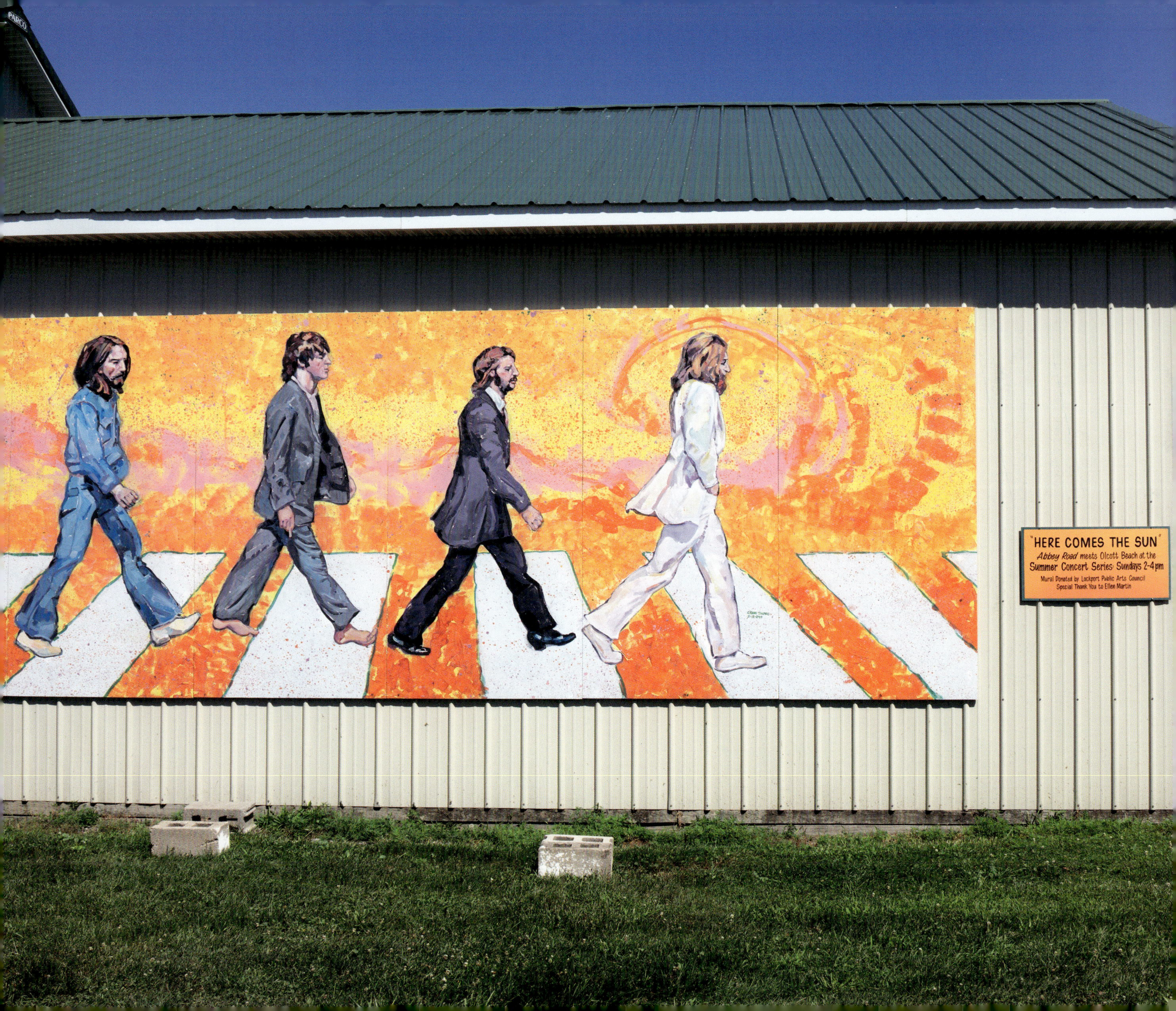
"HERE COMES THE SUN"
Abbey Road meets Olcott Beach at the
Summer Concert Series: Sundays 2-4pm
Mural Donated by Lockport Public Arts Council
Special Thank You to Ellen Martin

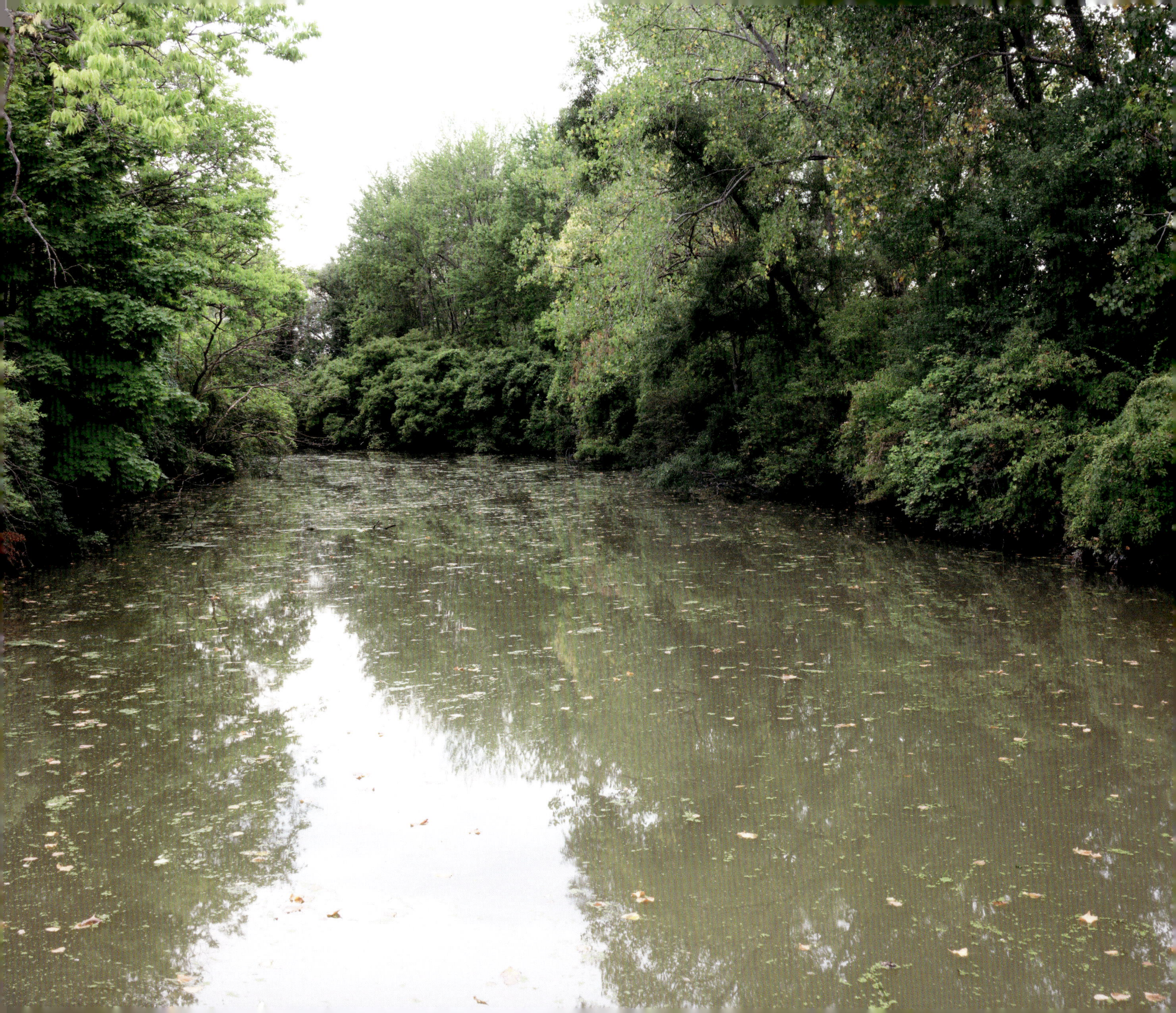

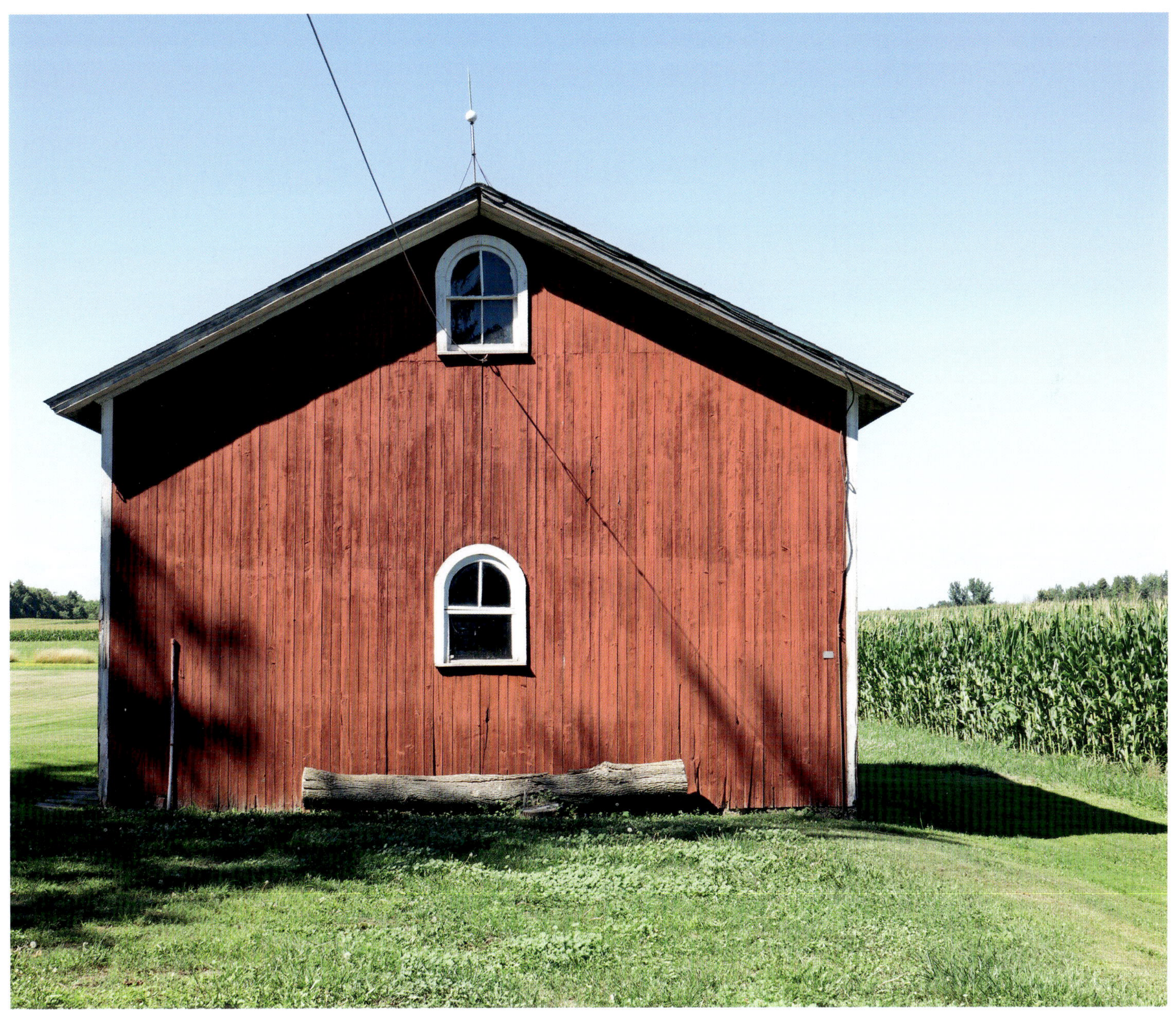

Red barn, Somerset, New York, 2022

Agricultural runoff, Ottawa County, Ohio, 2022

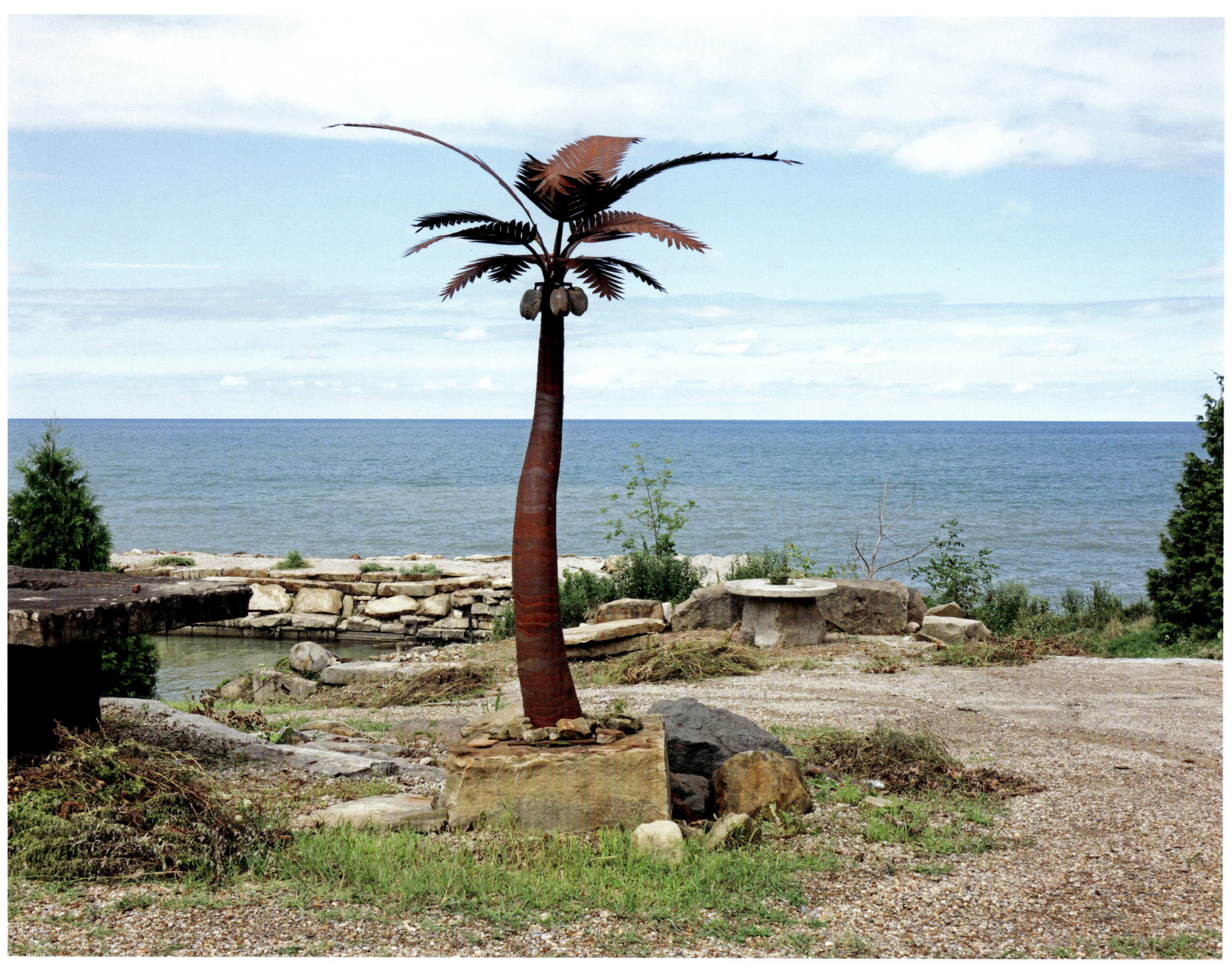

Metal palm, Lakewood, Ohio, 2022

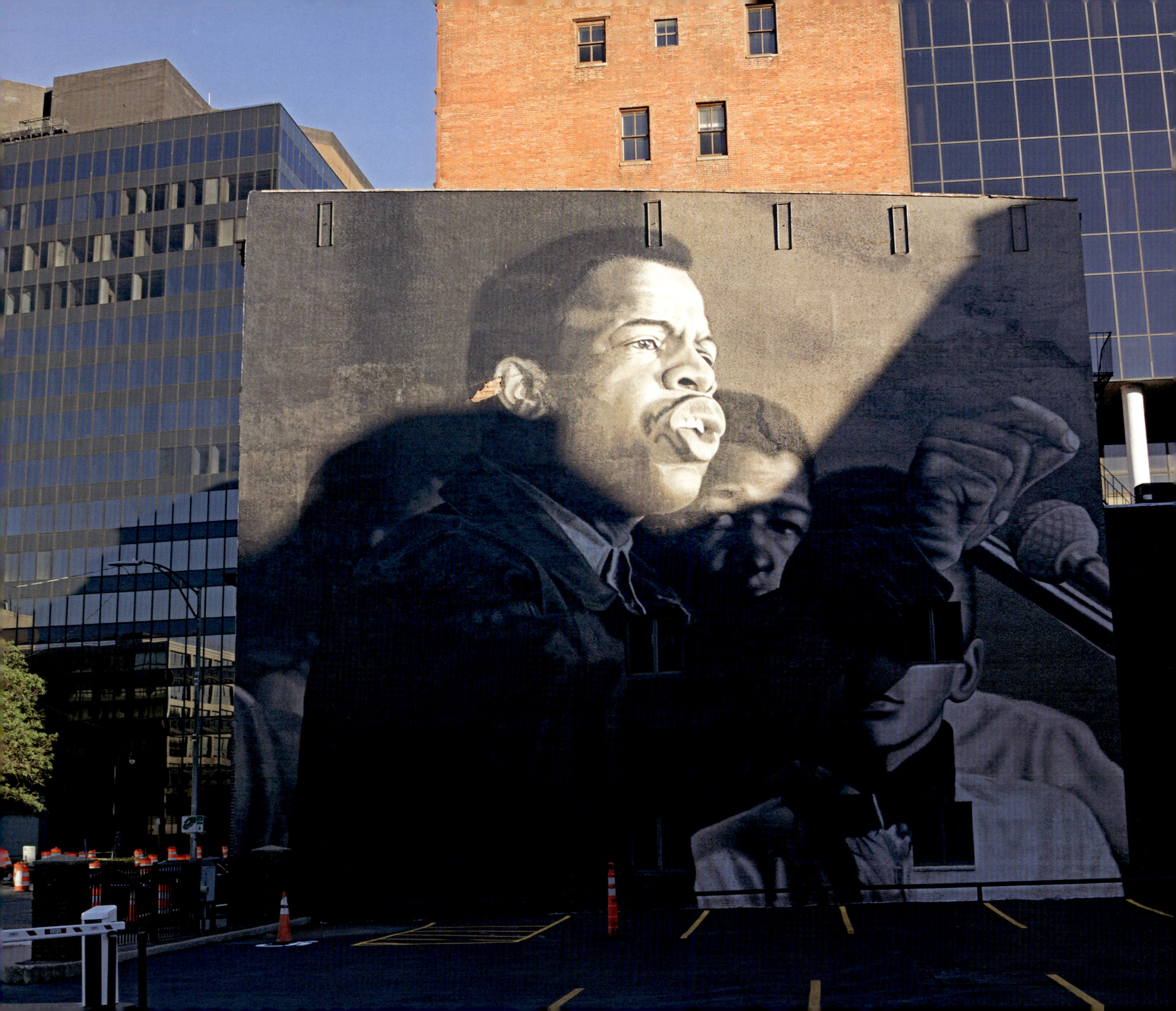

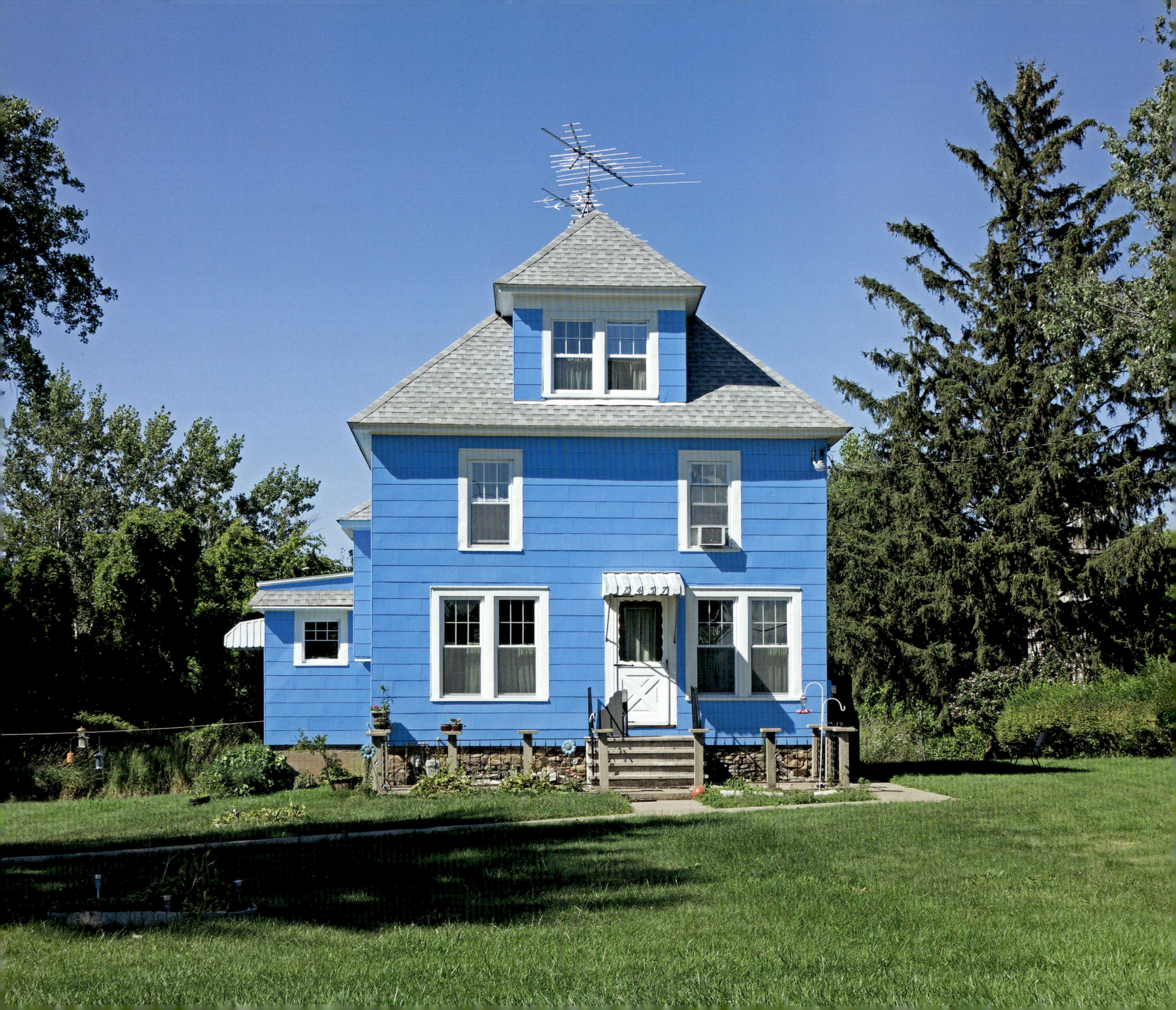
8437

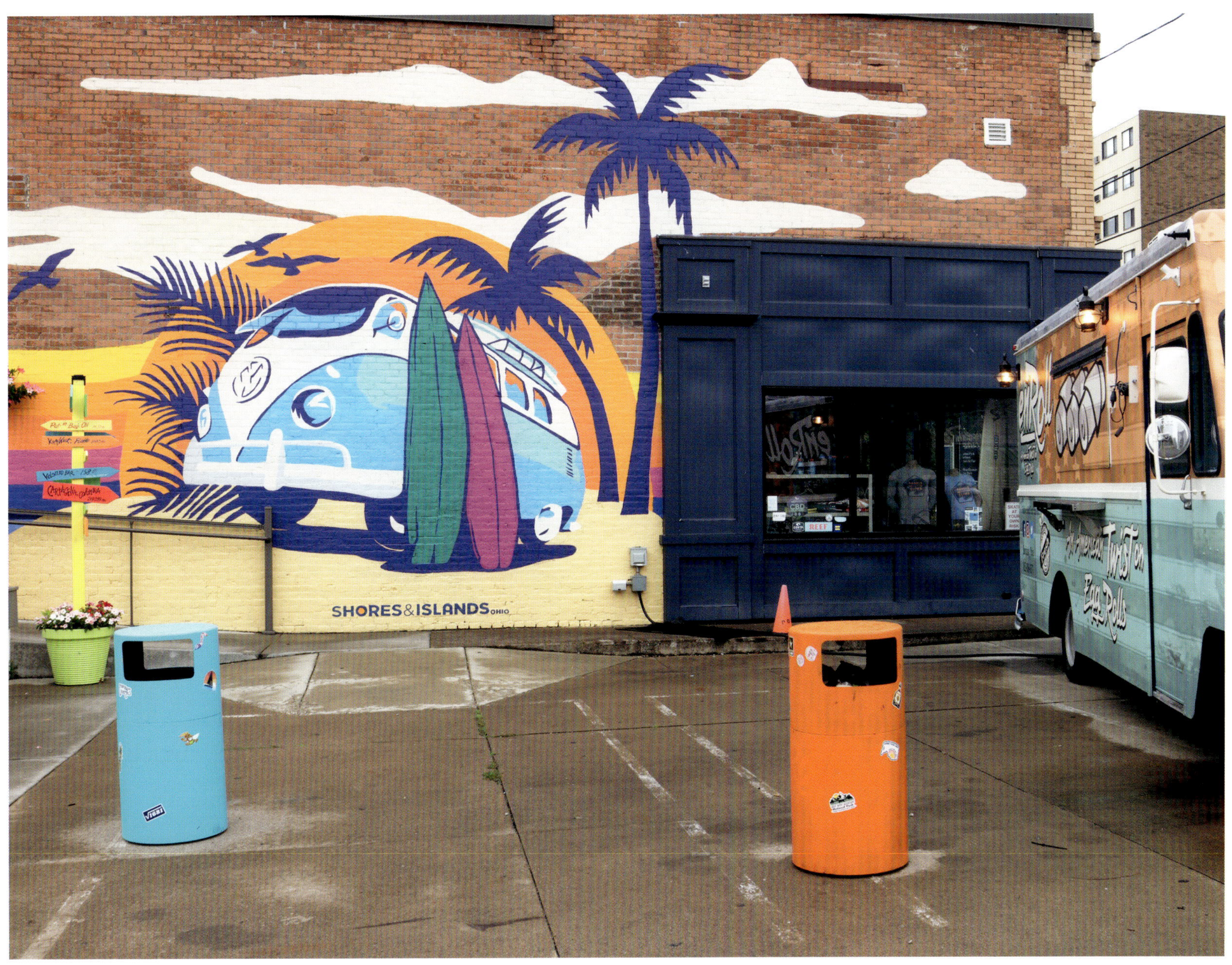

Food truck, Erie County, Ohio, 2022

Blue house, Sunset Beach, New York, 2022

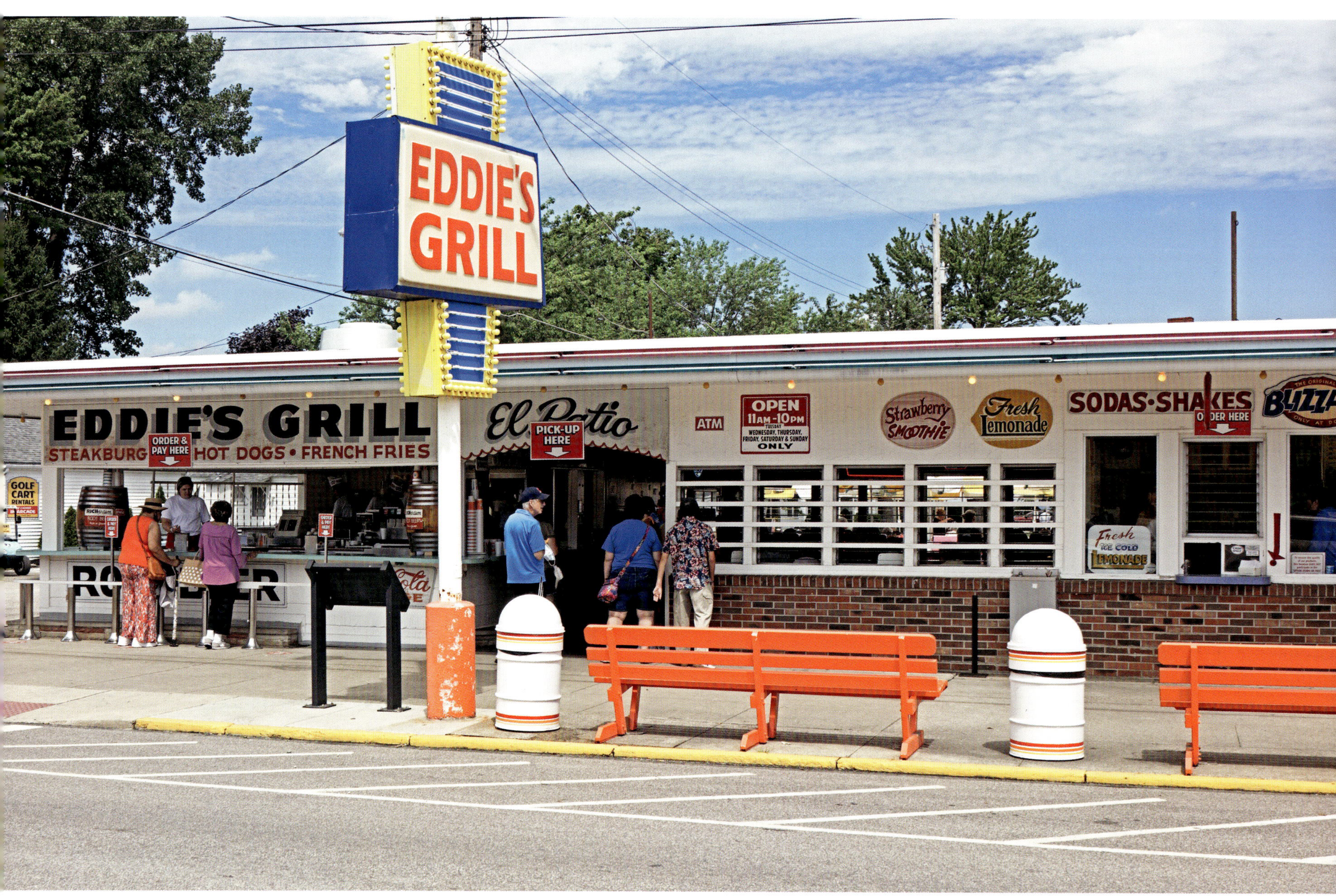

Diner, Ashtabula County, Ohio, 2022

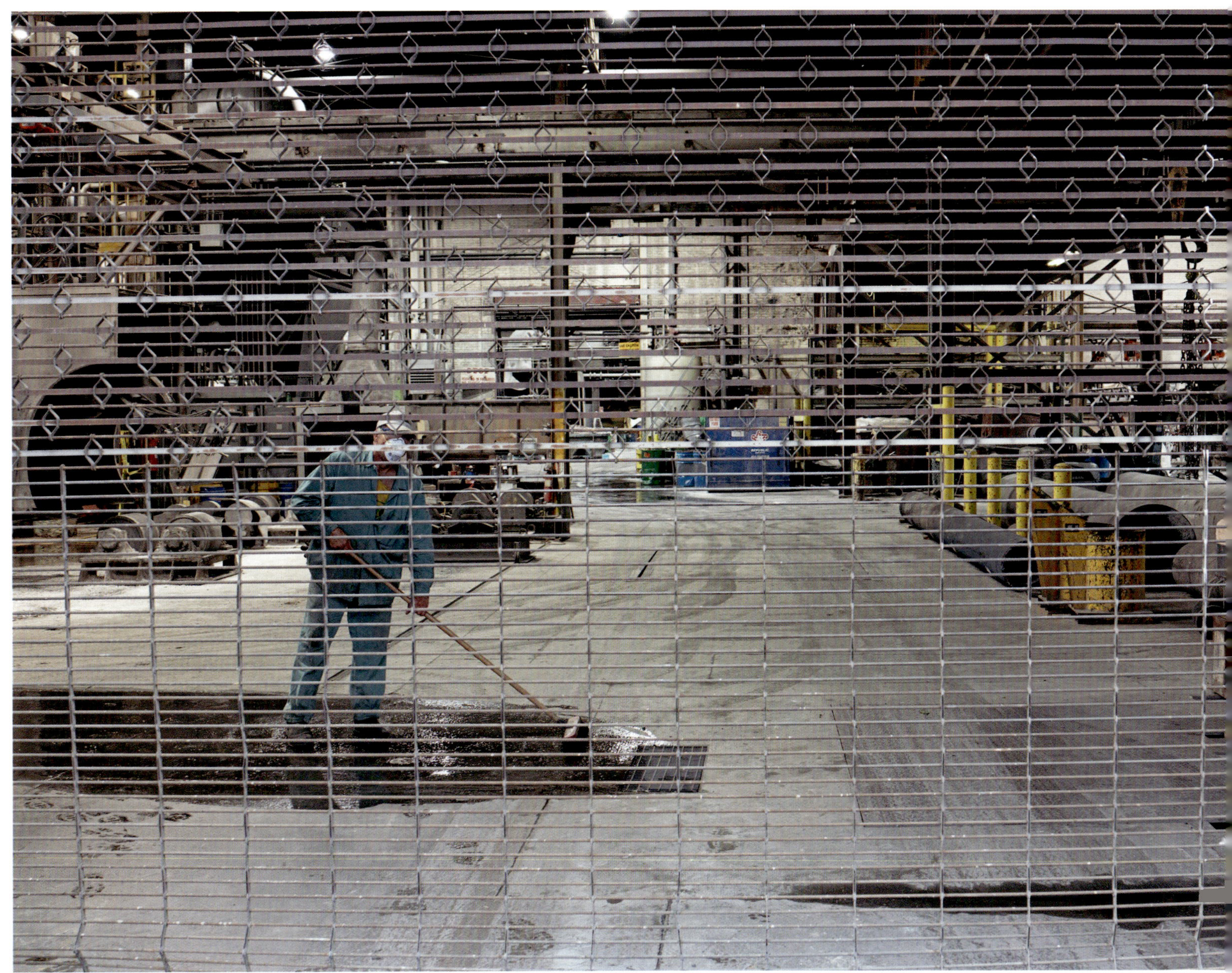

Steelworker, Sandusky, Ohio, 2022

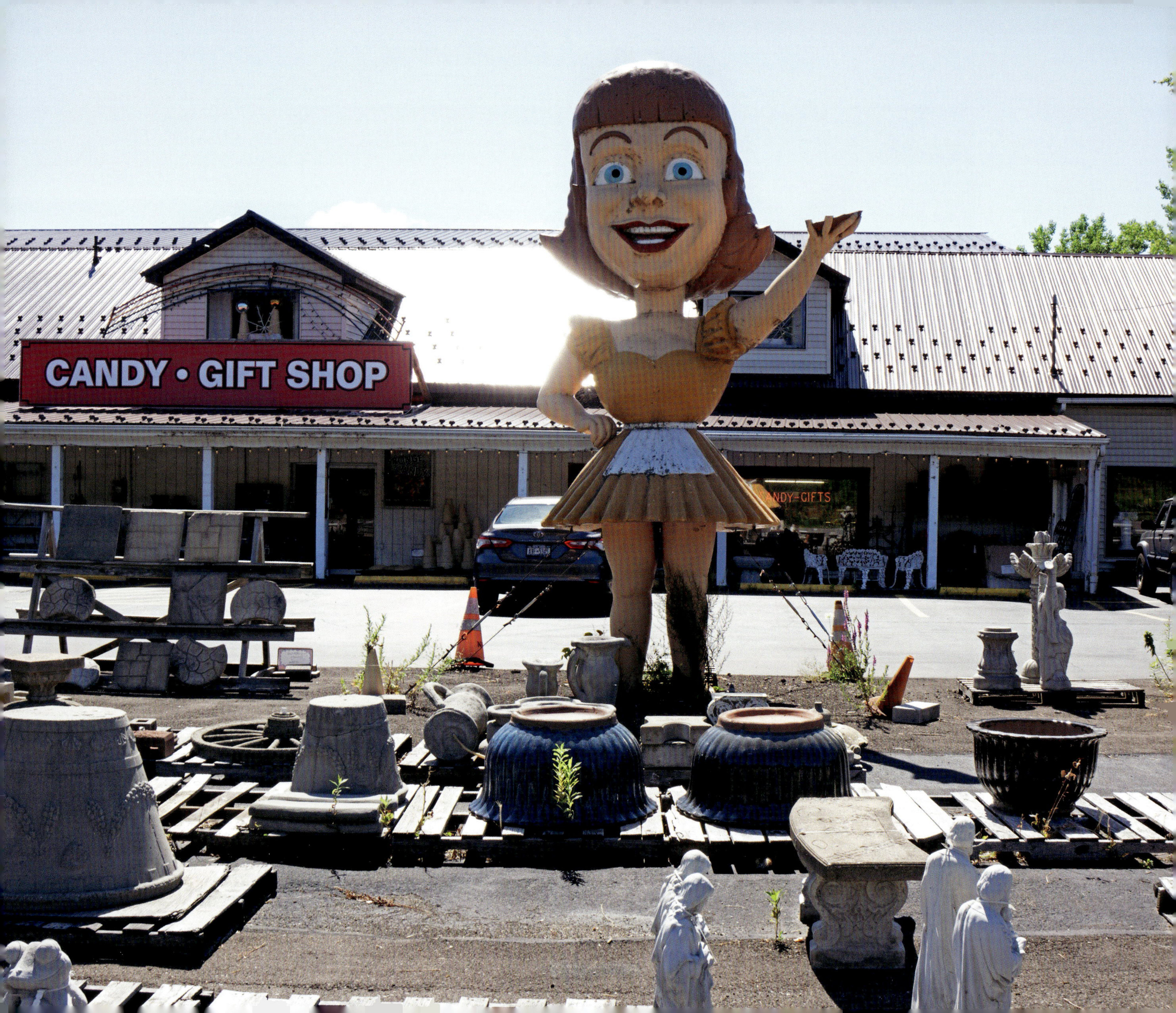
CANDY • GIFT SHOP

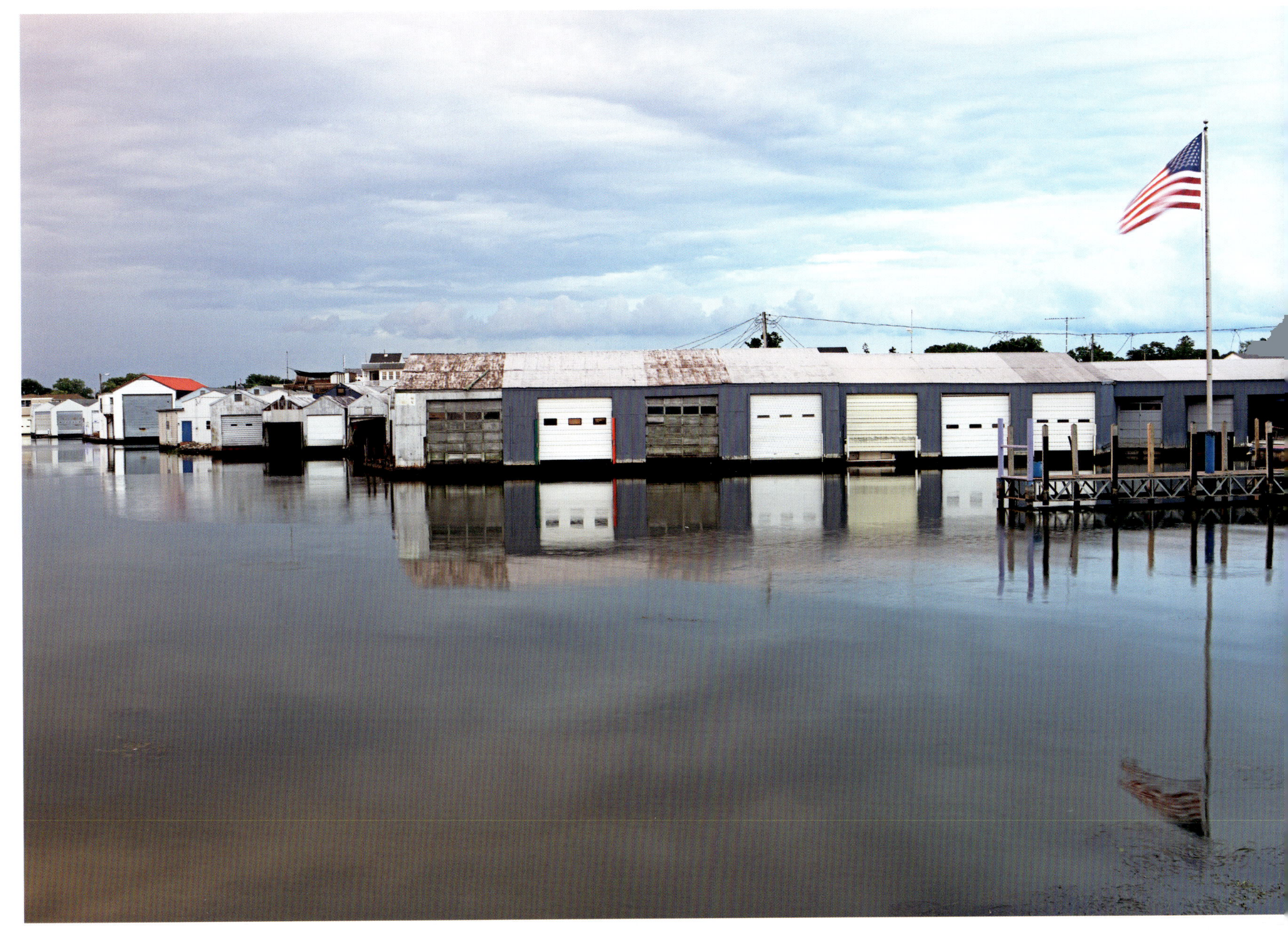

Boathouse, Erie County, Ohio, 2022

Gift shop, Angola-on-the-Lake, New York, 2022

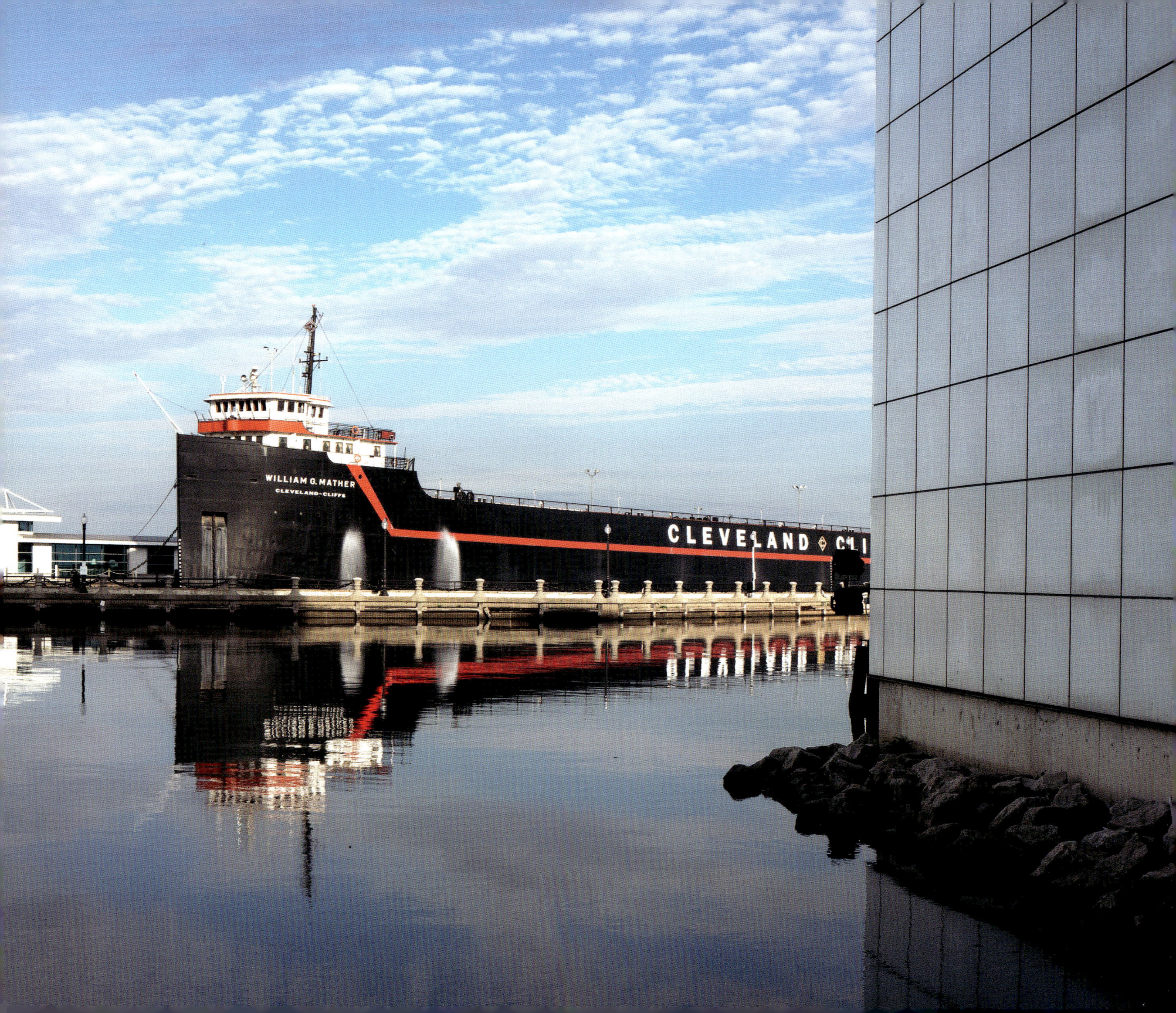
WILLIAM G. MATHER
CLEVELAND-CLIFFS
CLEVELAND

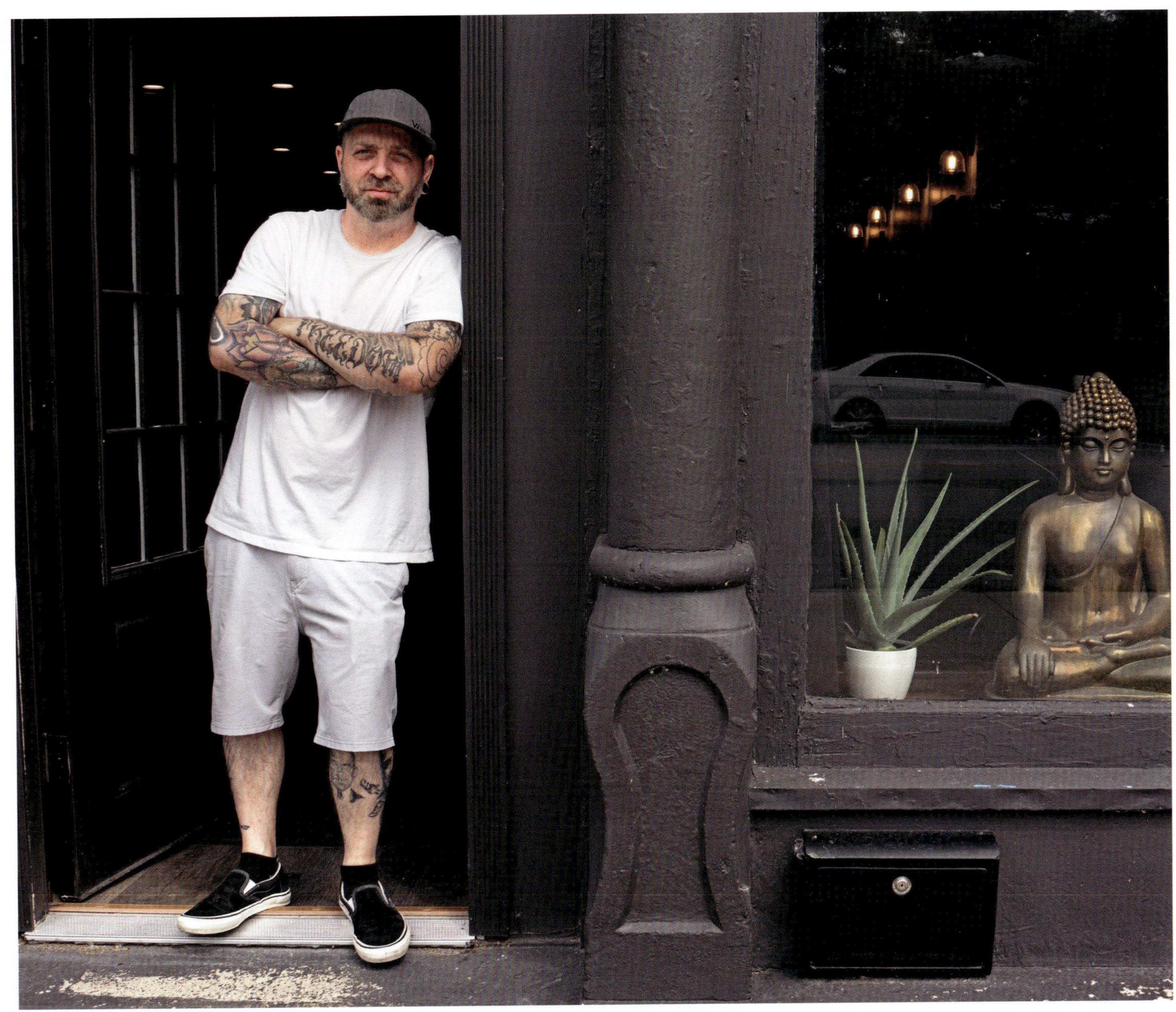

Rob (tattoo artist), Sandusky, Ohio, 2022

Great Lakes freighter, Erie, Pennsylvania, 2022

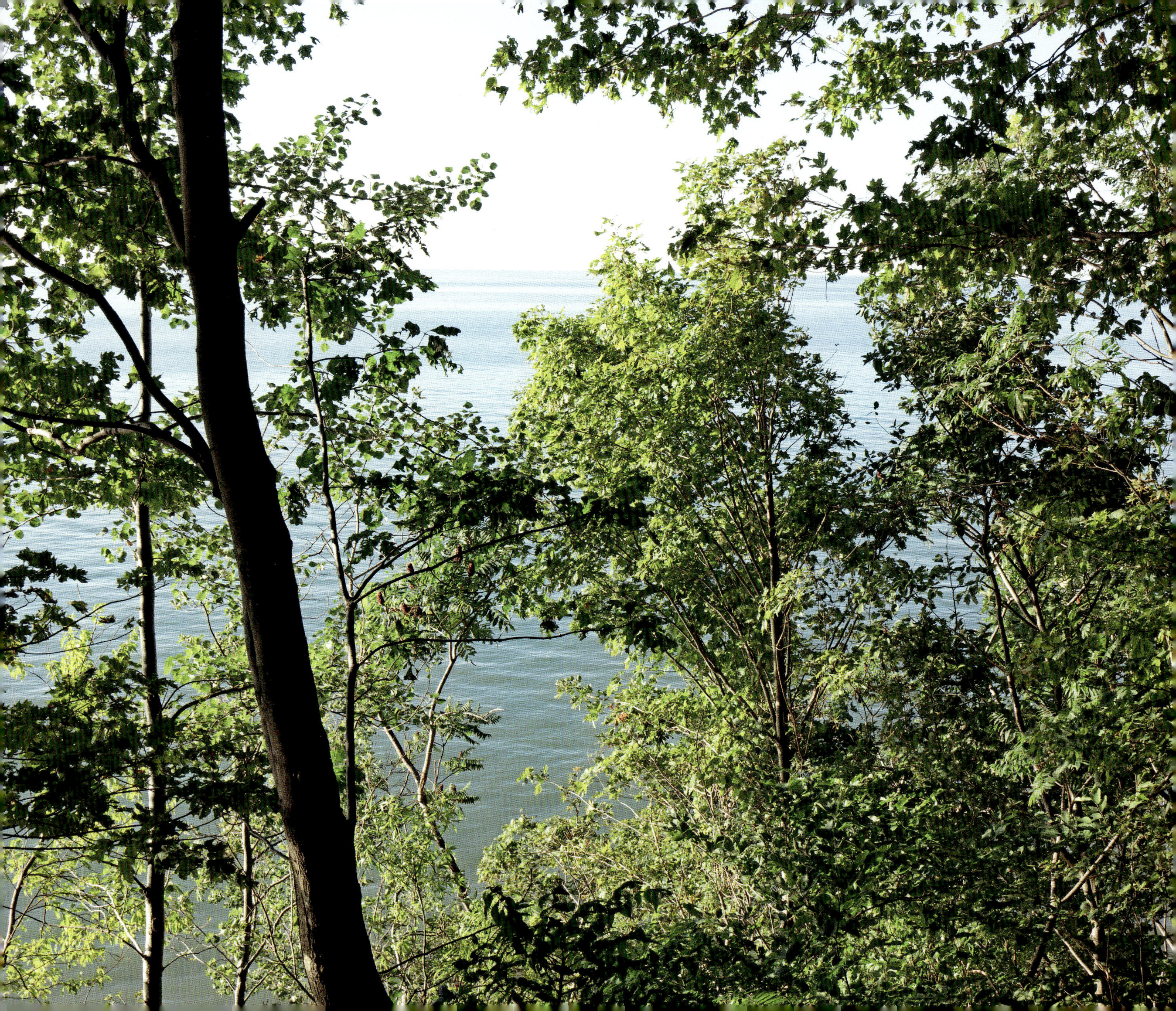

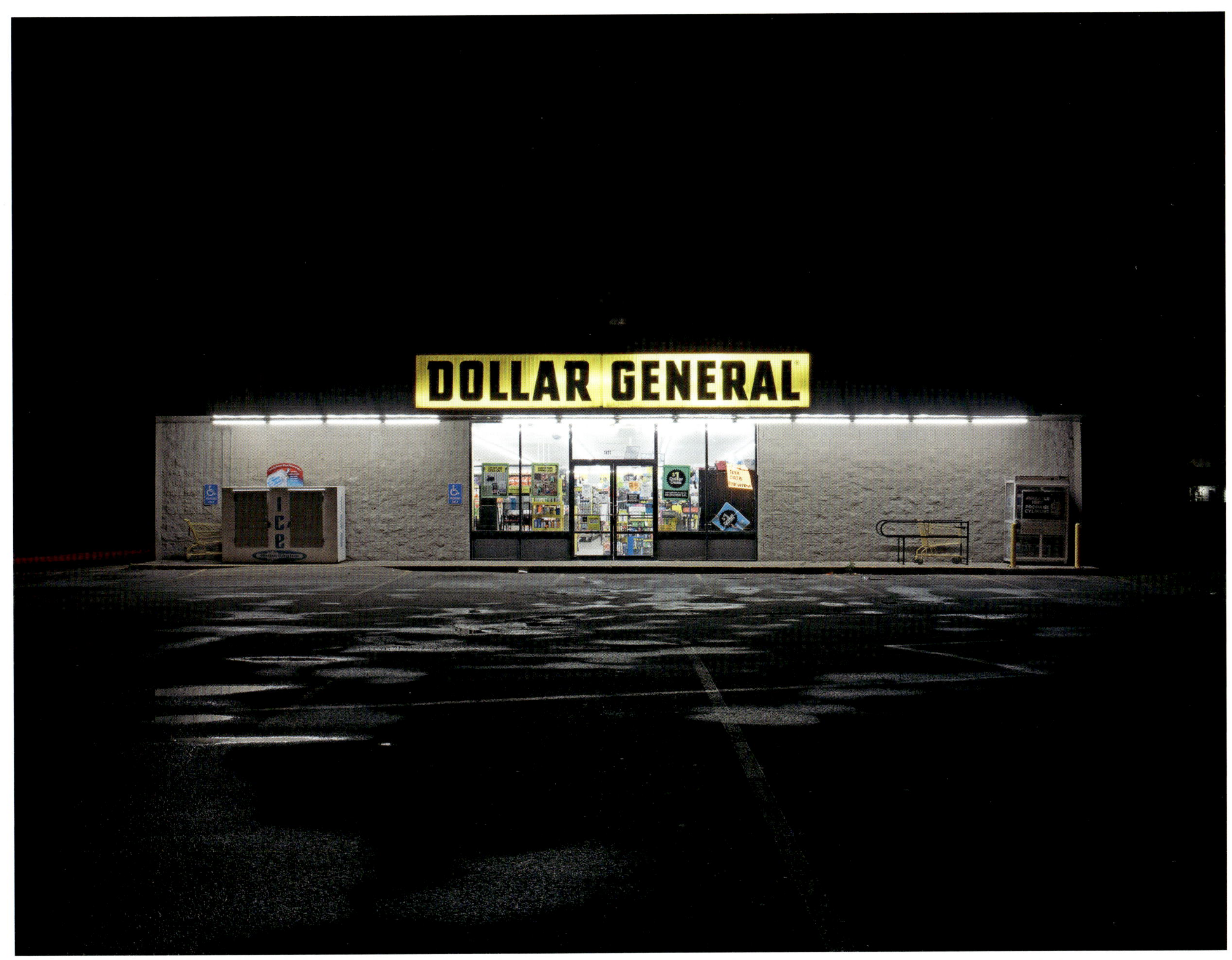

Convenience store, Sandusky, Ohio, 2022

Erie Bluffs, Pennsylvania, 2022

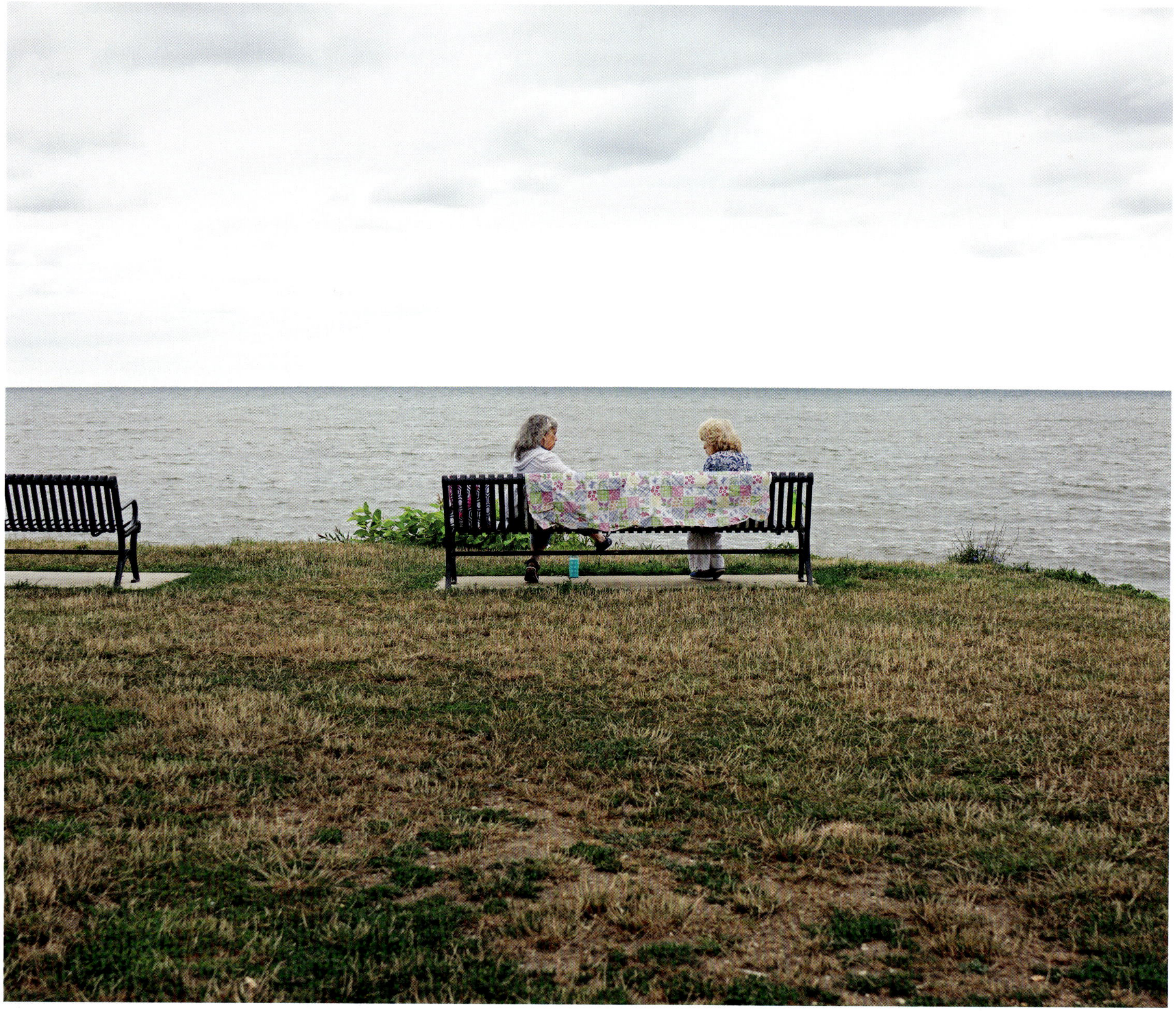

Lakeside park, Vermilion, Ohio, 2022

Passing storm, Sandusky Bay, Ohio, 2022

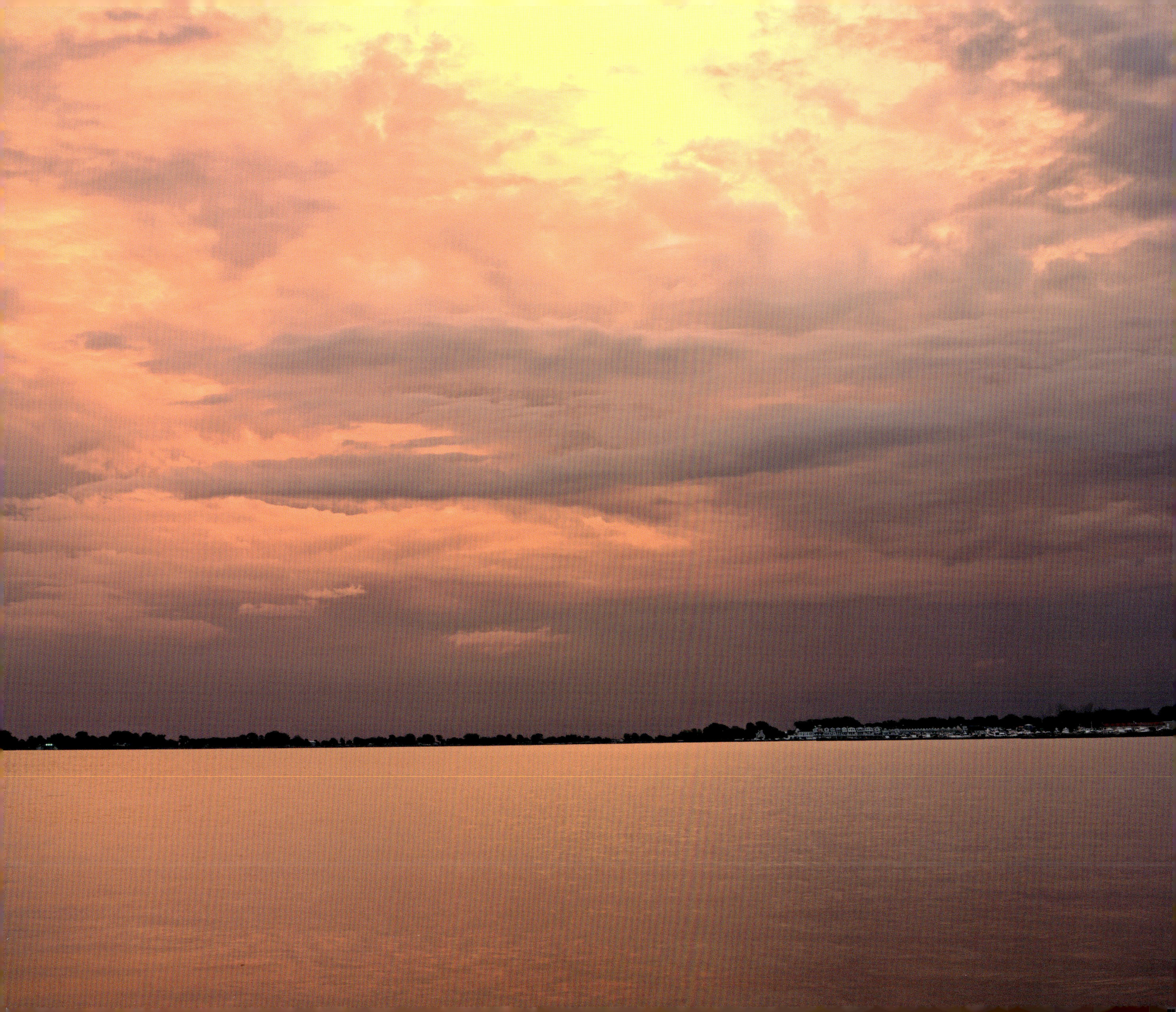

AUTUMN

LAKE HURON

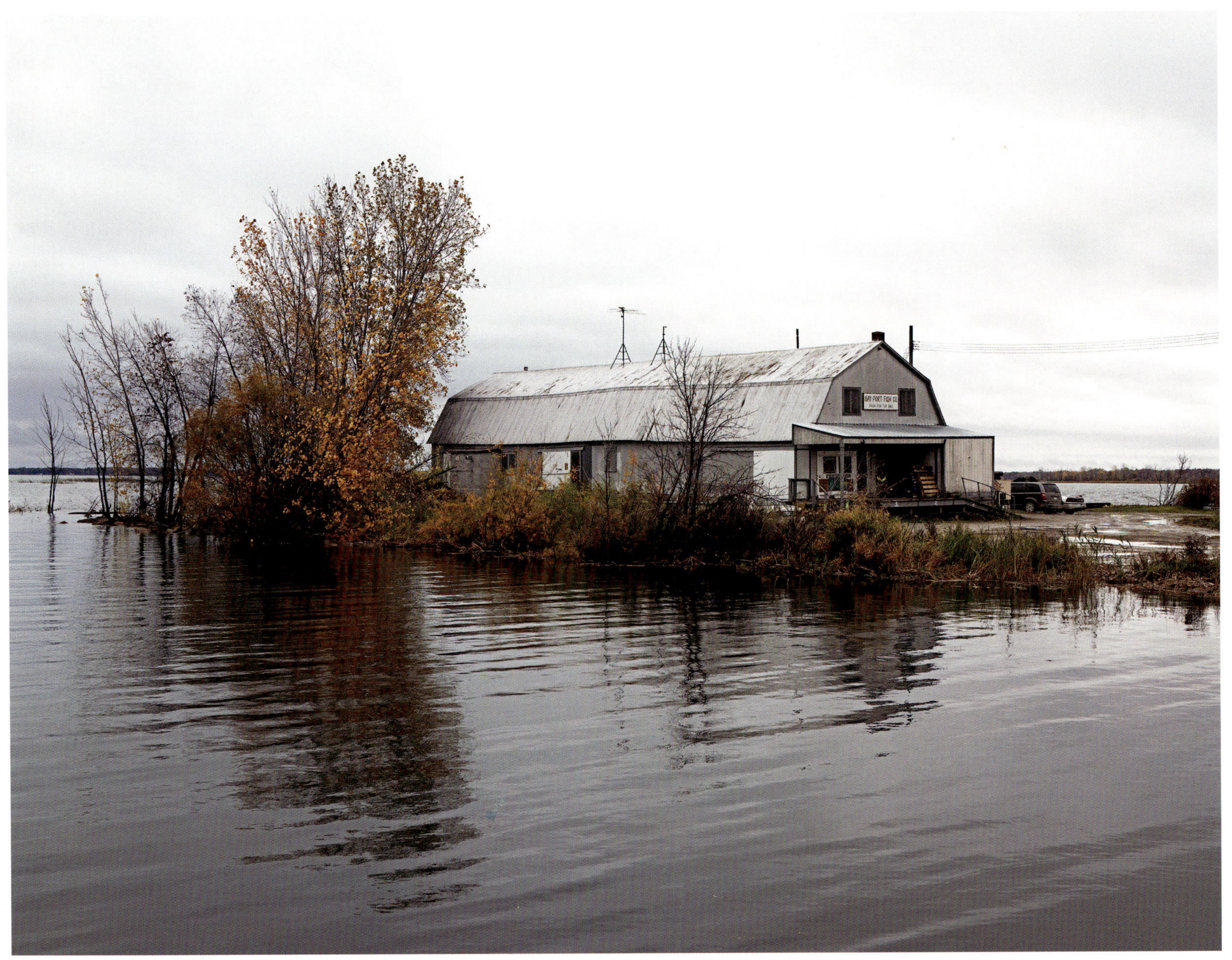

Bay Port Fish Company, Saginaw Bay, Michigan, 2020

Birch trees, Sand Point, Michigan, 2020

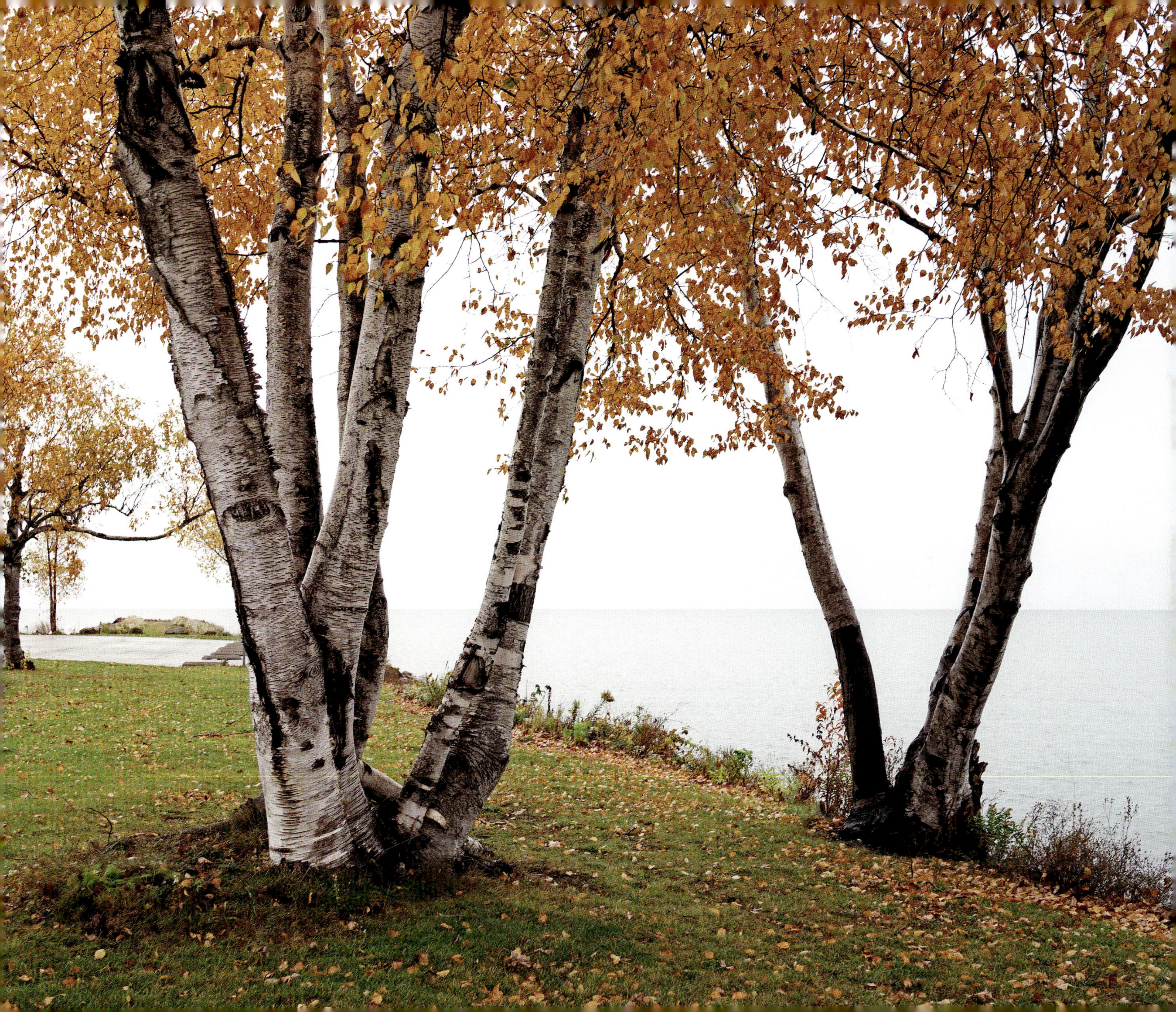

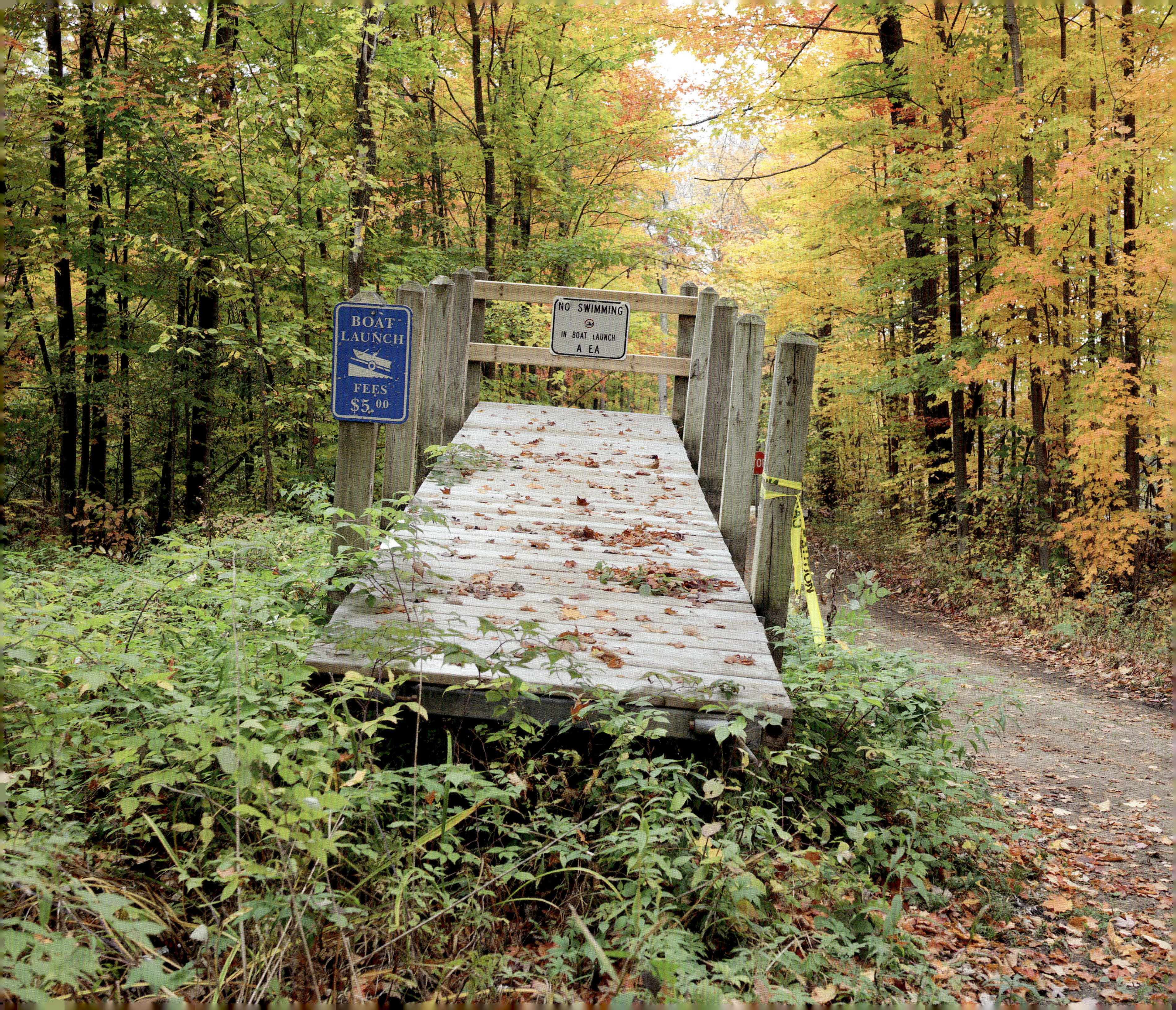
BOAT
LAUNCH
FEES
$5.00
NO SWIMMING
IN BOAT LAUNCH
A EA

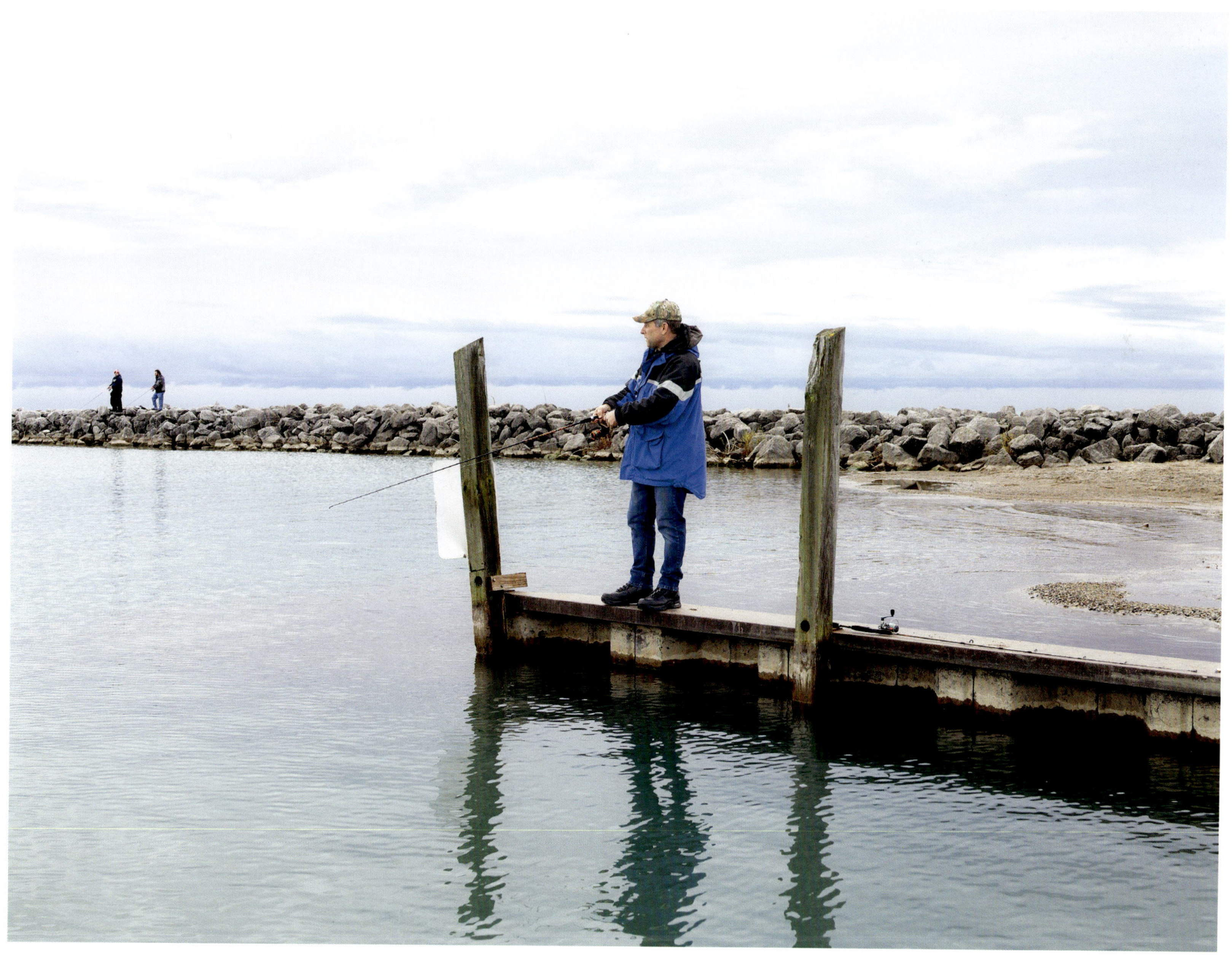

John (fisherman), Lexington Harbor, Michigan, 2020

Boat launch, Lakeport, Michigan, 2020

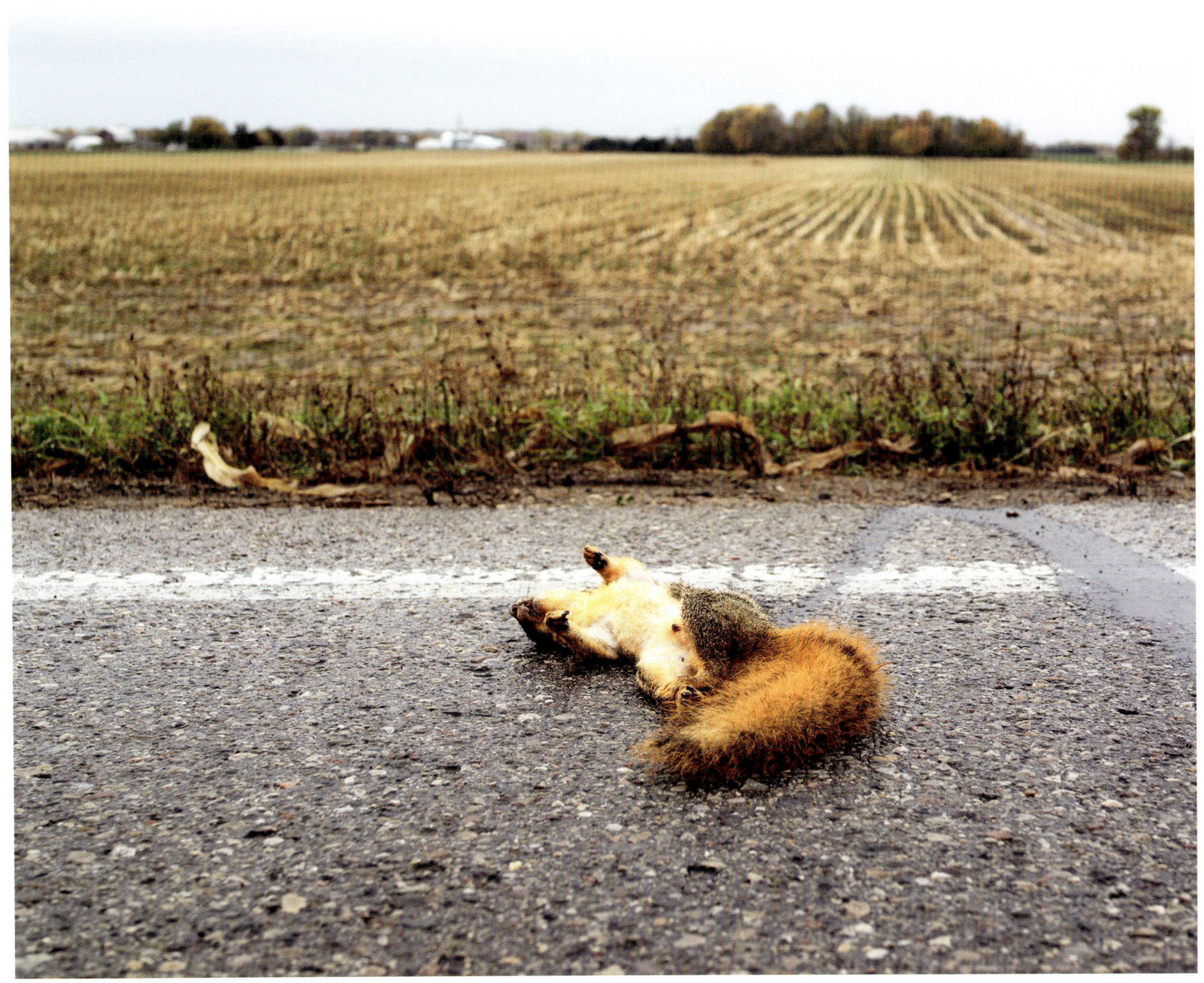

Roadkill, Grindstone City, Michigan, 2020

Sanilac County, Michigan, 2020

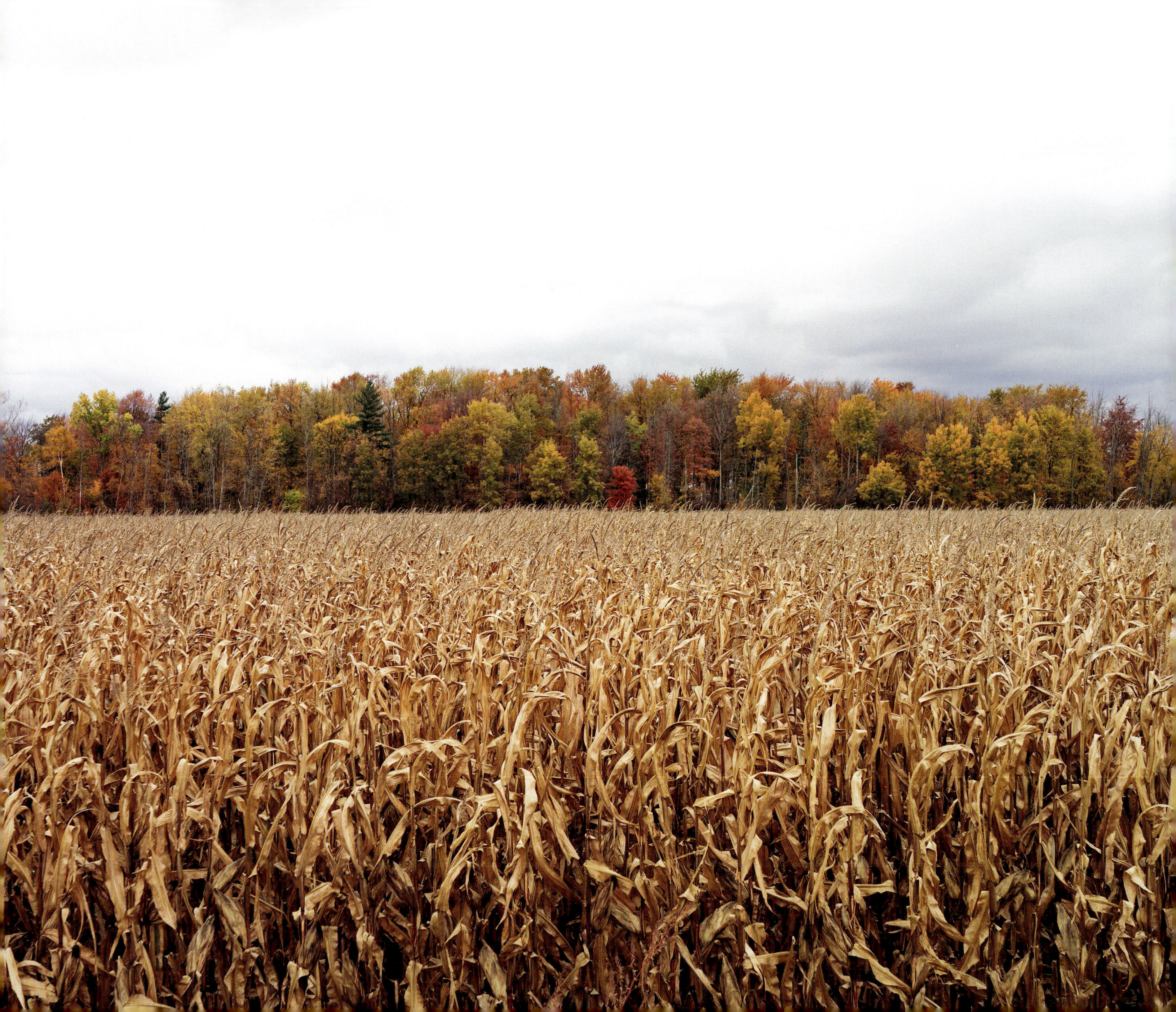

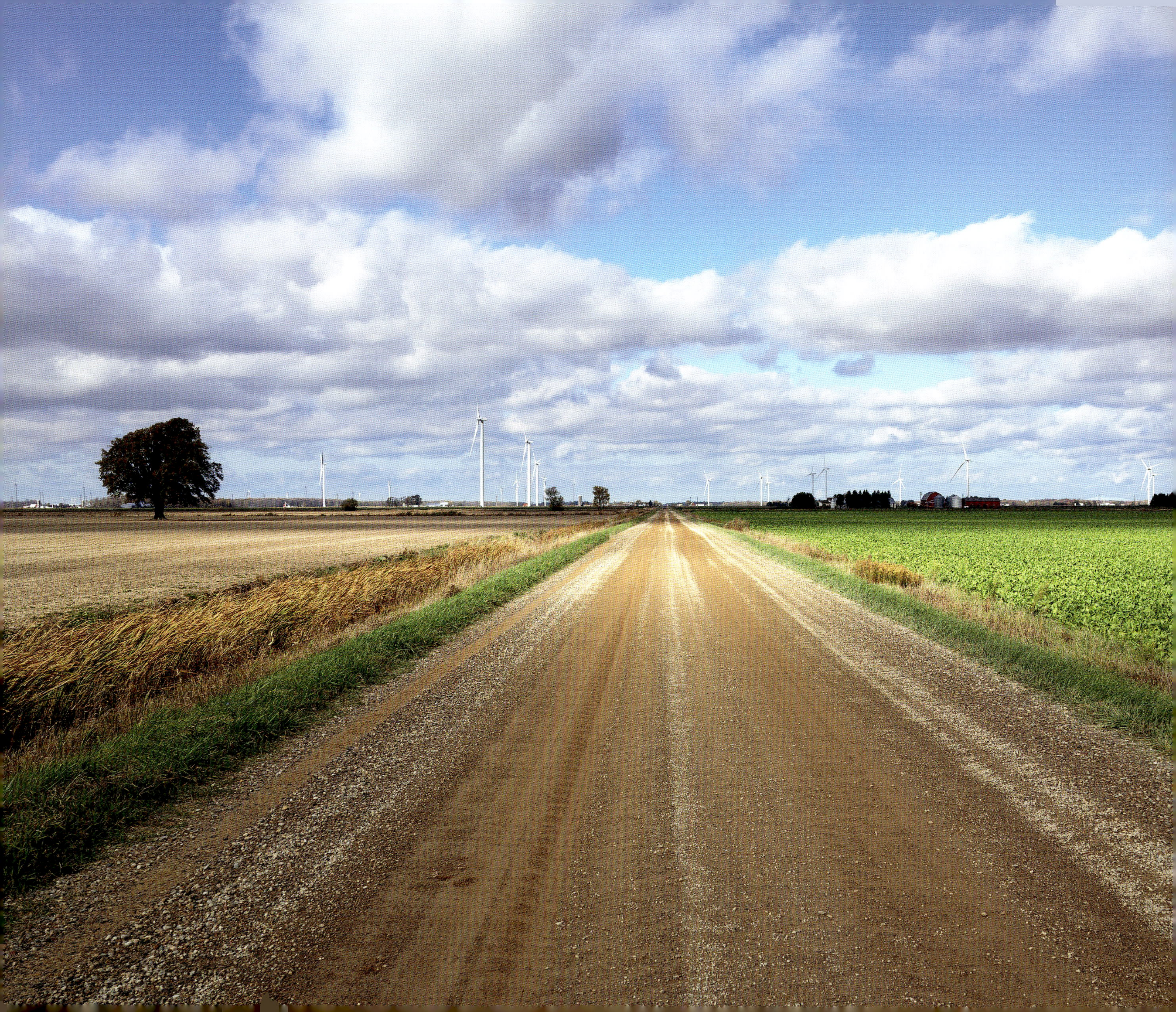

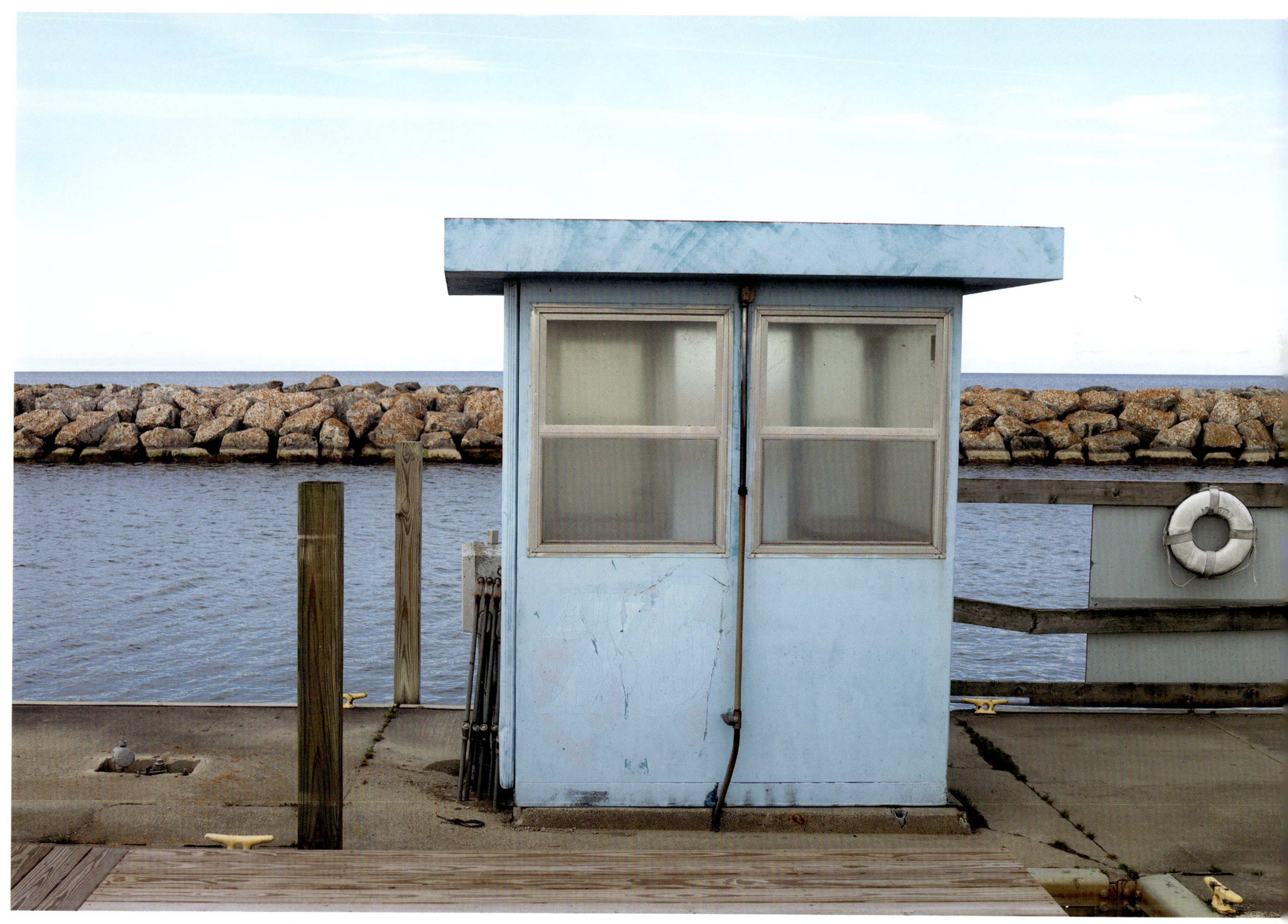

Marina, Huron County, Michigan, 2020

Huron County, Michigan, 2020

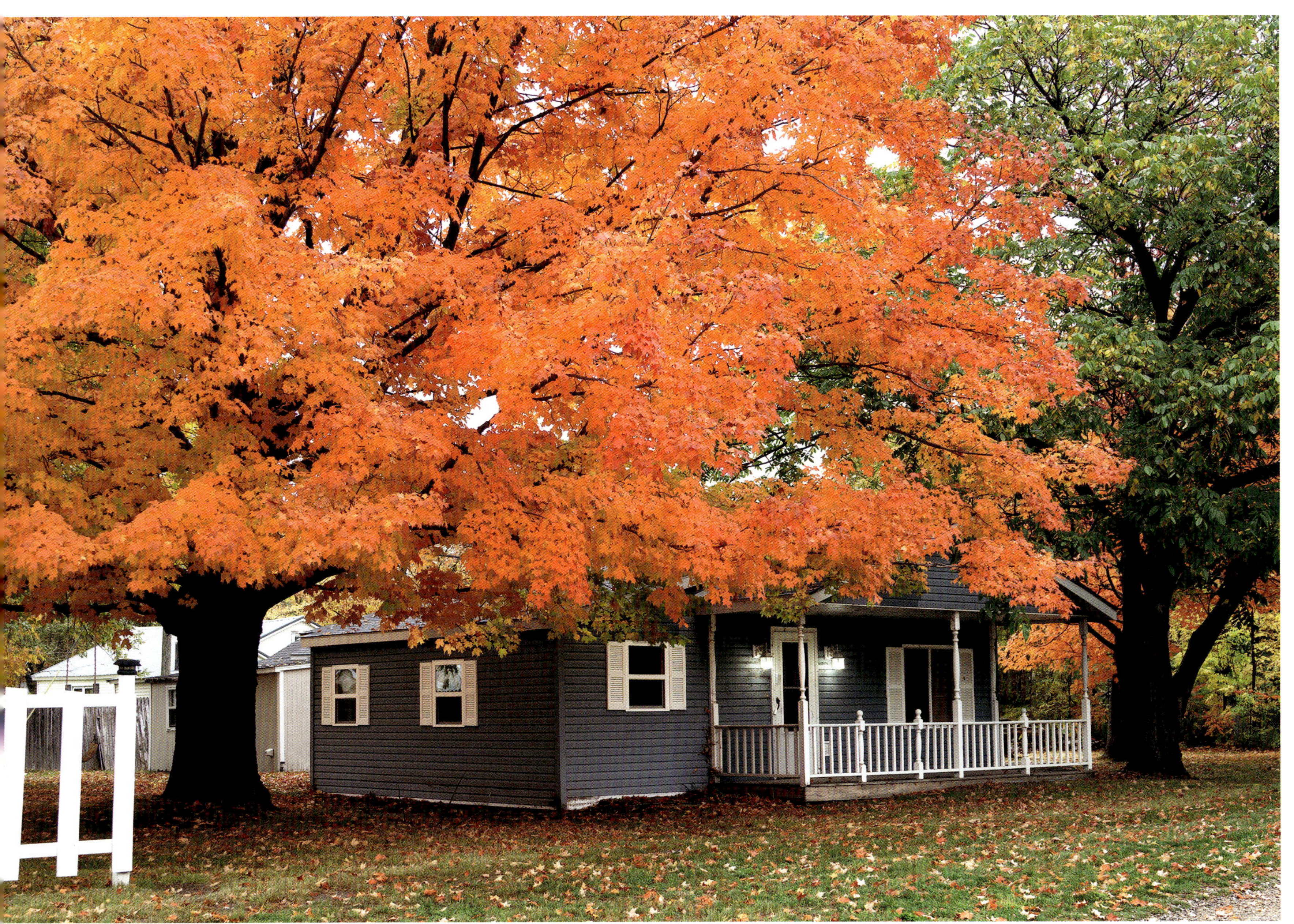

Autumn leaves, Forester, Michigan, 2020

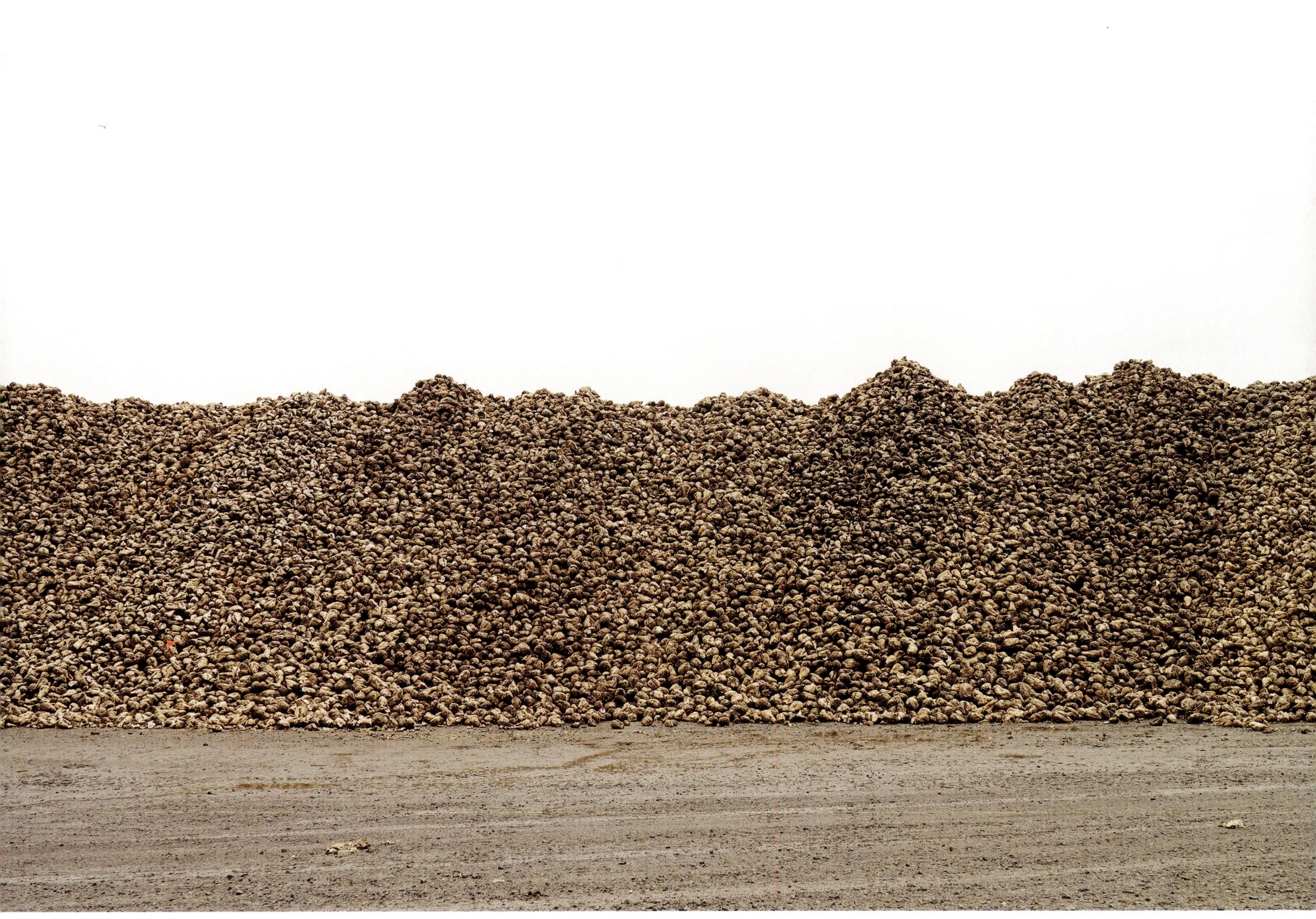

Sugar beet harvest, Sebewaing, Michigan, 2020

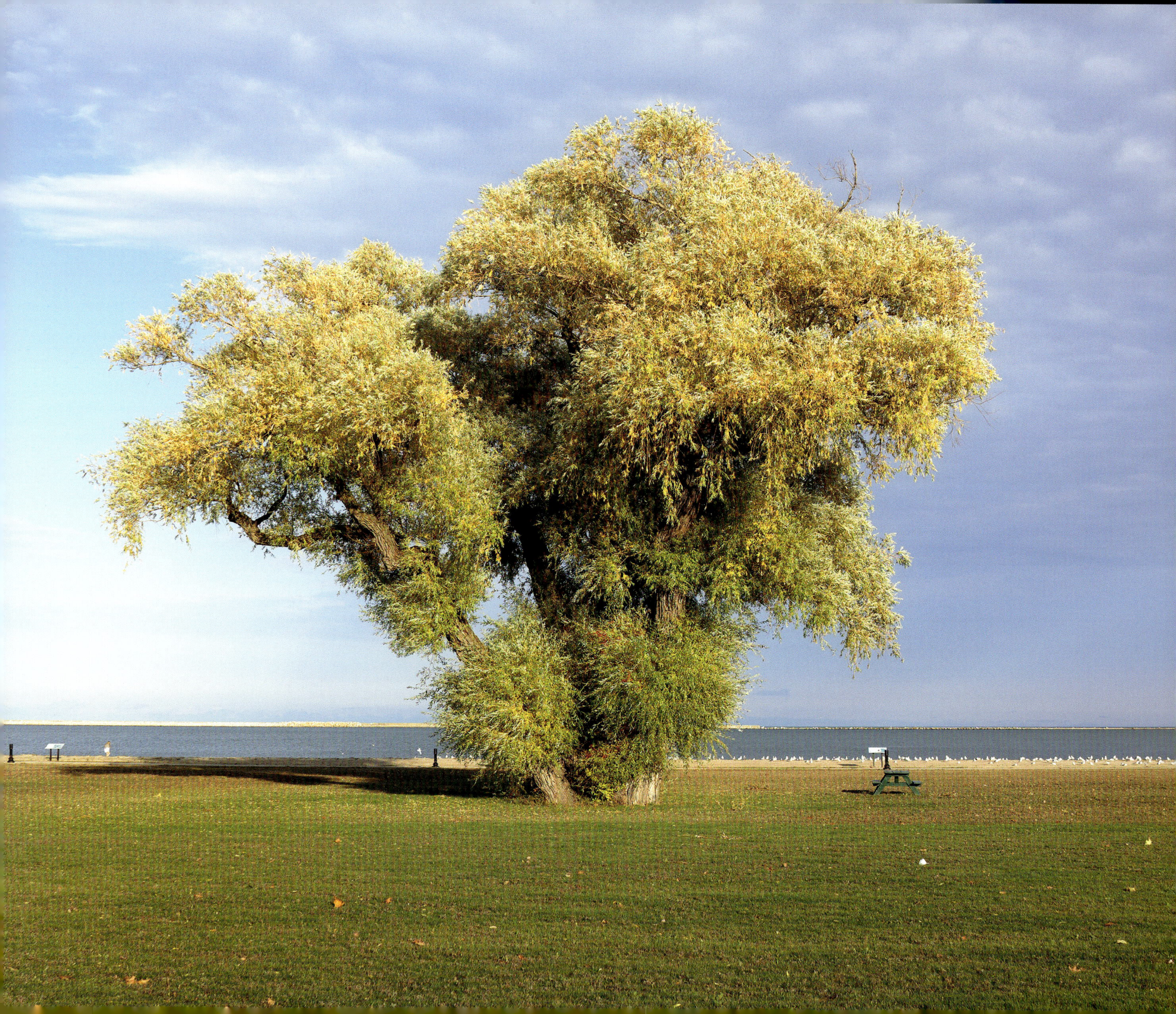

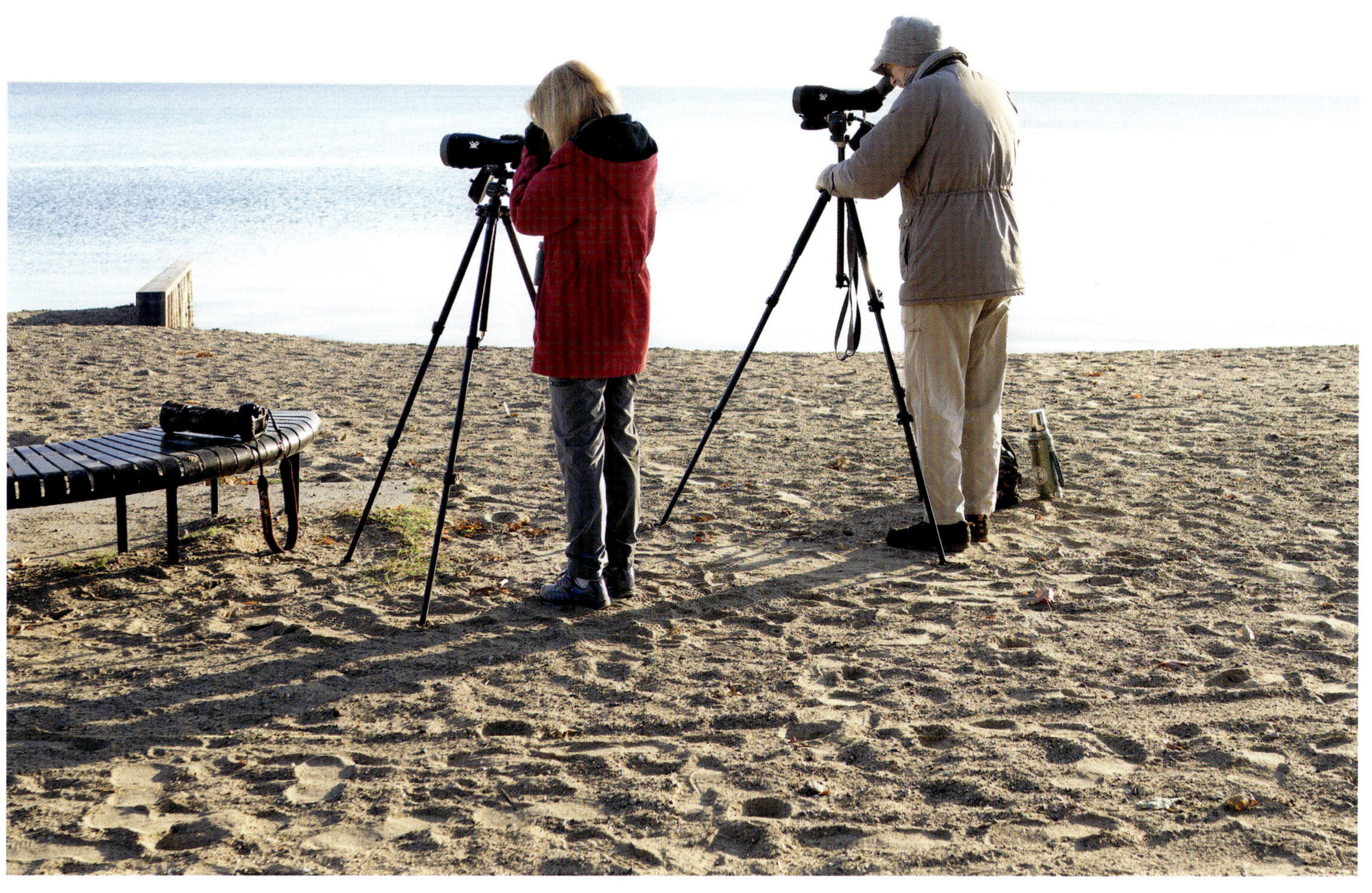

Birders, St. Clair County, Michigan, 2020

Willow tree, Harbor Beach, Michigan, 2020

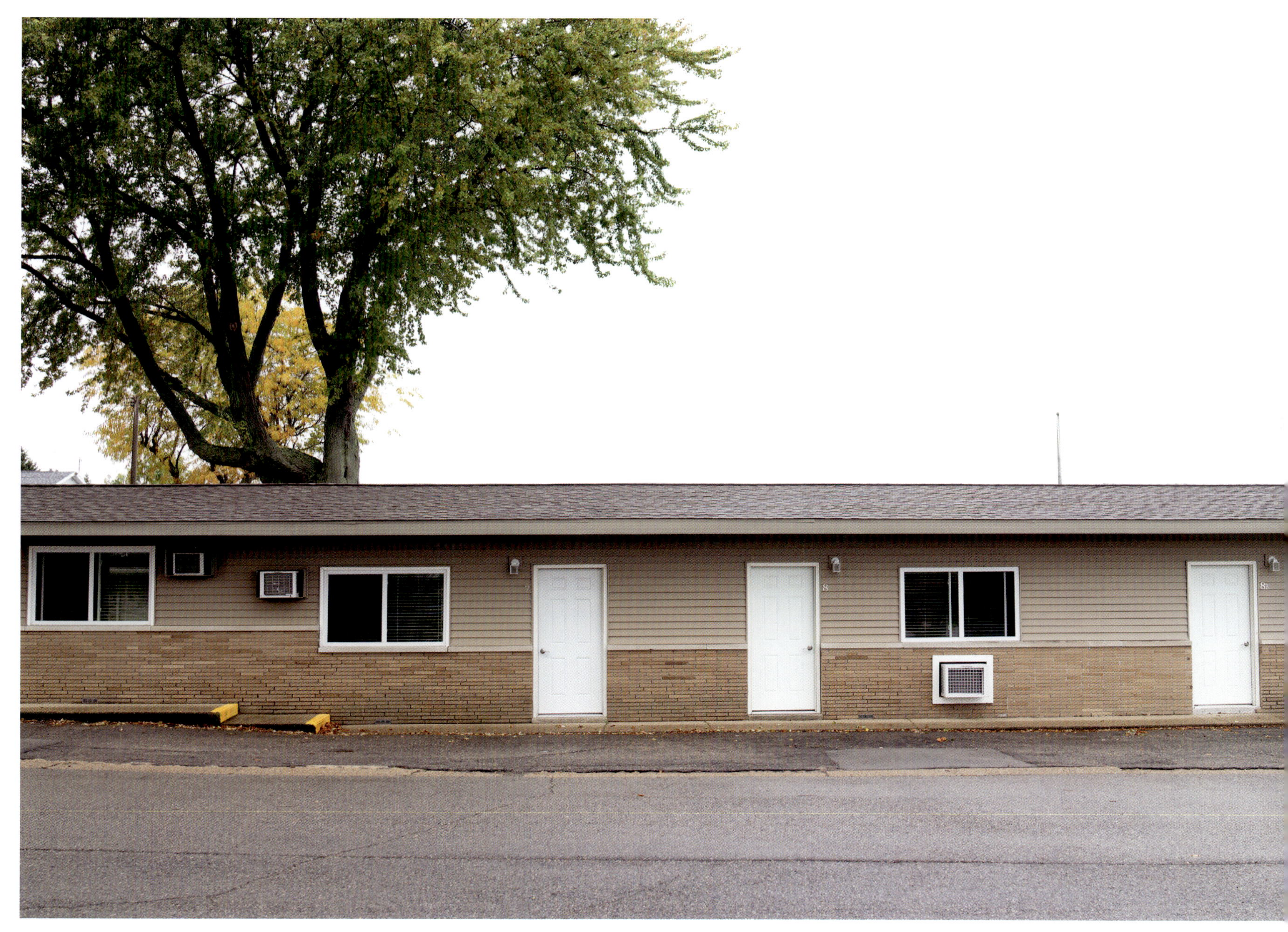

Lakeside motel, Grindstone City, Michigan, 2020

Whiskey Harbor, Huron County, Michigan, 2020

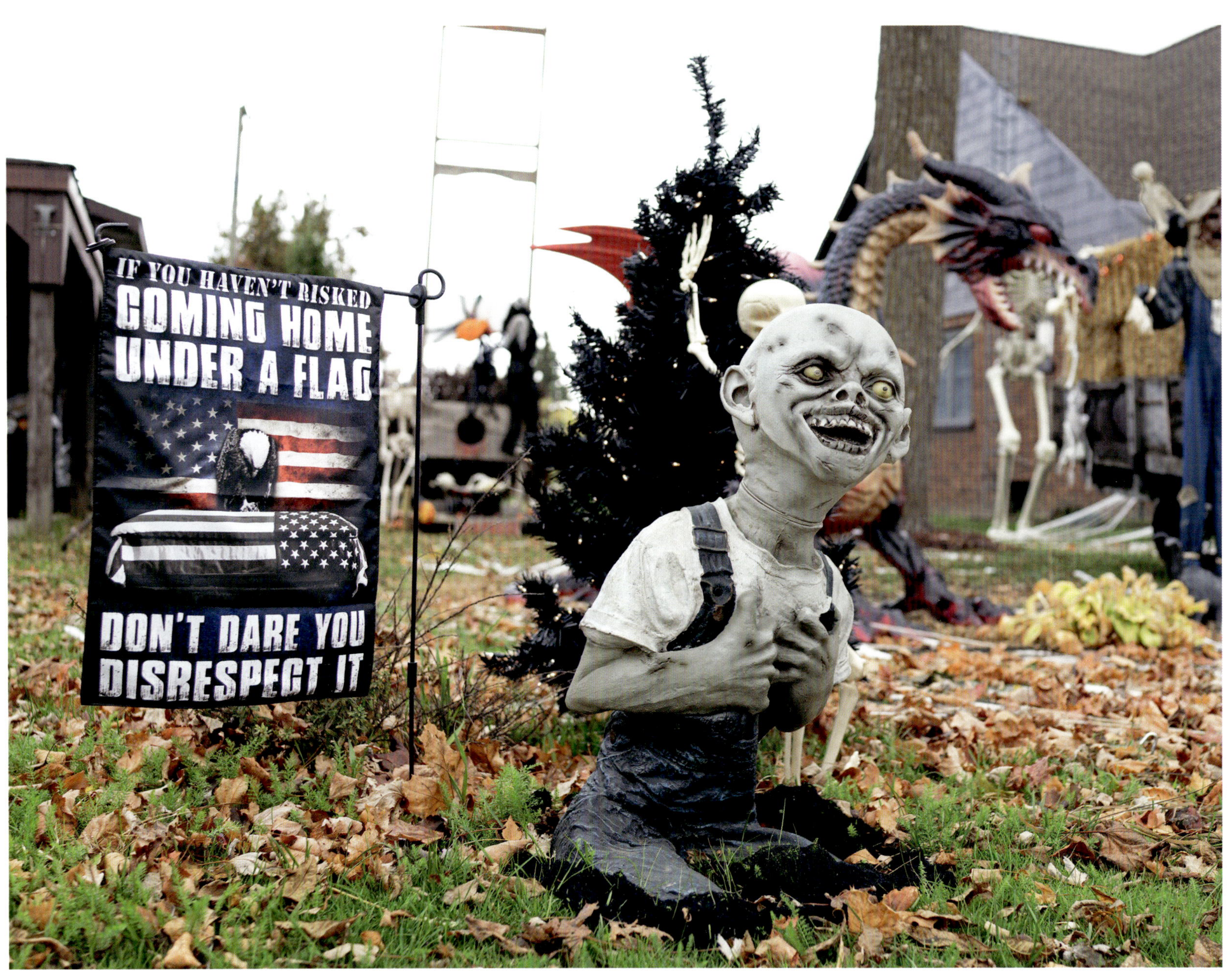

Yard decorations, Lexington, Michigan, 2020

St. Clair County, Michigan, 2020

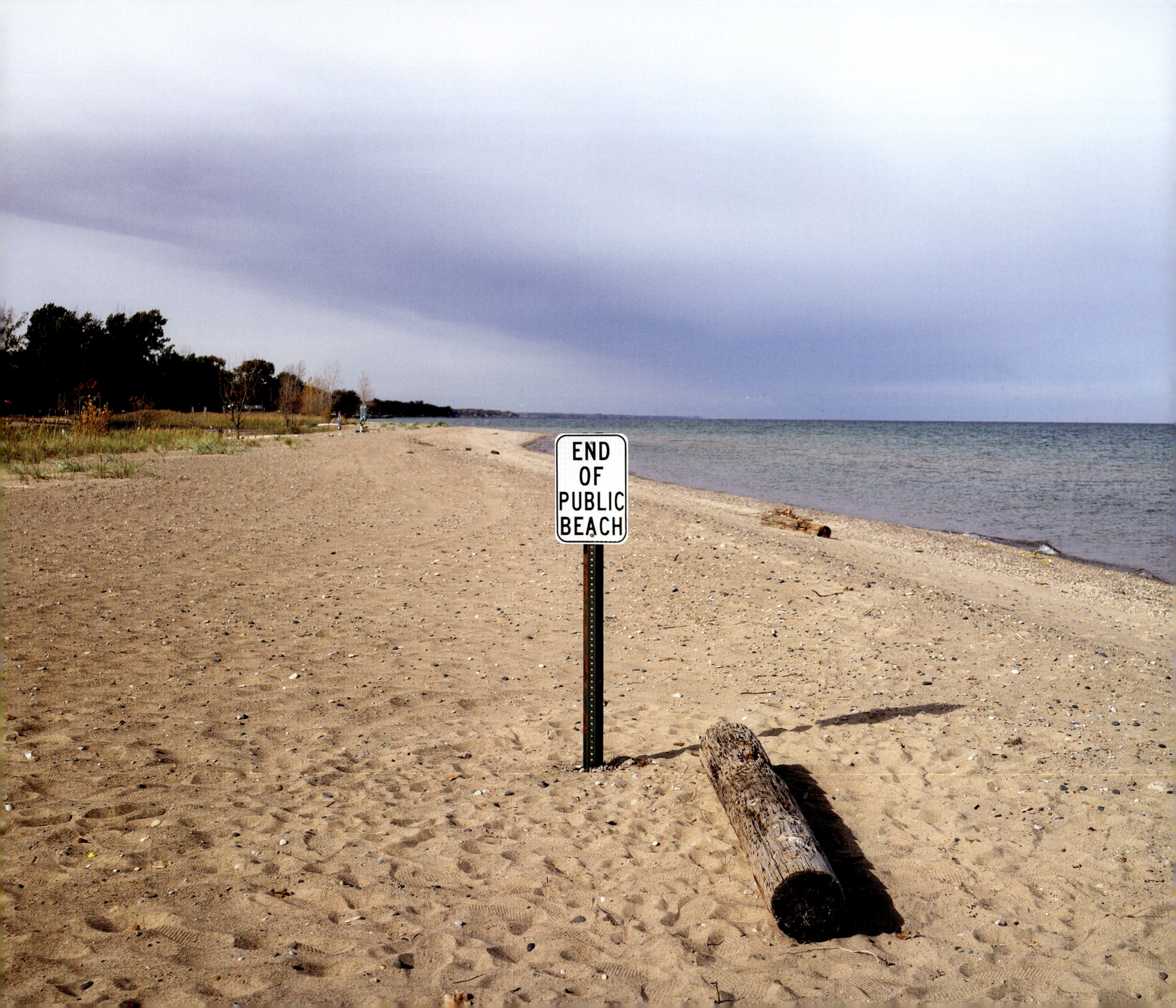
END
OF
PUBLIC
BEACH

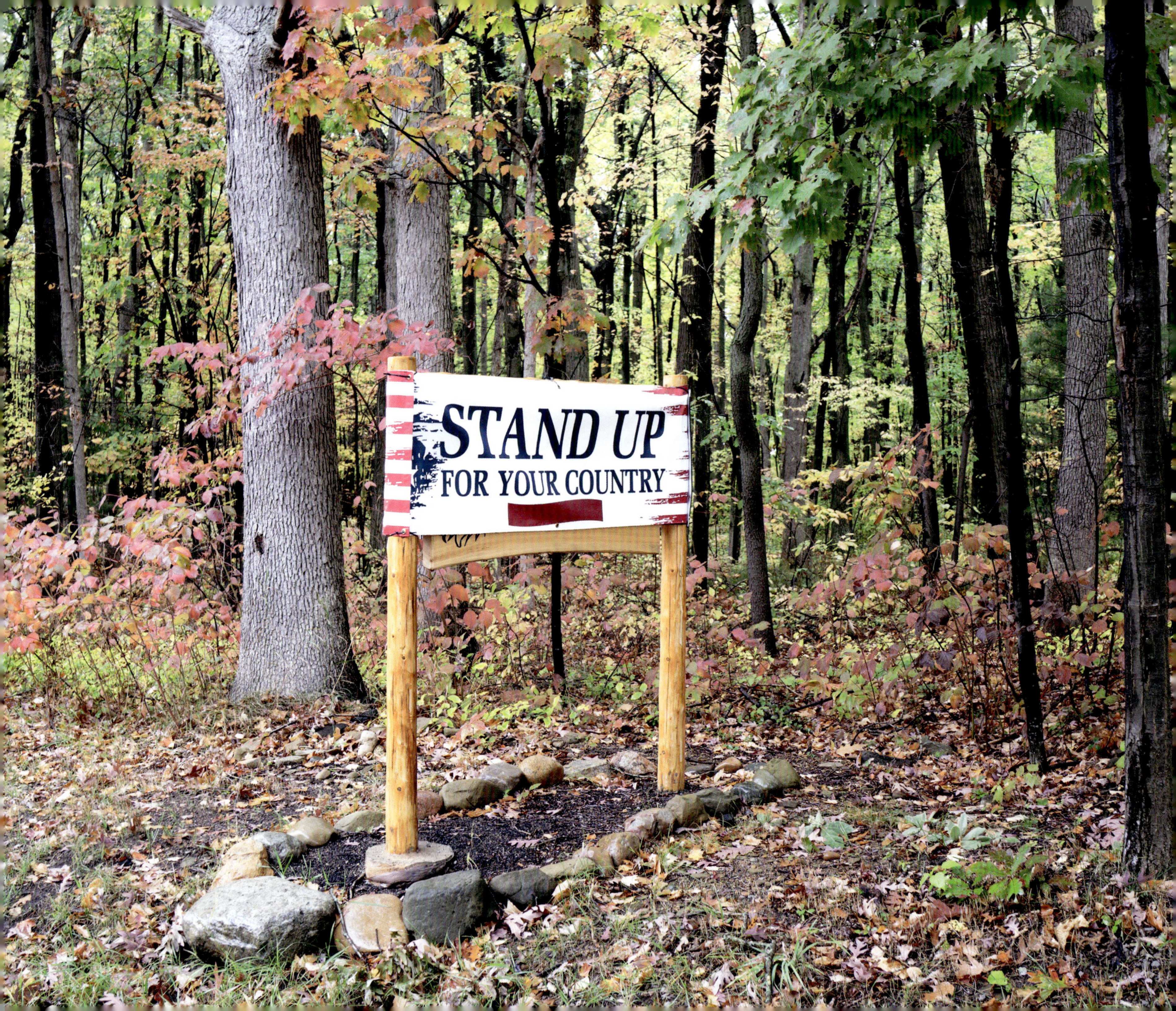
STAND UP
FOR YOUR COUNTRY

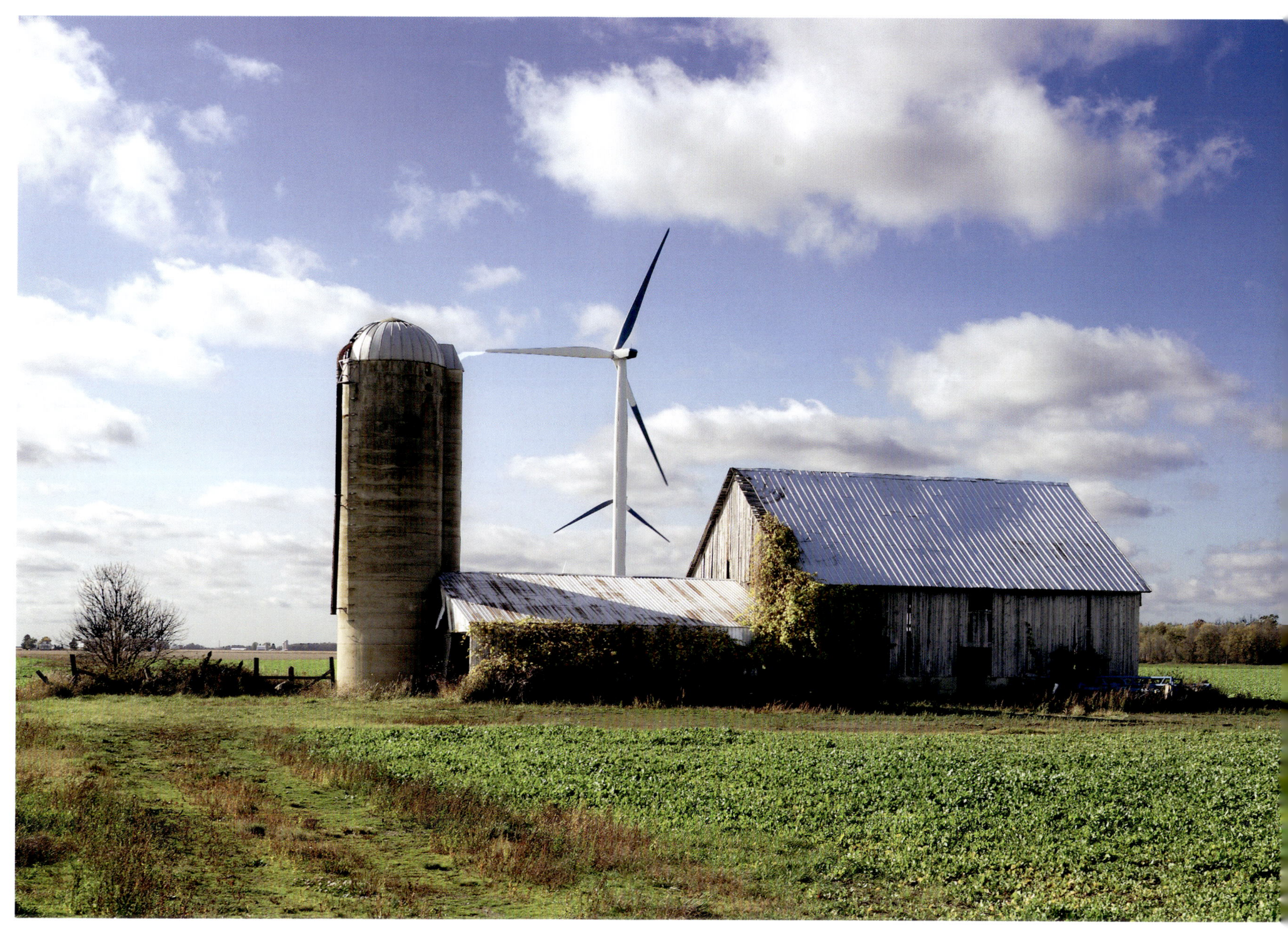

Barn and windmills, Huron County, Michigan, 2020

Sanilac County, Michigan, 2020

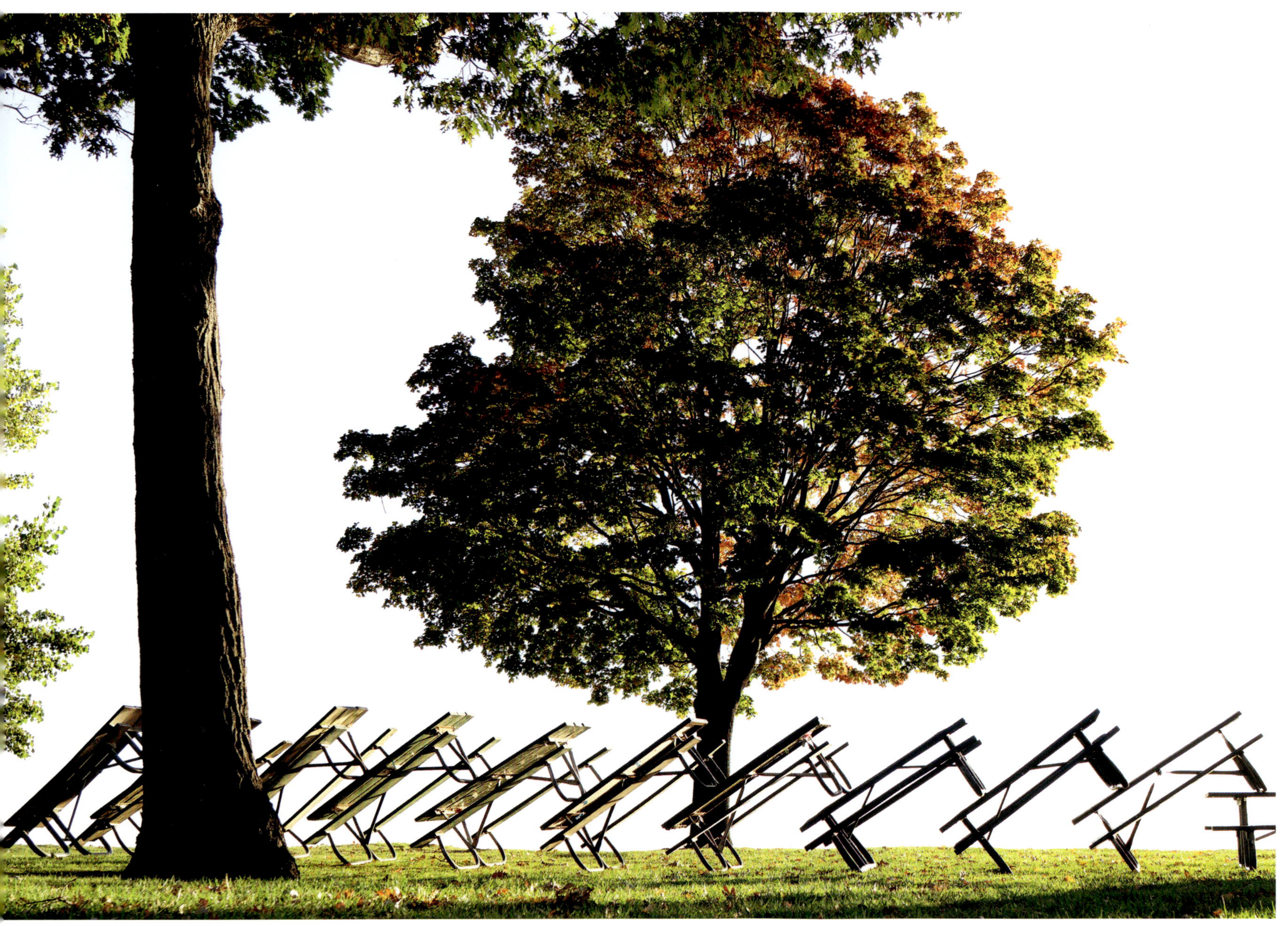

Season's end, St. Clair County, Michigan, 2020

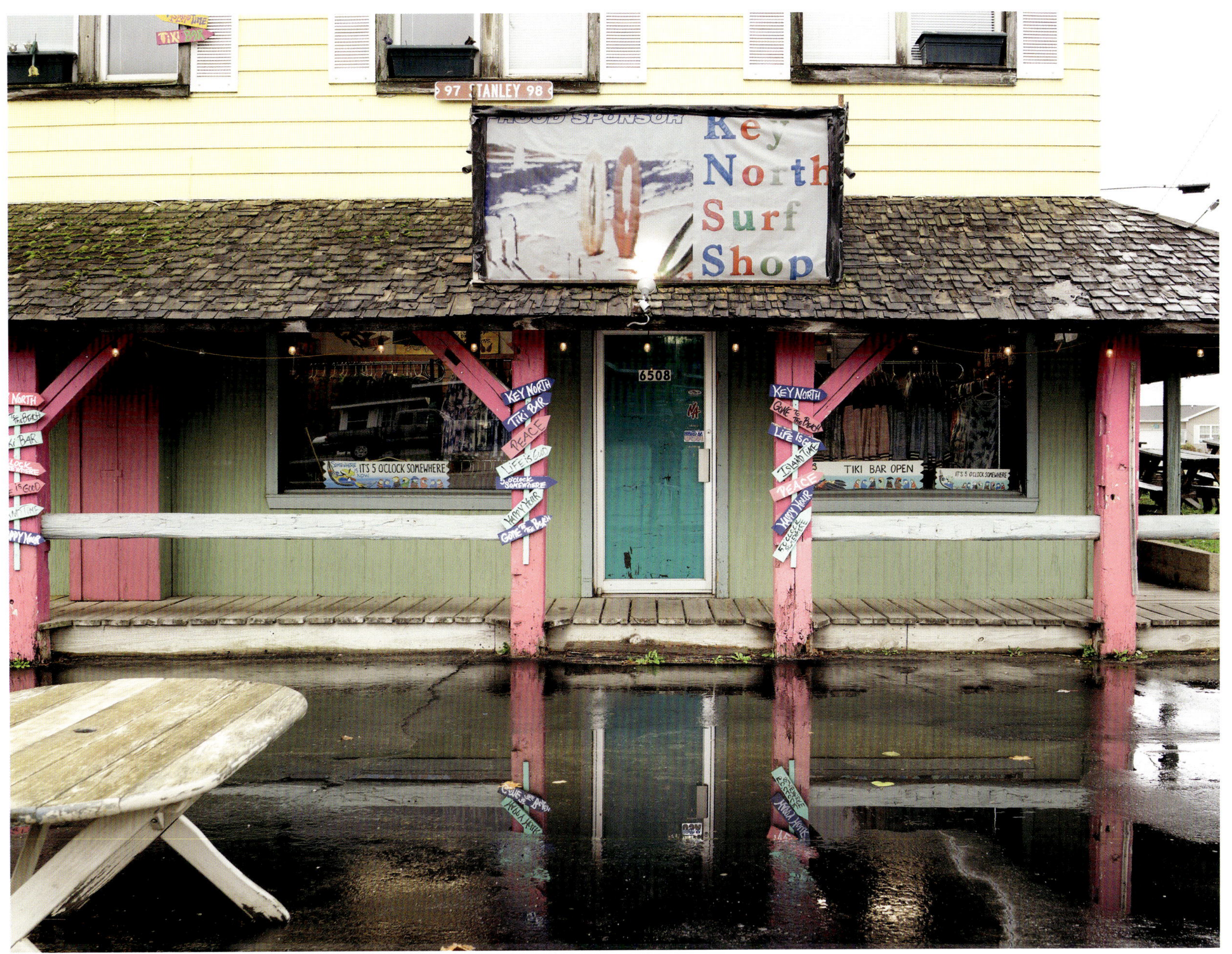

Surf shop, Caseville, Michigan, 2020

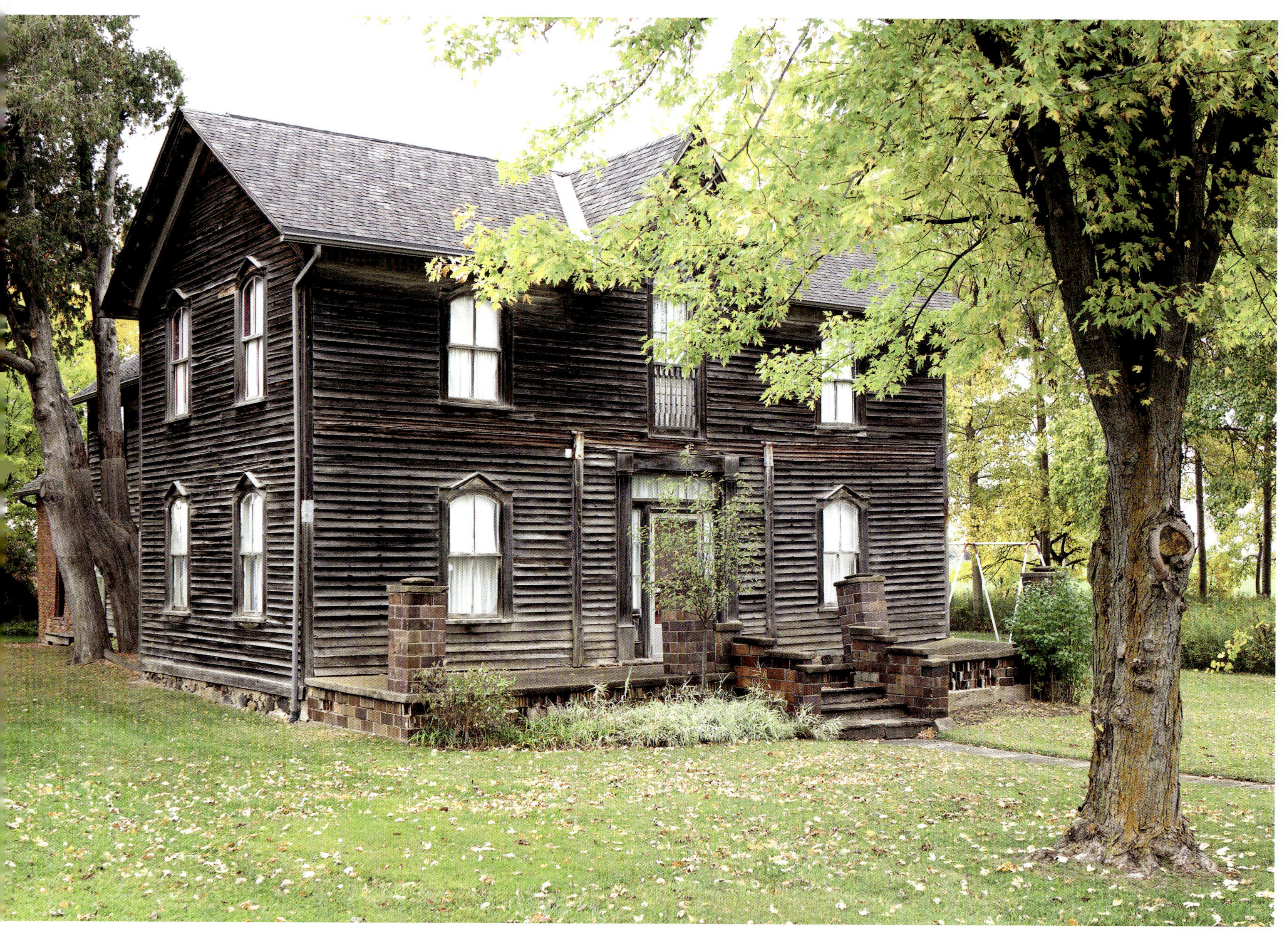

Abandoned farm, Sanilac County, Michigan, 2020

City park, Port Huron, Michigan, 2020

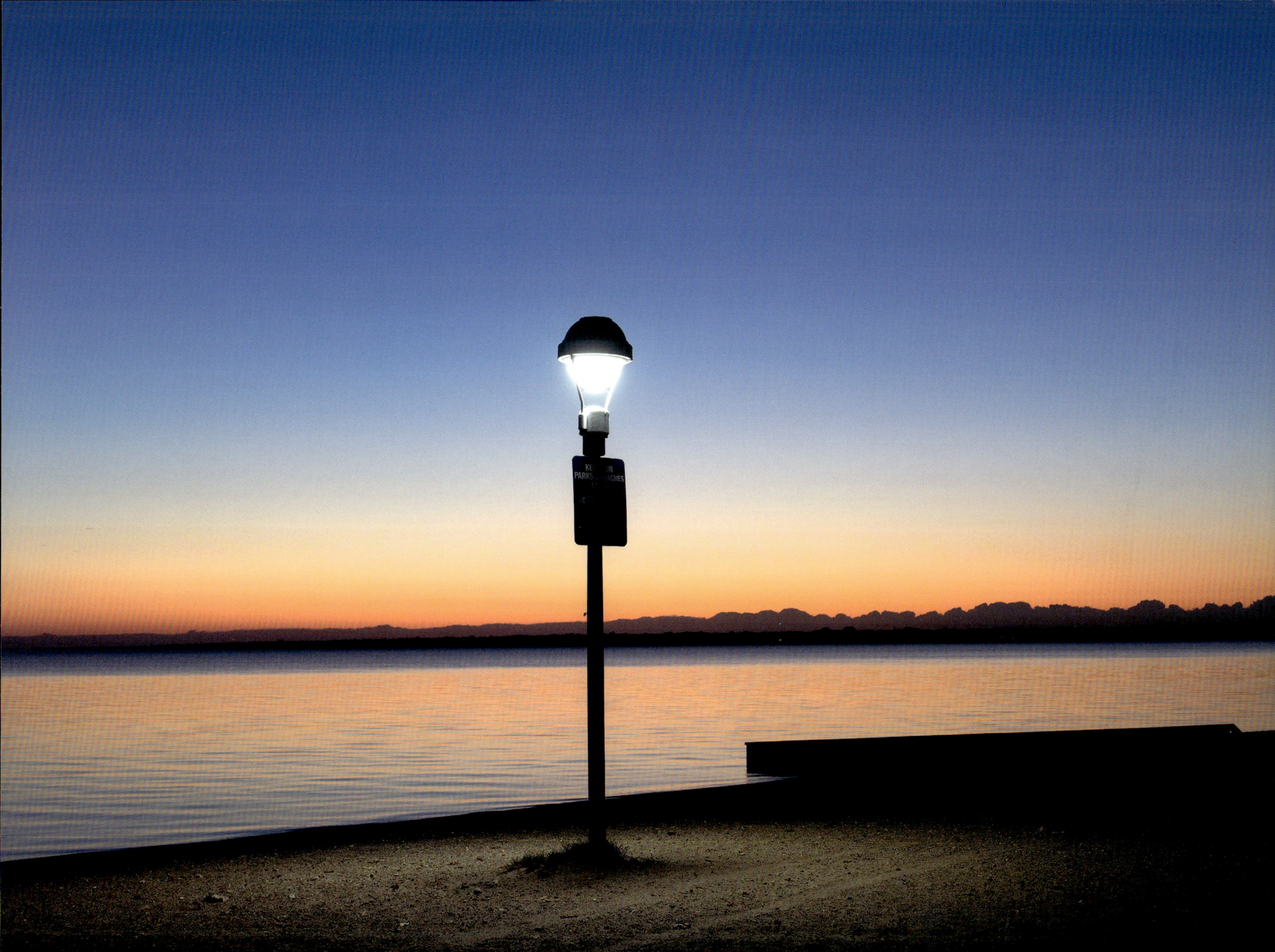
PARKS

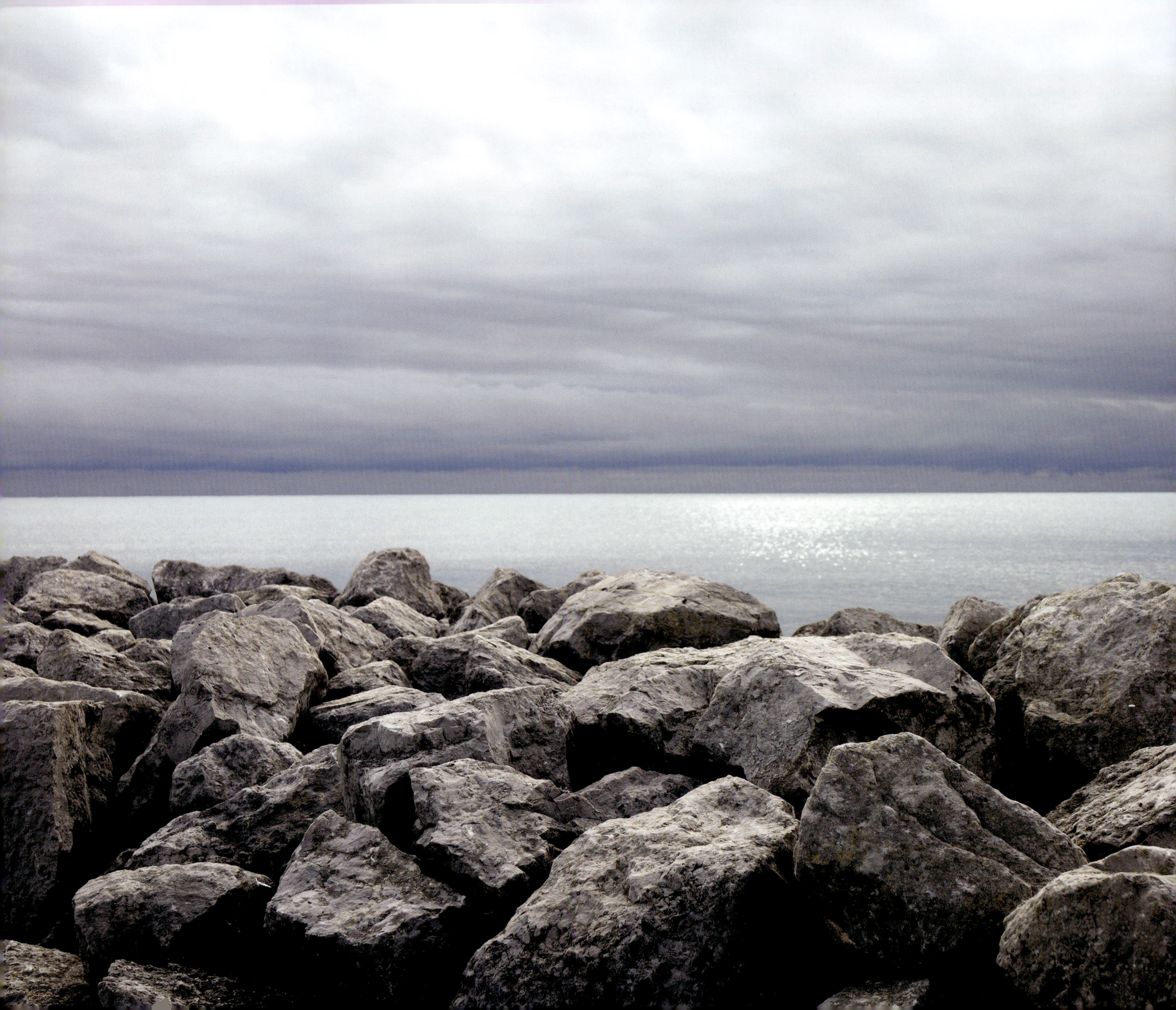

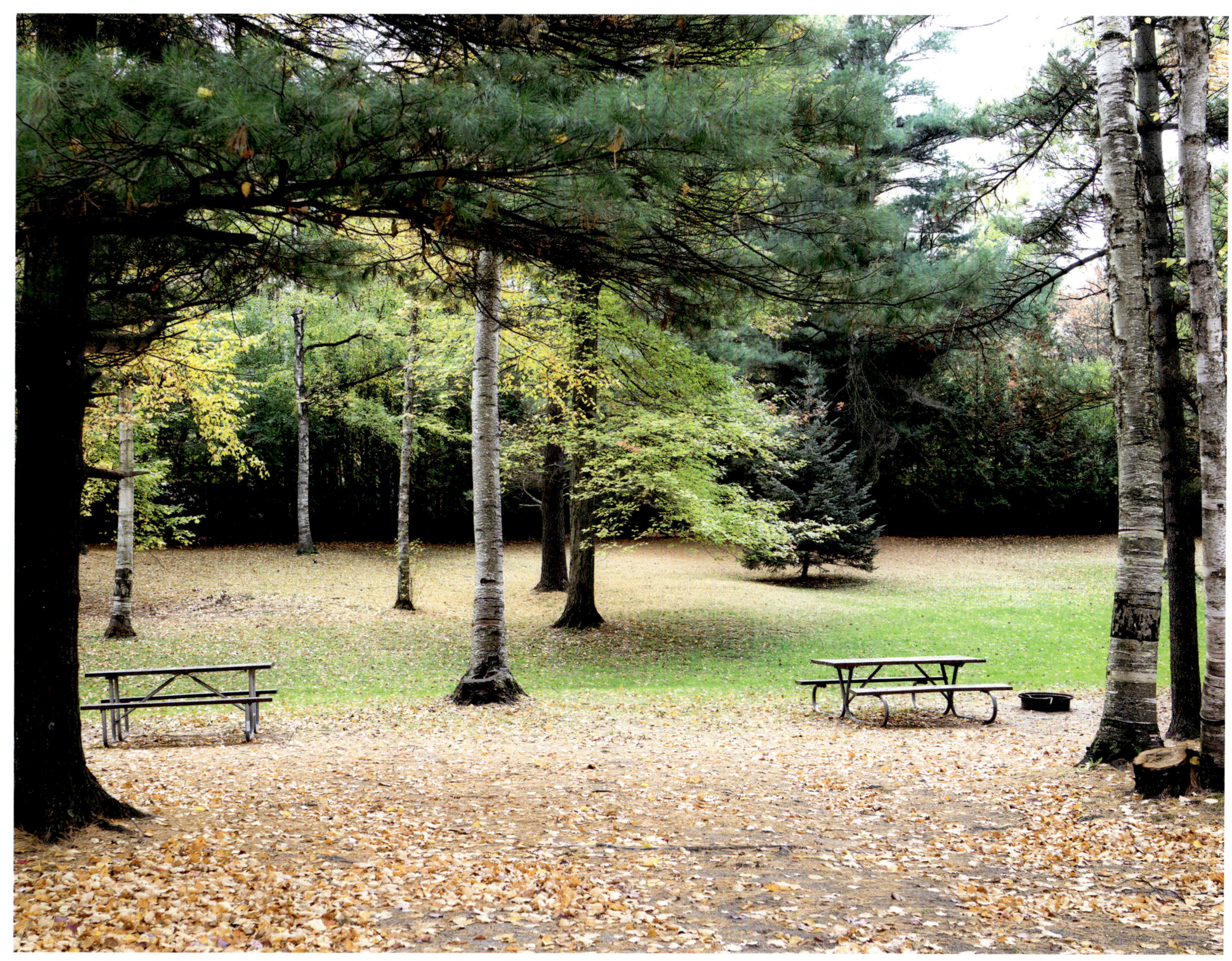

Roadside park, Huron County, Michigan, 2020

Breakwall, Port Sanilac, Michigan, 2020

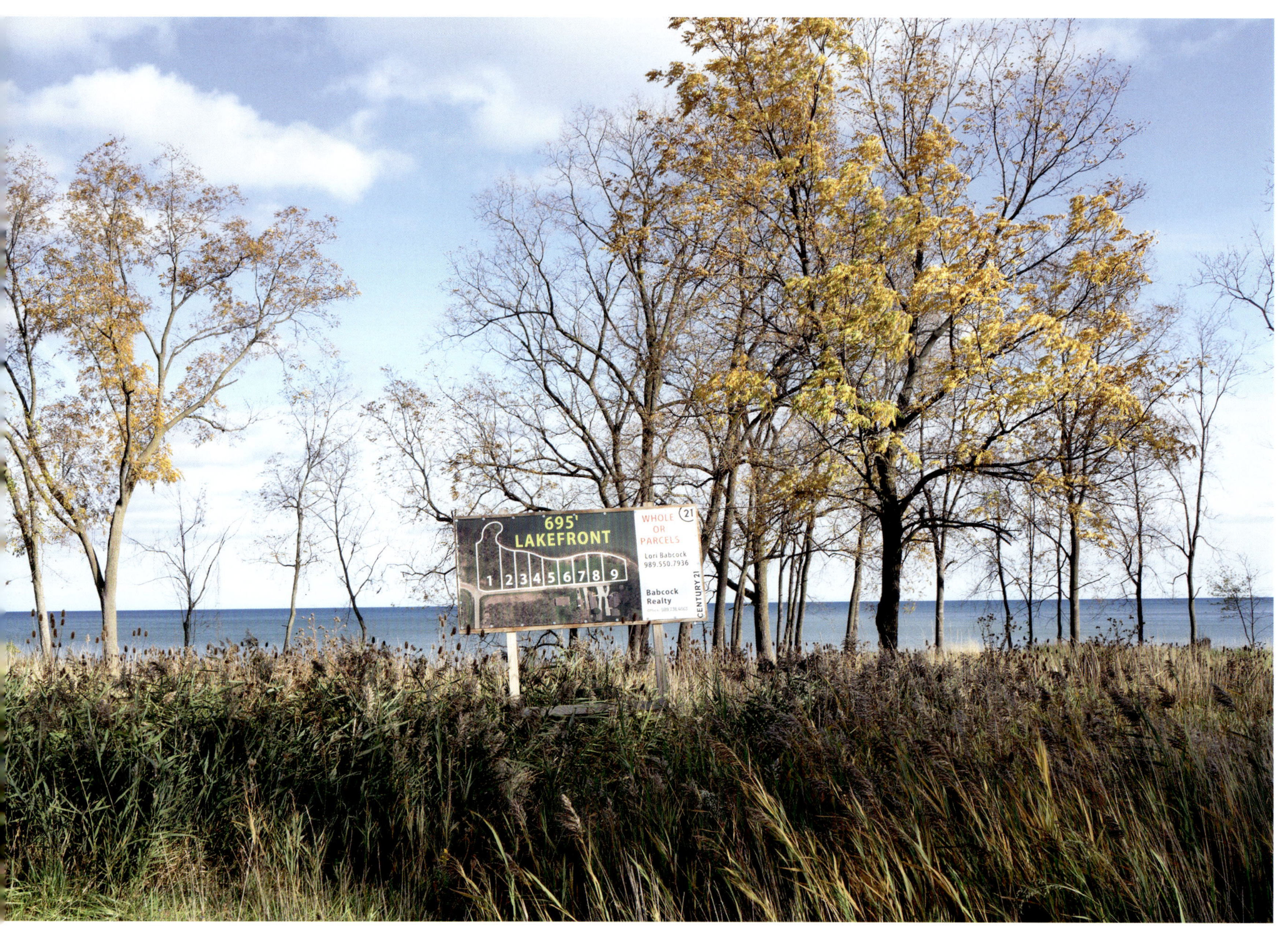

Waterfront land sales, Sanilac County, Michigan, 2020

Tropical cabana, Port Huron, Michigan, 2020

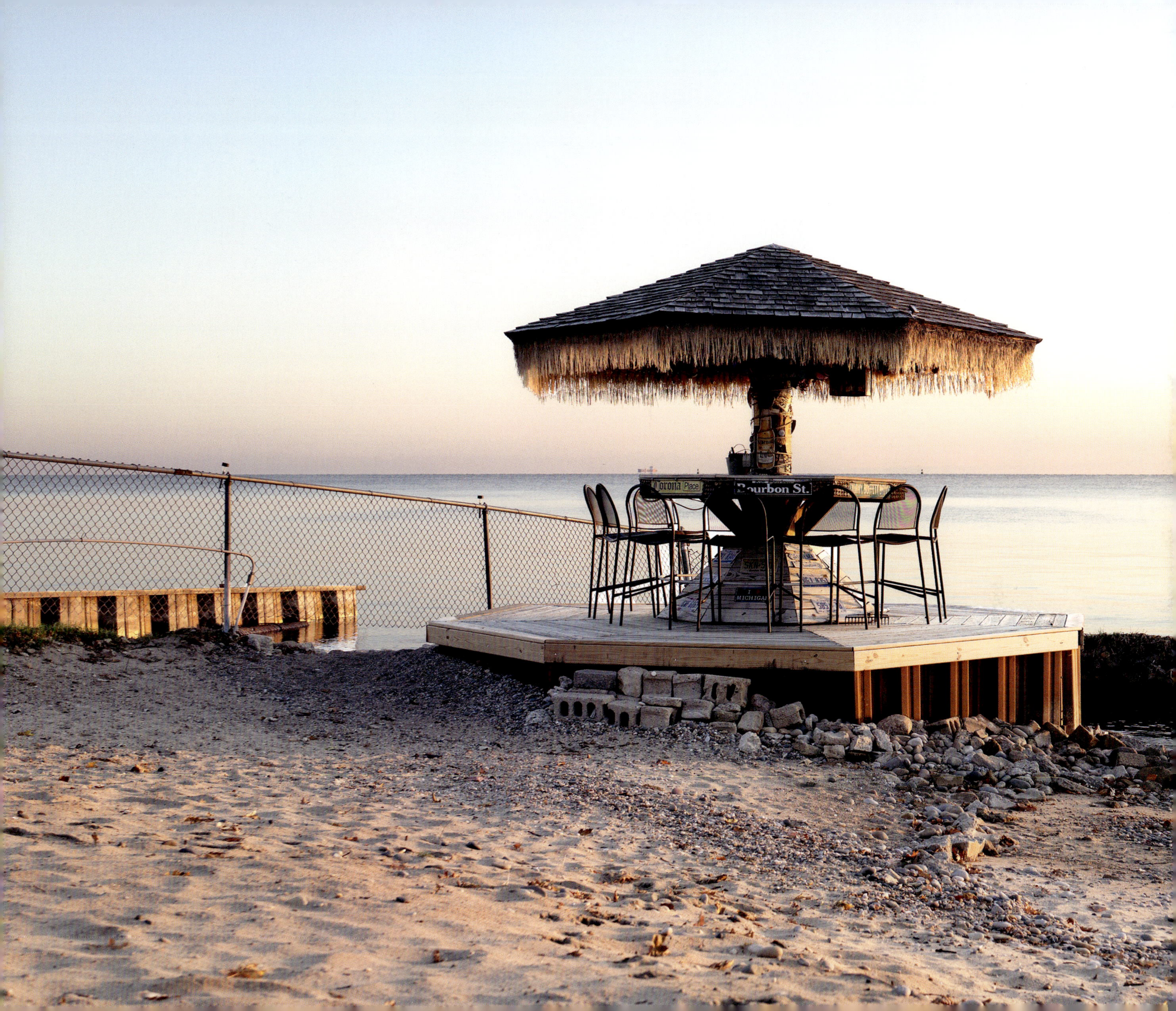
Corona Place
Bourbon St.

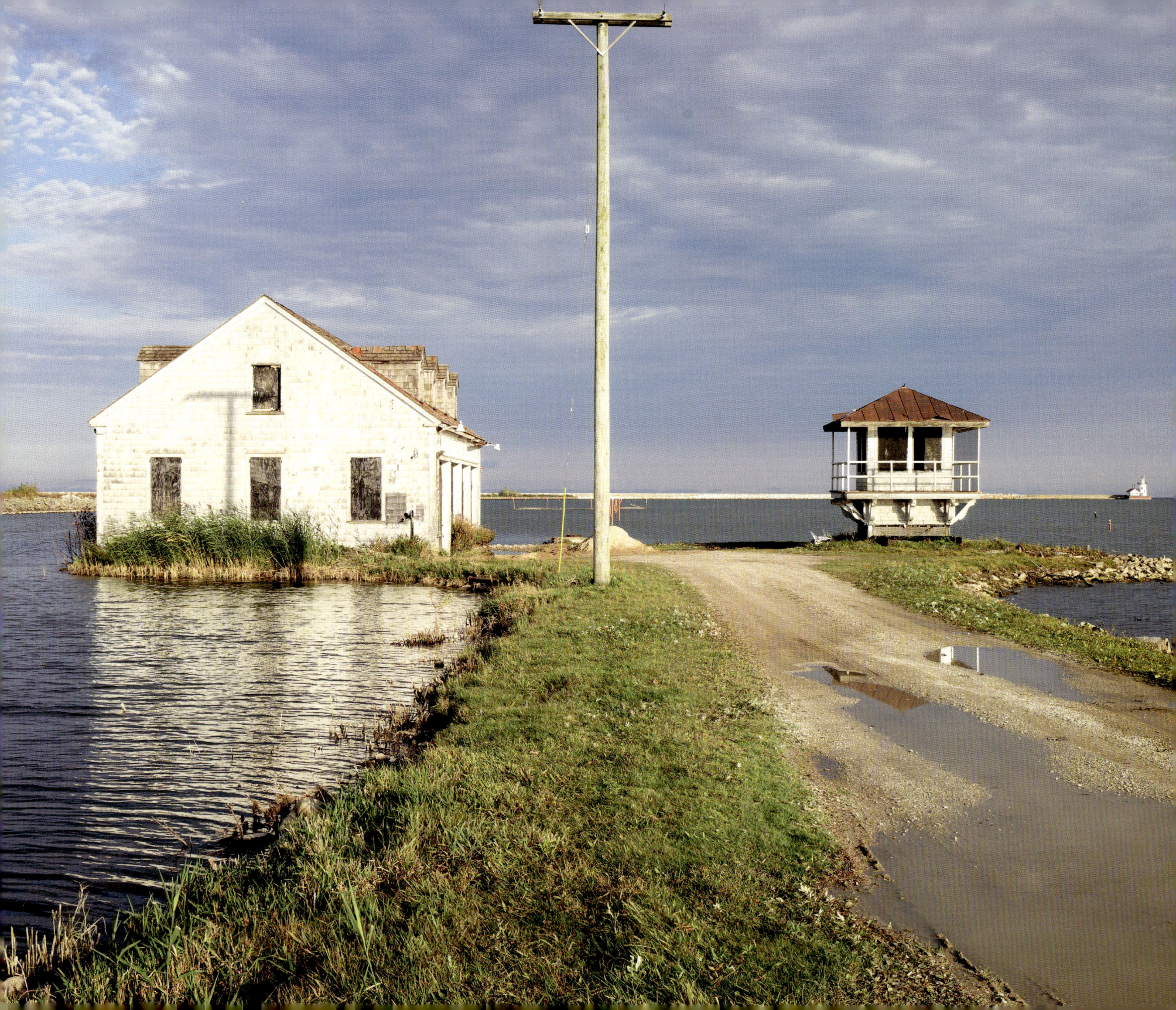

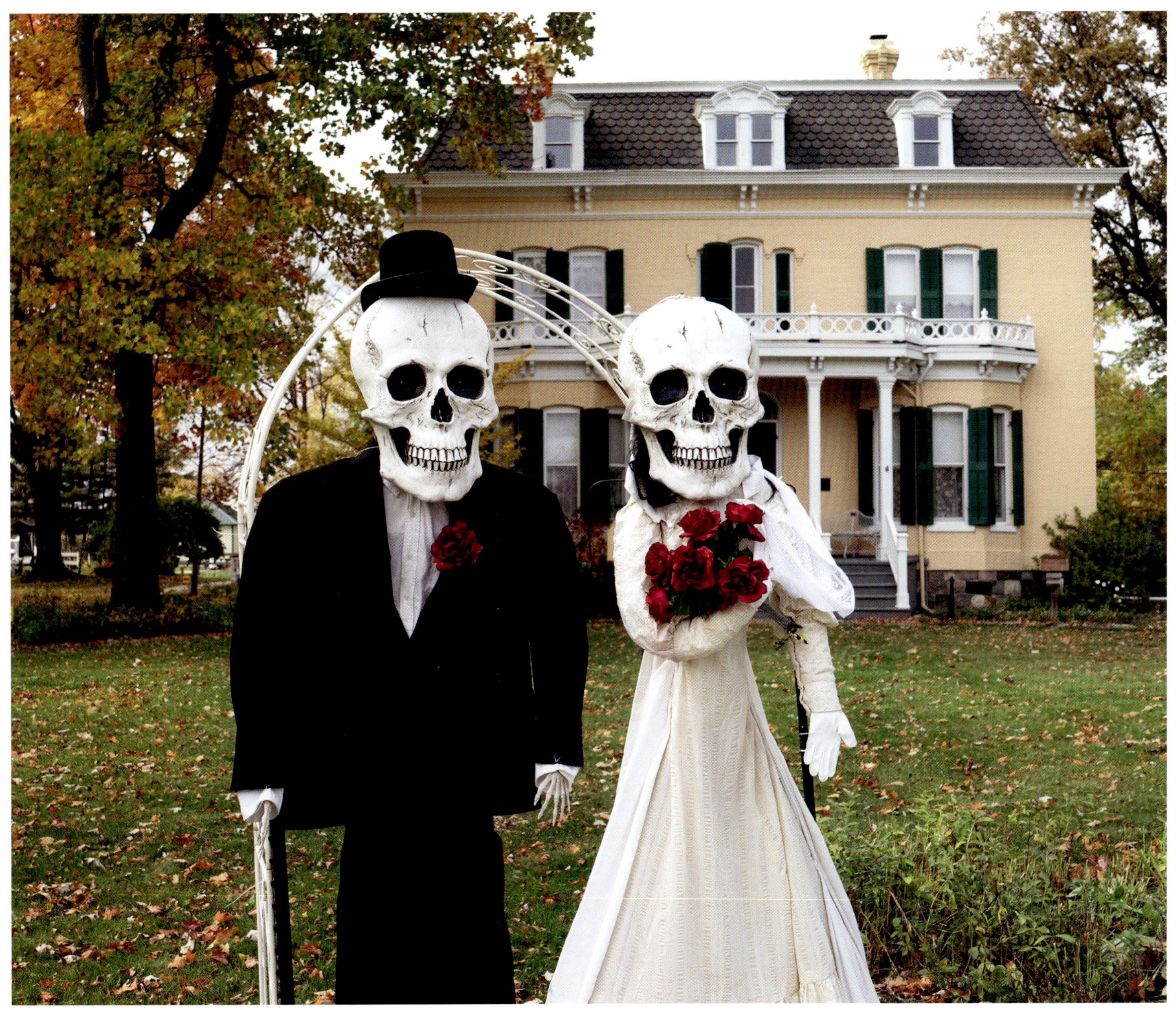

Halloween, Sanilac County, Michigan, 2020

Abandoned Coast Guard station, Huron County, Michigan, 2020

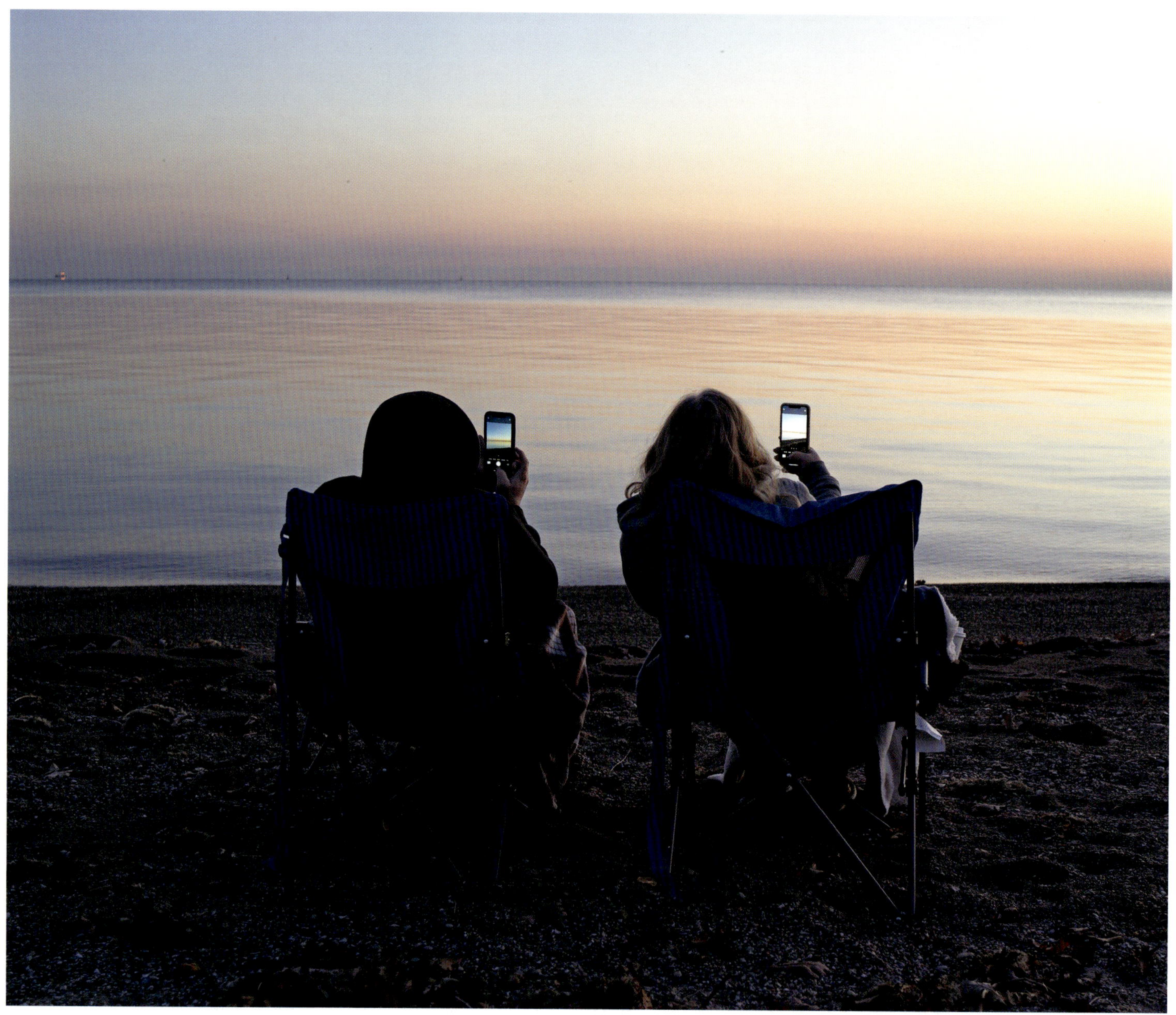

Sunrise, St. Clair County, Michigan, 2020

Schmucker Creek, Huron County, Michigan, 2020

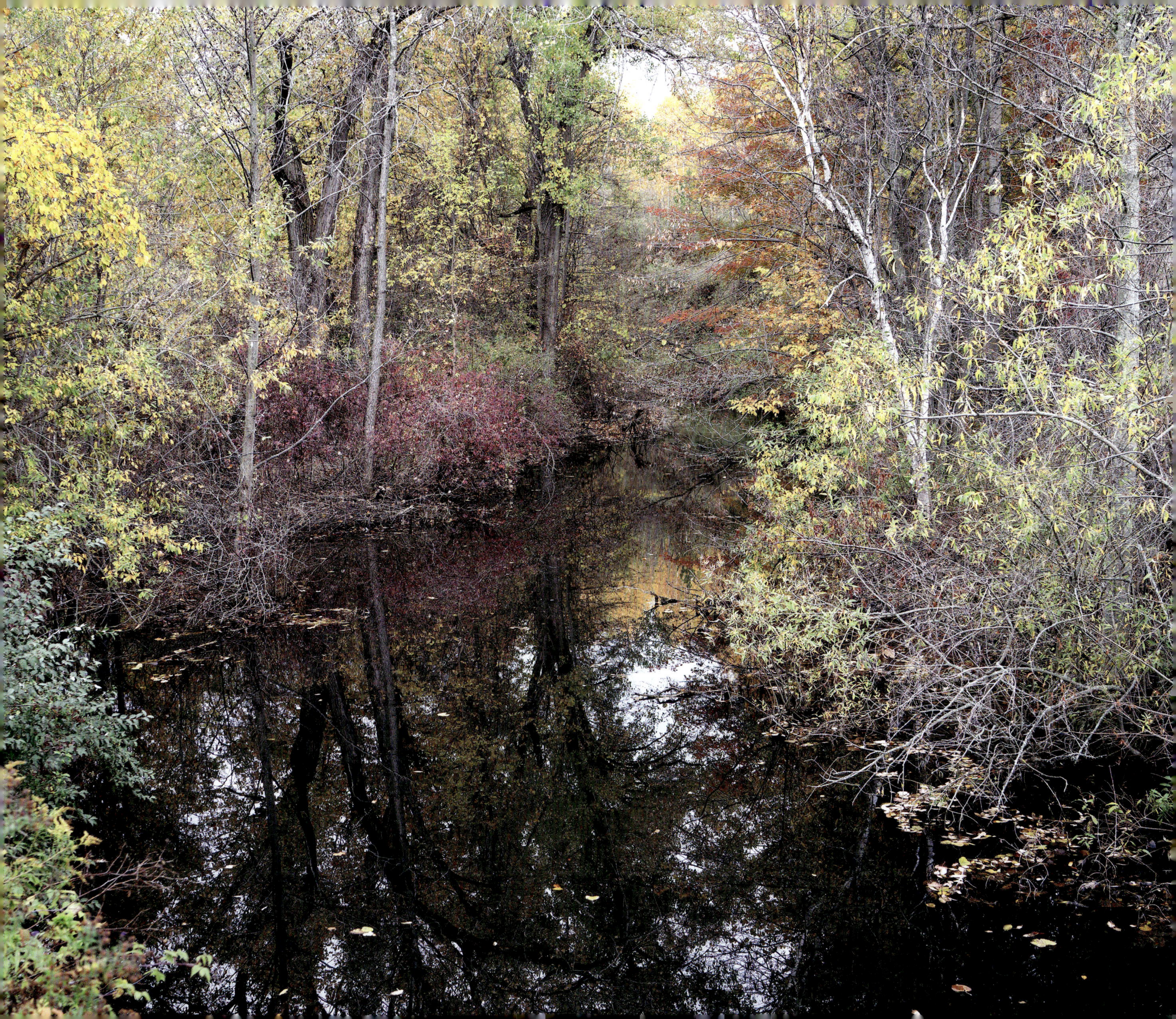

CONNECTING WATERWAYS

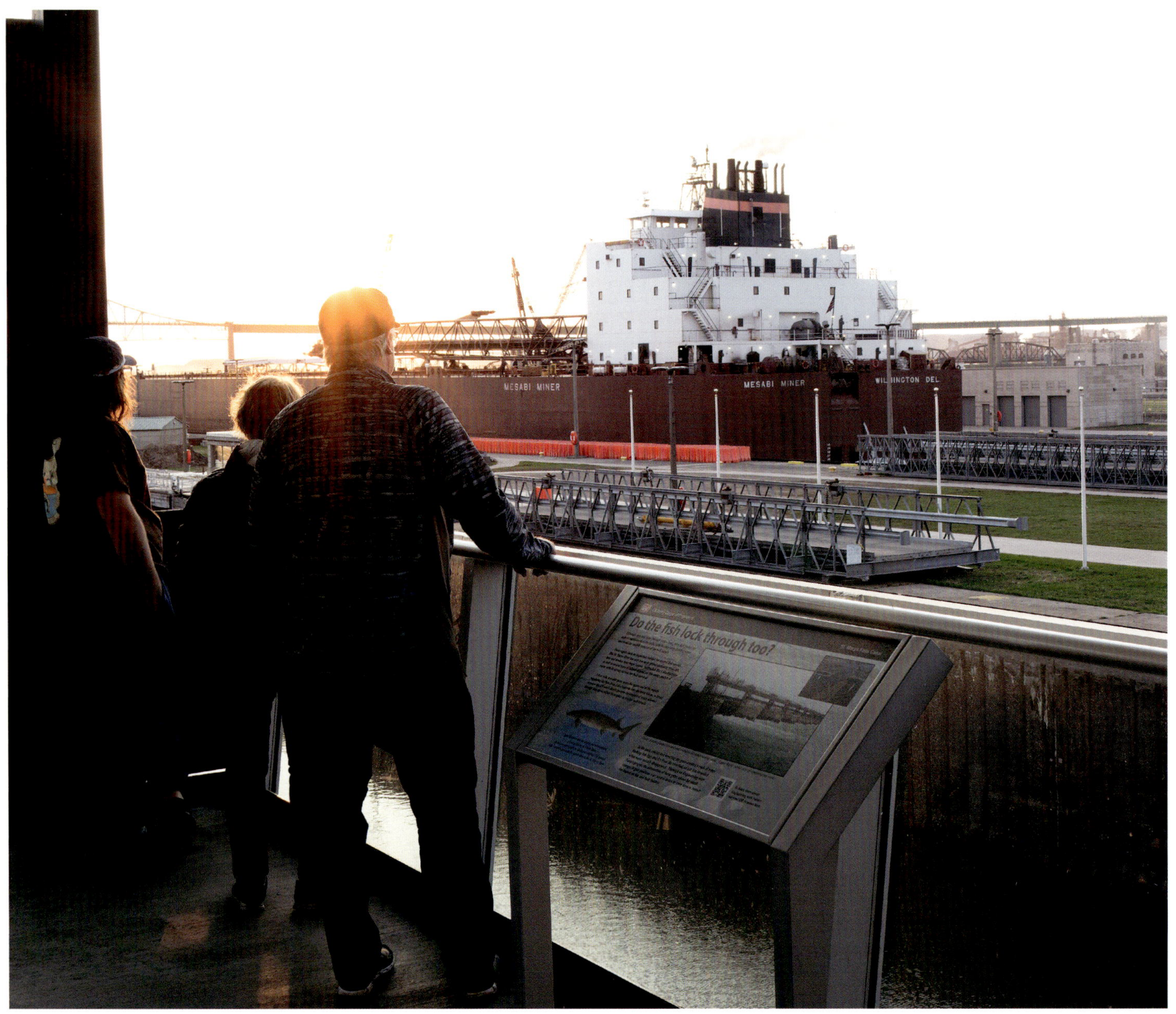

Viewing platform, Soo Locks, Michigan, 2023

Straits of Mackinac, Michigan, 2022

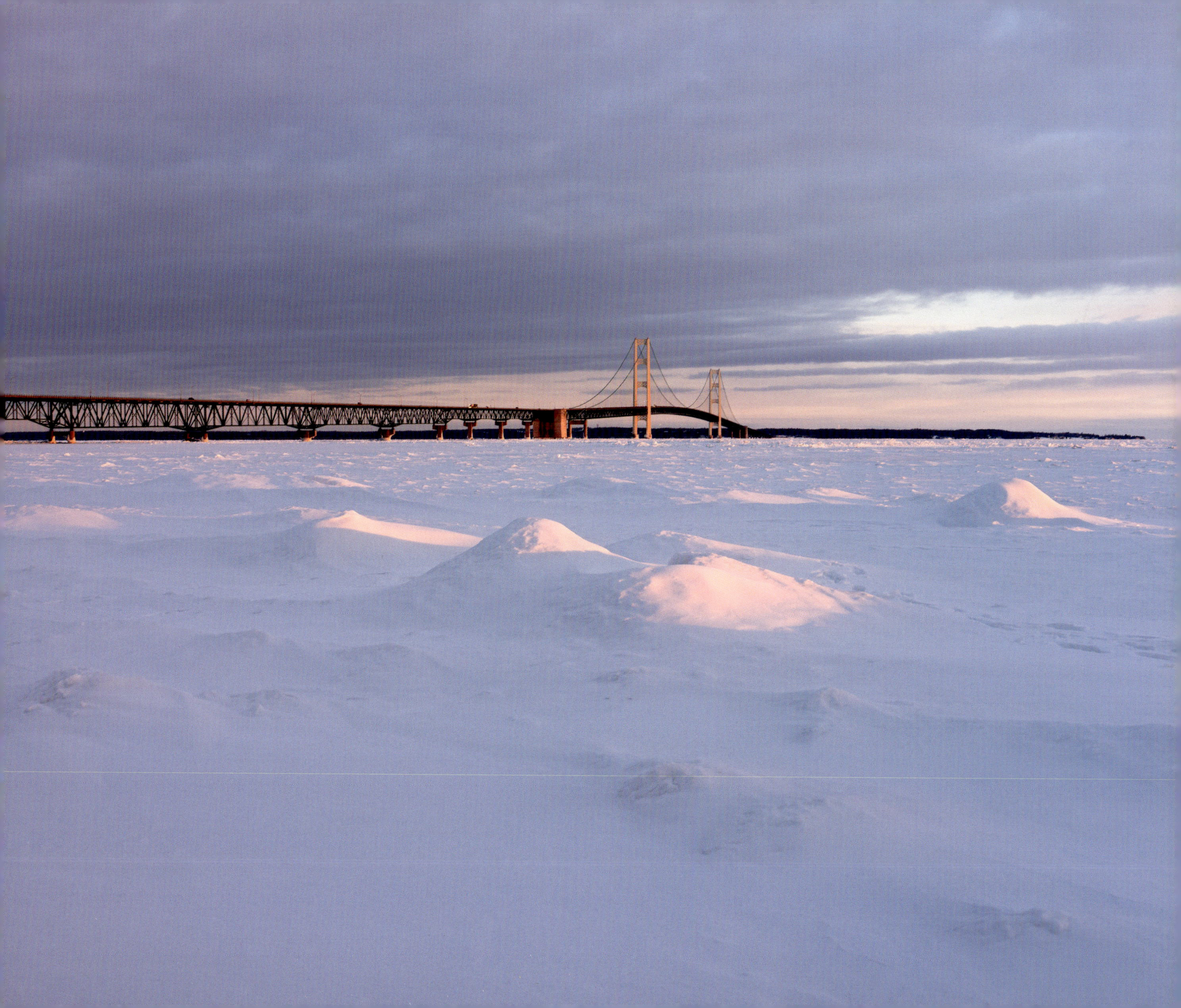

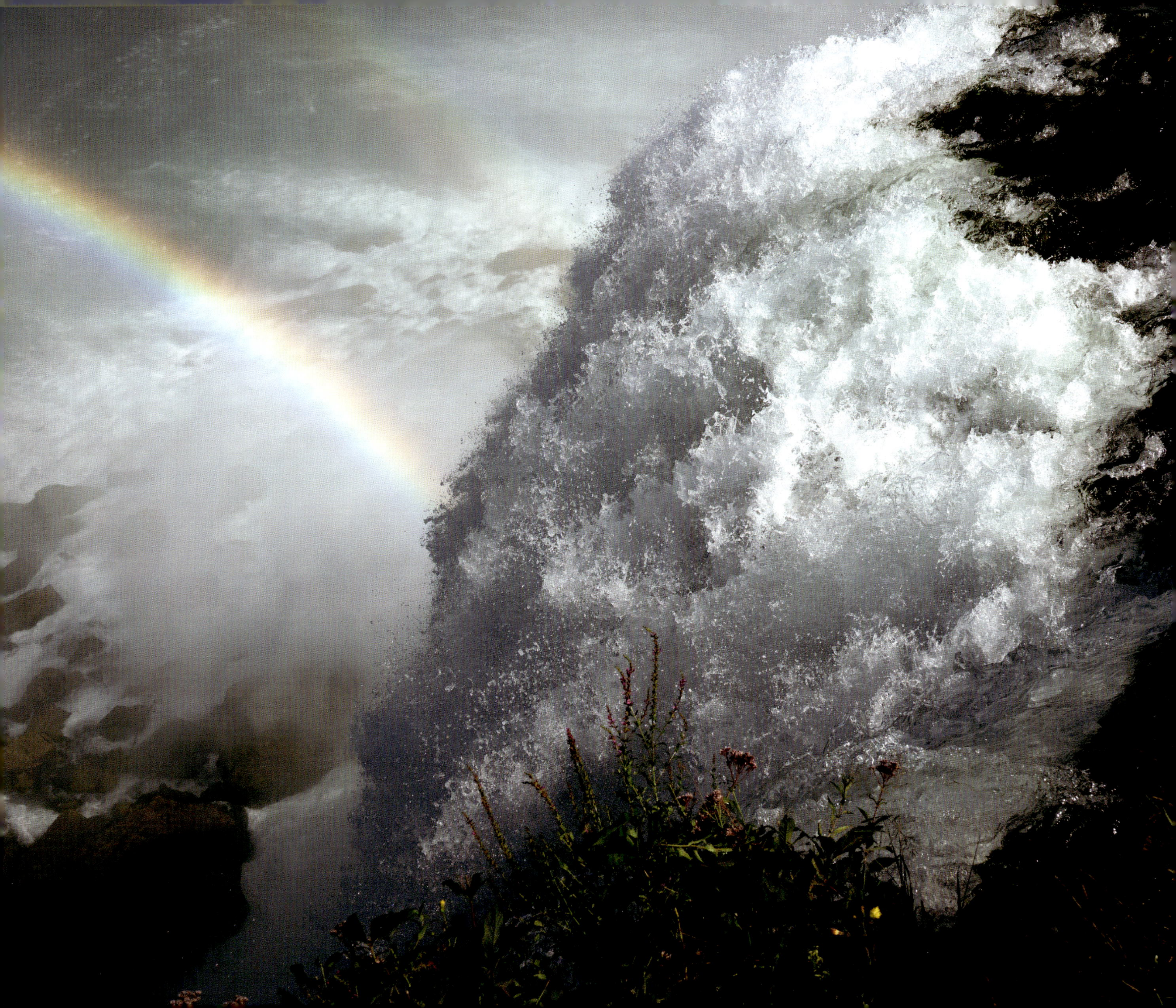

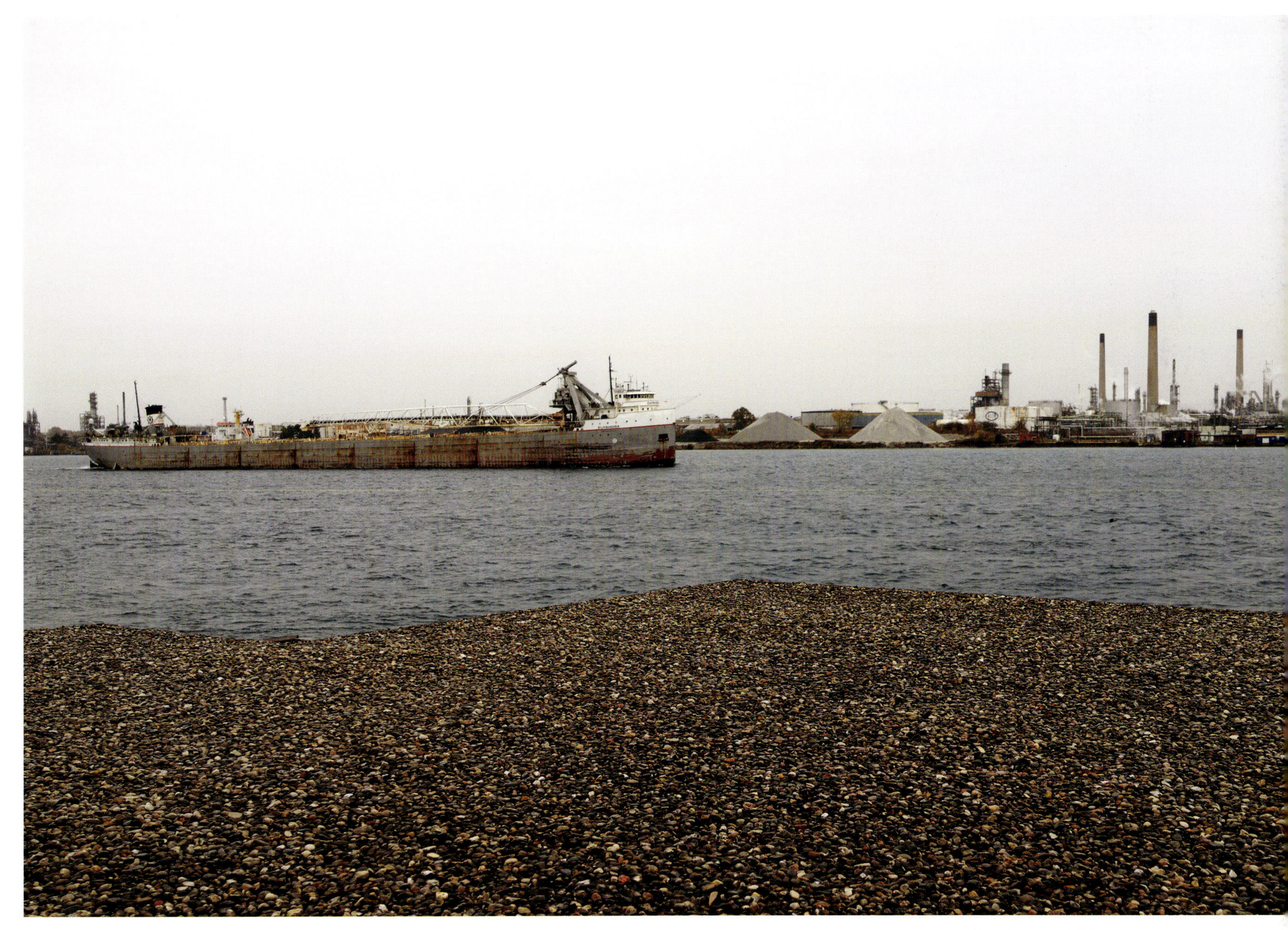

St. Clair River, Michigan, 2020

American Falls, Niagara River, New York, 2022

AFTERWORD

I was born and raised in a small town on the shore of Lake Huron, and although I've lived my adult years at a distance from it, the lake has never left me. In significant ways, I became the person I am because of it. In summers, I learned to swim and to fish in its water, and on winter days, when the ice was right, to skate across its glistening surface. Images of driftwood bonfires on the beach, underage beer parties, sunrises, hunting for Petoskey stones, and countless other adolescent experiences shape the memories that connect me to the lake. One of my most vivid childhood impressions is the sound of a foghorn. It meant a Great Lakes cargo freighter was making its way through the mist on the nearby waterway. Each time I hear the mysterious sound, I'm transported back to my early life on Lake Huron.

There is one image of the lake, however, that rises above all the others: an empty horizon. The unbroken line where water meets sky, ever-changing with the hour of day, the season, the weather conditions, and yet always there, timeless, hinting at the vastness of both the lake and a world beyond. Whenever I visit my hometown, the first thing I do is head to the water. I find a stillness in the motion of the waves lapping at the shoreline, the whitecaps dancing across a choppy surface, but it is the sight of the distant horizon that affects me the most. I gain from it a profound sense of *spaciousness*.

When the COVID pandemic made international travel difficult, I set aside my overseas photography work and looked for something to do closer to where I live. My internal compass pointed north, to where I had spent my youth. I had never considered the idea of a Great Lakes photography project before, but it became a likely prospect. I could reach the lakes in a day's drive from my home in the Kentucky hills. The region was deeply familiar but also different enough from Appalachia to offer a new adventure. And the Great Lakes culture was one I could easily slip back into. It would be a homecoming for me.

In autumn 2020, I set out from my brother's house in Port Huron to follow the watery outline of Michigan's thumb district. The towns I passed through—Lexington, Port Sanilac, Harbor Beach, Caseville, Port Austin, and others—were ones I'd visited many times in the past. The route I traveled was the same one my father had driven on our family outings. The landscape was filled with old memories. It was early November, a time of the turning of seasons, and while the parks located along the lake were still open for camping, they were mainly empty of visitors. It was getting colder at night and I often found myself alone with just my truck, camera, and tent. It was a quiet time. The frosty colors of fall lingered among the maple and birch groves along the road. The summer motels were closed. Most of the tourist shops were shuttered.

I was three days into my journey when my brother called to ask where I was. I told him. And then I said that I should be able to make it to Harbor Beach in a couple of days. He laughed. Normally, it takes an hour to drive the distance from Port Huron to Harbor Beach.

My route north along US 25 was a narrow corridor between lake and farm. Looking east, I saw the shoreline, water, sky. To the west were dairy farms spotted with hay bales, and acres of corn waiting to be harvested, their stalks withered brown with drooping ears and faded silken tassels. A steady flow of beet trucks traveled on the dirt roads, indicating the sugar harvest was underway. Wind turbines soared above the weathered silos, their shiny blades slicing the air to farm the westerlies. Populating the countryside were homesteads, barns, community granaries.

While farm life in the thumb's interior is removed from the lake by only a mile or so, it feels far away from the shoreline, which is given over almost entirely to water-based recreation, summer homes, tourism, light industry. It's surprising how little interaction takes place between the two realms, as if the societies they support inhabit different worlds. The dairy farm on which my mother was raised, for example, is located only a few miles inland from Lake Huron, and yet rarely did she or any of her siblings spend much time on the lake. Farm chores occupied their lives. My father grew up within sight of Lake Huron, but he never learned to swim.

As I engaged more fully with the Great Lakes in this project, I navigated travel routes that zigzagged between pastoral and marine landscapes, but never did I venture more than a few miles from the lakeshore. In a few localities, the farms extended to the water's edge, resulting in telling juxtapositions. In one setting on Lake Ontario, I came across a farmer using his tractor to tow a city sailor's catamaran onto the beach. In numerous places along Lake Erie, I watched slow-moving streams, silty and clogged with aquatic plants, enter stretches of water devoid of fish. Nitrogen and phosphorous runoff from the heavily fertilized fields created algal blooms and dead zones that threaten the lake's ecology. The interplay of lake and agriculture was readily visible along the south shore of Lake Ontario, where a microclimate, known as the lake effect, extends only a few miles inland but supports the cultivation of highly specialized fruit orchards and vineyards.

The Great Lakes shoreline is diverse, with its beaches, farms, forests, cities, and lifestyles. I visited Lake Superior in the middle of winter, when air temperatures rarely exceeded the single digits, and discovered not only incredible ice caves but a band of ice-bearded surfers who ride the waves generated by winter storms. On the eastern shore of Lake Michigan I came across the Third Coast Surf Shop, where a customer could purchase both snowshoes and a surfboard. Many stretches of the Great Lakes shoreline host RV campgrounds inhabited by people who spend their winters in Florida. These seasonal "snowbirds" have re-created in their northern parks a mini tropical world of fake palm trees, seashells, pink flamingo statuary, pastel colors, and thatch-roofed cabanas. In a lakeside park in Ohio I watched a foursome tee up at a makeshift driving range and send their golf balls flying into Lake Erie. While these anomalies attracted me, it was everyday life and the vernacular landscapes it produces that interested me the most.

Not far into my travels, I discovered each lake has its own personality. I organized my efforts accordingly. Lake Huron settles most deeply into my memory, with its associations with my early life and past adventures, and I thought it a fitting candidate for the quiet, pensive months of autumn. The winter, meanwhile, could only mean Lake Superior. This northernmost lakeshore is locked in ice and snow for many months of the year. I mentioned the ice-bearded winter surfers, but they are a few hardy souls. More commonly, people living along Lake Superior find winter fun by fishing for walleye, salmon, and trout through holes they augur in the ice, by snowmobiling and afterward visiting a local tavern, or by racing their trucks fitted with iron spikes across the frozen lake surface. To paraphrase a Michigan sports announcer, living on Lake Superior in the winter is not for nervous people.

Springtime brings flowers and fruit blossoms and the promise of warmer weather to residents of Lake Michigan. It's a time of rebirth and awakening. The tulip gardens of Holland, Michigan, connote love and renewal and are in such colorful abundance that they immediately bring to mind the town's European namesake. Farther north, the cherry trees bloom in mid-May, turning the rolling hills around Grand Traverse Bay into a carpet of white and pink orchards. The summer months bring warmer water temperatures, and the beaches along Lake Erie and Lake Ontario in July fill with sunbathers, sailors, and Jet Skis. The humid air takes on the scent of a hundred barbecues. The parking lots swarm with convertible cars, recreational vehicles, and motorcycles.

I came away from this project with more than photographs. I gained a better understanding of the Great Lakes. Taken together, they contain one-fifth of the earth's surface freshwater; are home to tens of millions of Americans; support industries, hamlets, and megalopolises; and provide places to contemplate nature. At the same time, the demands we place on the Great Lakes are intensifying. Many local commentaries lament that we are loving them to death. Indeed, over the past century the lakes have withstood a barrage of environmental insults and yet, as a testimony to their resiliency, remain largely intact. Moving forward, many communities now understand that balancing our reliance upon the Great Lakes with their natural recuperative abilities is critical for the lakes' future as both habitat and a resource for humankind. While contemplating these challenges during my photographic journeys, I also witnessed much of the Great Lakes' beauty and diversity and consider myself lucky to have the good fortune to have done so.

DAVID ZURICK

ACKNOWLEDGMENTS

This book results from a lifetime association with the Great Lakes. I want to take this opportunity to thank all the folks who have shared lake-based adventures and friendships with me over the years. I'd like to specifically thank the following people and entities for providing invaluable assistance during the course of this photography project: Adrian and Royal; Apostle Islands National Lakeshore; Bad River Band; Bay Port Fish Company; Bob and Jeff; Bob and Sayge; Carole Pence; Chris Andrews; Colin and Laura Murphy; Dallas Winston; Department of Natural Resources, State of Michigan; Fisherman Scott; Ice Road Racers; Jacob Rodgers; Jake the Trapper; Jim and Tony; John Siemen; Lily, Theo, and Opal; Lucky; Marblehead Lighthouse; Middle Bass Island State Park; Mr. Smith's Coffee Shop; Mystic Queen; Paul and Elsa Pearson; Rain Walker; Red Cliff Band; Rob Ballman; Ruggles Beach Mobile Home Park; Sajeel; Sean, Chris, and Jason; Turtle Joe's; Tyler Woodman; Valerie and Sterre; Wagoner County Park; and Washburn Bait and Tackle.

Thanks to my brother Doug, for painting the Great Lakes map, and to Teryl.

Thanks to my brother Steve, who knows the Great Lakes as only a waterman does, and to Janet, for providing me with a home away from home in my old hometown on Lake Huron.

Thanks to my sister, Linda, and to Rick, who shares my fondness for lake rocks and has been so gracious as to point out a few collecting spots.

Thanks to Jerry Dennis for writing the kind of penetrating essay that only a lifelong Great Lakes resident, someone who intimately knows and deeply loves the lakes, could do.

Thanks to my editor, Megan Stielstra, whose professionalism, enthusiasm, and bright, shining kindness have made this project such a great joy.

As always, my greatest gratitude goes to my wife and life partner, Jennifer—thank you for giving me the space, the time, the love, and the support to follow my muse.